CAPTIVE HEARTS
CAPTIVE MINDS

"*Captive Hearts, Captive Minds* is must reading for everyone who wants to understand the powerful appeal that cults exert over so many ordinary people, and do so in so many disguises, with so many subtle tactics. Although cults enter the national consciousness only when their charismatic leaders openly defy government officials or when they engage in suicidal or abusive actions that are media-worthy, cults are an insidious part of the very fabric of our society—and will become more dominant as we approach the millennium year of 2000. This book's wisdom is vital reading for us all."
Philip G. Zimbardo, Ph.D.
Professor of Psychology, Stanford University

"In a time of dangerously increasing irrationality, it is not surprising—though it is tragic—that cults attract so large a number of adherents. The cult problem is not just one more addition to the depressingly long list of difficulties our society faces. Because it is symptomatic of our mindless approach to the many complexities of life, the issue should concern us all. I strongly recommend this penetrating and insightful study."
Steve Allen
Author and Entertainer

"I wish every cult member, and every family of a cult member, struggling to free himself from the trauma of membership in a destructive relationship could read *Captive Hearts, Captive Minds*. It offers the powerful healing medicine of understanding."
Eugene H. Methvin
Senior Editor, *Reader's Digest*

"*Captive Hearts, Captive Minds* is an invaluable tool for anyone trying to manage their own recovery from a cult experience. The book works on many levels—offering practical advice, sharing personal experiences from other former members, and providing in-depth information and sources for the serious researcher on cults and mind control. The authors' well-thought-out approach to recovery encompasses a wide range of issues while reflecting respect, sensitivity, and encouragement to their readers."
Cynthia S. Kisser
Executive Director, Cult Awareness Network

CAPTIVE HEARTS, CAPTIVE MINDS

Freedom and Recovery from Cults and Abusive Relationships

Madeleine Landau Tobias
and
Janja Lalich

Hunter House

For further information contact:
Hunter House Inc., Publishers
P.O. Box 2914
Alameda CA 94501-0914

The authors are grateful for permission received to reprint or adapt from those works listed below or acknowledged elsewhere in the text:
The cartoon on page 166 by William Hamilton is reprinted by permission of Chronicle Features, San Francisco, California.

Library of Congress Cataloging-in-Publication Data
Tobias, Madeleine Landau.
Captive hearts, captive minds : freedom and recovery from cults and abusive relationships / Madeleine Landau Tobias and Janja Lalich.
p.   cm.
Includes bibliographical references and index.
ISBN 0-89793-145-9 (hard cover) : $24.95
ISBN 0-89793-144-0 (soft cover) : $14.95
1. Cults—Psychology. 2. Deprogramming. 3. Ex-cultists—Rehabilitation. 4. Ex-cultists—Mental health. I. Lalich, Janja. II. Title.
BP603.T62   1993
362.2—dc20   93-33938

Manufactured in the United States of America

9   8   7   6   5   4   3   2   1   First edition

Ordering

Trade bookstores and wholesalers in the U.S. and Canada, please contact:

Publishers Group West
4065 Hollis Street, Box 8843
Emeryville CA 94608   Phone: (800) 788-3123   Fax: (510) 658-1834

Special Sales: Hunter House books are available at special discounts for sales promotions, organizations, premiums, fundraising, and for educational use. For details please contact:

Special Sales Department
Hunter House Inc., Publishers
P.O. Box 2914
Alameda, CA 94501-0914   Phone: (510) 865-5282   Fax: (510) 865-4295

Project Credits

Project editor: Lisa E. Lee   Production Manager: Paul J. Frindt
Cover design by Jil Weil   Book design by *Qalagraphia*
Copyeditors: Bobbie Sumberg, Mary Lou Sumberg Editors: John Archer, Kiran S. Rana
Production Assistance: María Jesús Aguiló, Theo B. Crawford, Susan Burckhard
Photo of Janja Lalich by Barbara Maggiani
Marketing: Corrine M. Sahli   Promotion: Darcy Cohan, Robin Donovan
Customer Support: Sharon R.A. Olson
Publisher: Kiran S. Rana
Set in Galliard and Lithos by 847 Communications, Alameda CA
Printed by Gilliland Printing, Arkansas City KS

In memory of our mothers, who aren't here to share in our triumphs.
To the Pratt Street gang, whom I shall never forget . . . M. L. T.
To Shelly Rosen, who put me on the path to healing . . . J. L.
To all those who left . . . and to those who will leave
this book is for you.

Important Note

The material in this book is intended to provide an overview of the issues surrounding recovery from cultic relationships and experiences. Every effort has been made to provide accurate and dependable information and the contents of this book have been compiled in consultation with clinical professionals.

The reader should be aware that professionals in the field may have differing opinions, and change is always taking place. Since each case and each individual are different, the material contained herein is not offered as a uniform method for recovery, nor is it always successful.

Therefore, the authors, publisher, and editors cannot be held responsible for any error, omission, or outdated material.

In evaluating the alternatives available and appropriate courses of conduct, or if you have any questions or concerns about the information in this book, please consult licensed helping professionals, physicians, clergy, and legal counsel.

CONTENTS

The numbers in parentheses in the text refer to endnotes found on page 289.

FOREWORD

In the late 1960s and early 1970s increasing numbers of parents approached mental health professionals and clergy because their young adult children were joining offbeat groups and changing in ways that frightened the parents. The stereotypical story went something like this:

> My son had always been an "A" student, popular, with a lot of friends. Our family generally got along fine. He called home every week from college and loved coming home on weekends. He adored his younger sister, loved to play guitar, and was always cracking us up with jokes. Then in his junior year he began to attend the meetings of a group at school. At first I was pleased. I thought the socializing and group activities would help him mature.
>
> But quite rapidly he changed. He lost his sense of humor, began to reprimand his little sister for the silliest things, and was preaching to us constantly. He tried for a time to get us involved in his group, and insisted time and again that we would regret it if we didn't join. He cut off contact with his friends, except for one, whom he brought into the group, stopped playing the guitar, and paid so little attention to school that his grade point average dropped from 3.4 to 2.1. He stopped coming home for weekends, moved out of the dorm to live with members of the group, and virtually stopped calling home. He now says he's dropping out of school. Whenever I've been able to see him, he seems distant, like his mind is someplace far away. These changes in him have devastated our family. It's as though our son has died, as though someone has taken over his body. I don't know how, but I'm sure he's been brainwashed and that this group he is in is a cult.

Most parents who told variations of this story were rebuffed, however politely, by the vast majority of professionals to whom they turned for help. They were gently—and sometimes not so gently—told that they were overprotective, intrusive, domineering. Or they were told that it was just a phase their child was going through and everything would work out eventually.

Fortunately, a few professionals did begin to listen to the parents and to the small number of young people who had left these groups. These professionals realized that most of the cult joiners were relatively normal people from relatively normal families, who had been lured into powerfully persuasive environments that step-by-step eroded their independent, critical thinking and induced a state of dependency. This point of view runs counter to the unfortunately common misconception that cults are weird groups that attract crazy people. Sadly, even most former cult members share this misconception. They don't realize that they were in a cult because the group deceived them. As a result, they tend to overlook the role their cult experience plays in their current psychological or emotional difficulties and tend to be less prepared to deal with those difficulties. Quite often, the relatives, friends, and professionals to whom former cult members turn for help also subscribe to this misconception. This lack of understanding only compounds the difficulty of the ex-member's postcult adjustment.

Indeed, not understanding cults harms all of society. The most conspicuous recent example of this was in Waco, Texas, where the Branch Davidians, followers of David Koresh, immolated themselves. When agents of the Department of Alcohol, Tobacco, and Firearms first assaulted the Davidian compound and trapped Koresh between the humiliation of surrender, on the one hand, and his apocalyptic beliefs, on the other, those of us who understand cults shuddered. Our judgment about the probability of suicide was much different from that of the FBI, which chose the slow endgame of gas because it deemed suicide unlikely.

We would have judged the probability differently because we realize that a charismatic cult leader's capacity to control his followers' thoughts, emotions, and behaviors makes them, for all intents and purposes, a projection of the leader's psyche. If the leader is potentially self-destructive, so is the group (and those few who resist self-destruction will have it forced upon them). In the Branch Davidians there was only one relevant scale of suicide potential—David Koresh's—not one for each person. Contrary to what some FBI agents thought, and contrary to what the overwhelming majority of Americans thought, parents in cults are capable of permitting the murder of their own children. It happened in Jonestown. It happened in Waco. And it can happen again.

Although such tragedies alert society to the harm cults cause, individuals and families affected by cults learn that lesson firsthand. A growing body of research attests to the degree of distress among those who have left a cult. An important study found that during the postcult adjustment period 95 percent of former members scored high enough on a psychological test to warrant a psychiatric diagnosis. Their level of distress was higher than that of the average psychiatric inpatient. Unfortunately, most psychotherapists, pastoral counselors, relatives, and even ex-members look at the manifestation of these symptoms and ask, "What is wrong with _____?" Psychotherapists may try to determine what early childhood experiences may have motivated the person to seek suffering. Relatives who cannot understand why the person is unhappy may, in their frustration, blame him or her for being lazy, cowardly, stupid, or all of the above. The ex-members may further berate themselves by analyzing their unhappiness according to the cult's doctrines, which always places the cult on top and the member on the bottom. All these people unknowingly participate in victim blaming because they don't understand cults.

Based on the cumulative knowledge and research of those of us who study cults, we know that the majority of cult members eventually leave their groups. (Unfortunately, the sizable number who stay in their groups may remain exposed to even deeper psychological and physical harm.) The fact that many do leave is significant, however, in that it helps to explain what is wrong with cults. If we are to believe that cult members were unhappy before they joined, supposedly became happier after they joined, were continually pressured to remain, left anyway, and then were more distressed than ever after leaving, what could have impelled them to leave and to remain apart from the group? The inescapable conclusion seems to be that the cult experience is not what it appears to be.(1)

Cults are *not* what they appear to be. And, consequently, the cause of former cult members' suffering is not what *it* appears to be. Although not necessarily caused only by the cult experience, their pain is inextricably linked to that experience. And because deception lies at the heart of the cult experience, former cult members (and those who help them) must be educated about cults before they can see through the deception and adequately deal with the problems.

That is why this book is so important and timely. The authors speak from firsthand experience about postcult problems and what to do about them. Madeleine Landau Tobias is a psychotherapist and exit counselor who has worked with scores of former cultists. Janja Lalich has been researching cults since 1986 and is actively working with parents and loved ones of current cult members and meeting with former cult members in a local support group. Both authors are themselves former cult members: Madeleine spent 14 years in Eastern meditation and psychotherapy cults; Janja spent more than 10 years in a "feminist" left-wing political cult. Their personal experiences underline the often overlooked fact that cults are not necessarily religious. Cults are exploitative groups characterized by extreme levels of manipulation that induce dependency in members. And cults should be distinguished from "new movements," including those that may have bizarre belief systems, but are not exploitatively manipulative.

The authors' personal experiences also reflect changes that have occurred since the early 1970s, when the typical cult scenario was that described earlier. Former cult members seeking help today are no longer just teenagers or young people in their early twenties. They are of all ages. Many have been in groups for more than 10 years. Many have been married and even raised children in cults. Many do not have supportive families waiting for them to come out.

In 1992 and 1993 the American Family Foundation, a cult research and educational organization, sponsored recovery workshops for ex-cult members. The participants' average age was 36. More than two thirds had left the cult groups on their own, without a family-inspired intervention. Some had been ejected from the cult, for example, because they had begun to openly question certain doctrines or practices. And there were still many young former members, even some whose experiences resembled the story told earlier. But the age ranges, educational levels, and social backgrounds now represent a cross-section of America.

Cults are more common than most people realize. Most, like the Branch Davidians, are small, with no more than a few hundred members, although some have tens of thousands of members. Although the precise level of harm experienced by cult members is not known for sure, research and experience show that a large minority, if not a majority, are seriously impacted—both psychologically and physically. Most misconstrue their problems, and very few receive appropriate professional assistance.

That is why it is so important for former cult members to have books that can help them. Sometimes, unfortunately, such books may be all the support they can find. Those who read this book will gain valuable insights about their cult experience, the distress they have felt since leaving, and how they can heal themselves.

I also hope that psychotherapists, pastoral counselors, and friends and relatives of former cult members will read this book. If they do, they will avoid the victim blaming and misconceptions that intensify ex-cult members' feelings of inadequacy, discouragement, and confusion.

During the early years of the cult phenomenon, my colleague Dr. John Clark called the phenomenon an "impermissible experiment." He said that cults were manipulating people's personalities in ways that would make ethical social psychologists blanch. Dr. Clark recognized that at heart the cult problem is an ethical one. It highlights how much human beings can be damaged when they are treated like objects to be manipulated instead of like persons to respect and honor.

This book can help those who have been subjects of this impermissible experiment understand the psychological abuse they have suffered and rediscover the self-respect that is the birthright of everyone of us.

Michael D. Langone, Ph.D.
Executive Director, American Family Foundation
Editor, *Cultic Studies Journal*

ACKNOWLEDGMENTS

We gratefully acknowledge the help, encouragement, and loving support of all the people who kept us going from the time of conception of this book through completion—in particular, all the former cult members who never stopped asking, "How's the book coming?" and saying, "Hurry up and finish it." Because of their enthusiasm, this project stayed alive.

Michael Langone of the American Family Foundation (AFF) earns our deepest thanks. Most recently, Michael read each word and each line, critiquing and cajoling as needed. We also thank Carol Giambalvo, who gave her immediate attention, constructive advice, and enthusiasm to each chapter. Both Carol and Michael responded at the speed of light, sending faxes across the country to meet our deadlines. Thanks also to Lorna and Bill Goldberg for reading chapters and for their encouragement.

Our appreciation goes to Kiran Rana and the staff at Hunter House, our publisher, and most especially to Lisa Lee, who recognized the value in this project from the time it was first presented to her.

A special thanks to Herbert Rosedale, who took time off from his busy schedule as an attorney and as president of the AFF to read the manuscript, giving us advice and support. We also thank numerous friends and colleagues, most notably Dr. Margaret Singer, Patrick Ryan, Joe Kelly, Kevin Garvey, Anna Bowen, Betty Rich, and Father Hud Richard.

With deep-felt regard, we thank those former cult members who added a special, personal element to the book by generously contributing their stories. And we will never forget the countless others who managed to leave their cults, from whom we have learned so much.

With gratitude we acknowledge our sharp-minded and sharp-eyed editors, Mary Lou Sumberg and Bobbie Sumberg, who brought clarity and energy to our ideas, and John Archer and Kiran Rana, who with great sensitivity gave the manuscript its final touch.

Finally, Madeleine cannot thank enough her family, Ed, Allison, and Jason, for their love, patience, and support—for standing by her first during the cult years, then through the ups and downs of recovery, and finally while immersed in the frantic world of writing a book. And with a heartfelt sigh, Janja thanks her partner, Kim, for her encouragement and support, her boundless tolerance, and her love.

INTRODUCTION

Captive Hearts, Captive Minds was written to give former cult members, their families, and professionals an understanding of cultic techniques and the aftereffects of these techniques, as well as to provide an array of specific methods and aids that may help to restore normalcy to ex-cult members' lives.

Cults did not fade away, as some would like to believe, with the passing of the sixties and the disappearance of the flower children. In fact, cults are alive and thriving, though they have to a certain extent "cleaned up their act." If there is less street recruiting, it is because many cults now use professional associations, campus organizations, and self-help seminars as their main sources of new members. Today we see older people, middle-aged people, and even multigenerational families being recruited into a wide variety of groups, focused on everything from therapy to business ventures, from New Age philosophy to Bible-based beliefs, from martial arts to political change.

Most cults don't stand up to be counted in a formal sense. Currently, the best estimates are that there are about 5,000 such groups in the United States—some large, some very small. Noted cult researcher and clinical psychologist Dr. Margaret Thaler Singer estimates that "about 10 to 20 million people have at some point in recent years been in one or more of such groups."(1) The national office of the Cult Awareness Network reports that it receives about 18,000 inquiries a year.(2) These are not small numbers.

A cult experience is rarely pleasant, as those of you who are ex-cult members no doubt know—or you wouldn't be reading this book. More often than not, leaving a cult environment requires an adjustment period, not only to reintegrate into "normal" society but also to put the pieces of yourself back together in a way that makes sense to you. When you first leave a cultic situation, you may not recognize yourself. You may not know how to identify the problems you are about to face. You may not have the slightest idea who you want to be. The question we often ask children, "What do you want to be when you grow up?" suddenly takes on a new meaning for adult ex-cult members.

This process of assessing what happened and sorting out how to get your life back on track may or may not include professional therapy or pastoral counseling. The healing or recovery period varies for each individual, with ebbs and flows of progress, and times of great insight as well as great confusion. How you approach your postcult transition will be up to you, but certain factors will play into it. One is the length and intensity of your cult experience. Another is the nature of the group or person you were involved with—where they fall on the scale of mildly harmful to extremely damaging, or nonviolent to violent. For most of you, recovering from your cult experience will not end after the exit counseling which may have helped you to leave, nor will it end after the first few weeks or months away from the group. On the contrary, depending on your circumstances, aspects of your cult involvement may require some attention for the rest of your life.

Given this, it is important to find a comfortable pace for your healing process. In the beginning, especially, your mind and body may simply need a rest! Now that you are no longer on a mission to save the world or your soul, relaxation and rest are no longer sinful. In fact, they are absolutely necessary for a healthy, balanced, and productive life.

Reentering the noncult world can be painful and confusing. To some extent, time will help. But the passage of time and merely being physically out of the group are not enough. You must actively and of your own initiative face the issues of your cult involvement. Let time be your ally, but don't expect it alone to heal you. We both know ex-cult members who have been out of their groups for 7, 10, 15 years, who have never had any counseling or education about cults and mind control. These individuals live in considerable emotional pain and have significant difficulties in their lives due to unresolved conflicts about their group, their leader, or their cult experience. Often they are still under the subtle effects of the group's thought-reform program.

The degree and type of harm suffered by cult members may vary considerably. Thus, some leave with a minimum of distress and readjust rapidly to the larger society, while others suffer severe emotional damage requiring psychiatric care. The dilemmas facing people can be awesome and need thoughtful sorting out. Many have likened this period to being on an emotional roller coaster.

First of all, self-blame (whether for joining the cult or participating in it, or both) is a common reaction which can tend to overshadow every positive feeling. Added to this is basic identity loss and confusion. If you were recruited at any time after your teens, you already had a distinct personality, which we call the "precult personality." While in the cult, you most likely developed a new personality to adapt to the demands and ambience of cult life. We call this the "cult personality." And, if your cult was like most cults, by means of a deliberate thought-reform program (sometimes known as brainwashing), you were probably led to believe that your precult personality was all bad and your adaptive cult personality all good. Upon leaving the cult you don't automatically switch back to your precult personality, and may often feel as though you have two personalities! Evaluating these personalities—integrating the good and discarding the bad—is a primary task faced by most former cult members.

As you seek to redefine your identity you will want to address the psychological, emotional, and physical consequences of having been in a controlled and possibly violent environment. And as if all that weren't enough, there are many basic life necessities and challenges to meet and overcome. These include finding employment and a place to live, making friends, repairing old relationships, confronting belief issues, deciding on a career or going back to school, and possibly catching up with a social and cultural gap.

If you feel like "a stranger in a strange land," it may be a consolation to know that you are not the first person to have felt this way. In fact, that pervasive and awkward sense of alienation which both of us felt when we left the cults we were in was a motivating factor in writing this book. We hope that the information here will not only help you get rid of any shame or embarrassment but also ease your integration into a new life.

We were also compelled by the fact that people coming out of cults have such difficulty finding practical information. We, too, experienced that dilemma, for both of us faced one roadblock after another in seeking helping professionals knowledgeable about cults and postcult trauma.

•

This book is divided into four major sections:

Part One exposes the workings of cults and one-on-one cultic relationships; describes the dynamics of the thought-reform process and the effects of cult conversion; and presents, based on studies of the psychopathic personality, a profile of the cult leader. It is intended to help former cult members understand their cult involvement—how they got there, how they were manipulated and exploited, and how they can assess the damage they suffered.

The section opens with a letter written by a former cult member, Holly Ardito, to her group two years after leaving. Holly's letter expresses the sense of freedom experienced when a person is able to look back on the cult experience with confidence and calm. There are several other first-person accounts in this section including Janet Joyce's recollection of her recruitment into a psychotherapy/political cult, and another woman's vivid portrayal of a three-year cultic relationship. "Rachel" (a pseudonym), brings clarity to a subject that bears more attention—the one-on-one cult.

This part concludes with a discussion of the corrupted power dynamic typically found in cults. We use a 15-point profile to delineate some of the commonly recognized characteristics of cult leaders, illustrated with a case study of David Koresh. Some of the material in Part One is somewhat theoretical and may at first be difficult to grasp. We include it because we believe that a clear intellectual understanding of cults and thought reform is vital to recovery from a cult experience. If you have difficulty with these early chapters we suggest that you come back to them later when you have dealt with some of the issues that may be preventing you from tackling them at this time.

Part Two deals with healing from the trauma of a cultic involvement.(3) It begins with a personal account by Joseph Kelly, who spent 14 years in two different Eastern meditation cults. Joe tells us how he finally gathered the strength to leave, then found himself confronted with an array of postcult difficulties. The most commonly recognized aftereffects of involvement in a cult tend to fall within the general areas of survival and growth: physical, psychological, and spiritual health; personal decision making and intellectual pursuits; career and belief issues; and interpersonal relationships. Specific difficulties and dilemmas within each of these areas, illustrated with case examples and personal accounts, are addressed along with healing methods and tools that have proven helpful to recovery.

Part Three is comprised of nine first-person accounts of freedom and recovery from a cult experience. Former members from a variety of cults share their experiences of leaving their group and learning to cope and adjust to life on the "outside." In one way or another, these stories touch on every issue faced in postcult life—spiritual, vocational, social, physical, and psychological. Just as there is no typical cult member, there is no single path to healing and recovery. Each person is different and has a different experience. This is clearly borne out by the personal accounts included here.

Part Four deals with some special concerns. The topic of children in cults is sometimes difficult to face, for children tend to be the most exploited and, in some cases, the most abused persons within a cultic environment. We have addressed this issue from the point of view of the children and the parents. In Part Three, Rosanne Henry tells of leaving her daughter to be raised by her cult leader, and going back to free her six-year-old from the cult. Here Rosanne describes the issues the Henry family grappled with to help integrate "Ganga" into the family's life and the "real world." We also hear from 14-year-old "Jessica Kay," who as a child was subjected to psychological manipulation and sexual abuse by the man her mother engaged in a cultic relationship with. In addition to the personal accounts are practical advice and professional suggestions for the special needs of children coming out of cults. Part Four also includes cult-related therapeutic issues for the professional.

The very last part of the book offers a brief checklist of cult characteristics, useful in assessing new and old involvements, as well as resources for further exploration, reading, and personal support.

A matter we hope to shed light on in this book is the damage wrought by the "cult apologists." These individuals (mostly academics) take the stance that cults do no harm and that all reports of emotional or psychological damage are exaggerations on the part of disgruntled former members. Naturally, we disagree. We also find it unfortunate that there is so little public understanding and appreciation of the potential danger of cults to ordinary people. Certainly there are dangers and harmful consequences for the individual cult member. If there weren't, there wouldn't be a need for cult research and information organizations or for books such as this. There are also documented dangers to society in general from cults that carry out their beliefs in antisocial ways—sometimes random, sometimes planned—through terrorist acts, drug dealing, arms trading, enforced prostitution of the members, and other violent or criminal behavior.

From our perspective, a group or relationship earns the label "cult" or "cultic" on the basis of its methods and behaviors, *not* on the basis of its beliefs. Those of us who oppose cults are often accused of wanting to deny individuals their freedoms, of being against religion. Yet what we are fighting against is precisely the repression and stripping away of individual freedom that occurs in cults. *It is not beliefs that we oppose, but the exploitative manipulation of a person's faith and trust in other human beings.* Cults use deception, manipulation, and psychologically coercive methods of persuasion (which we call "thought-reform techniques") to attract, recruit, convert, hold on to, and ultimately exploit their devotees.

We also feel it necessary to clarify that in society today there are many noncult organizations that individuals believe in, dedicate their lives to, and through which they experience personal transformation. Many religious institutions, the military, and mainstream political parties are examples of such noncult organizations. We would not call them cults because they are publicly known institutions and are usually accountable to some higher body or to society in general. When people join, they have a clear idea of the organizations' structures and goals. Deceptive practices are not integral to the growth of these organizations or their ability to retain their members.

Cult membership, by contrast, is not voluntary. It is the result of a coercive and destructive psychological process based on deception, dependency, and dread. Cults attack and destroy a person's independence, critical-thinking abilities, personal relationships, and general physical, spiritual, and psychological state of being. That's the stuff that cults are made of.

We intend this book for the many individuals who have experienced trauma in a *group* situation or in a *one-on-one* cultic relationship. Because it is awkward to repeat the phrase "cult or cultic relationship," in many instances we have simply shortened it to "cult," meaning it to be inclusive of all types of cult experiences. In the same vein, we usually say "cult leader" or "leader" rather than "leader or abusive partner." Also, we use masculine pronouns when referring to cult leaders in general. This is not to deny that there are many female cult leaders but to acknowledge that the majority are male. Both male and female leaders are equal-opportunity victimizers, drawing men and women of all ages into their web of exploitation.

We have used case examples and personal stories throughout to illustrate the specifics of cult involvement, the aftereffects, and the healing process. Unless an example is otherwise noted, it is a composite based on interviews and our personal and professional experiences with hundreds of former cult members. In several instances, individuals chose pseudonyms to protect their privacy; this is indicated in the text by the use of quotes.

If you are a former cult member, you may find that you identify personally with some of the experiences, emotions, and difficulties discussed here. Other topics may appear quite foreign and unrelated to your experience. It may be helpful to look them over anyway, as there may be lessons or suggestions that could prove useful to your situation.

The keys to recovery are balance and moderation, qualities of life that were most likely absent in the cult. Give yourself a program for recovery that addresses *your* needs and wants, changing it as necessary to adapt to new circumstances and needs. The important thing is to do what feels right. After all that time in the cult spent squelching your gut instincts, it is now time to let your *self* speak to you—and this time you can listen and act. From now on, only you are responsible for setting and achieving your goals.

THE CULT PHENOMENON

Cults are primarily a social and cultural rather than a psychiatric or legal problem . . . . With greater knowledge about them, people are less susceptible to deception.
—Robert Jay Lifton

GREETINGS FROM
A FORMER MEMBER

HOLLY A. ARDITO

The Recovery Alliance, Inc. (RAI), bills itself as a self-help organization dedicated to the advancement of recovery for what the group refers to as "obsessive-compulsive" persons, such as alcoholics, compulsive eaters, and compulsive gamblers. RAI practices the 12 Steps of Alcoholics Anonymous (AA), but claims to do it in a way that is more "pure" than AA and other "Anonymous" fellowships. RAI believes that the 12-step programs have been watered down over the years and no longer practice the *true* program of recovery as it was intended by its founders.

RAI is structured as a nonprofit organization, with a board of directors and an organizational charter. Although the board elects a chairman, all the members' activities, beliefs, and direction evolve from the founding member, Donald Gilroy. Gilroy teaches that the "illness" that members are recovering from is centered in selfishness and self-centeredness. To recover, members must commit their lives to selfless self-sacrifice. They are subjected to, among other things, rigorous and tiresome fund-raising schedules, public humiliation, rigidly controlled diets, and other abusive conduct.

I wrote the following letter to RAI members two years after leaving the group.

March 7, 1992

Hi!

This week has marked two years since I left the Recovery Alliance, Inc. (RAI). I am writing this letter just to let you know what it's like on this side. I have so much to say that I could go on for pages, but I will try to keep this as brief as possible.

I have seen you guys several times—fund-raising, of course. I saw you selling T-shirts in Seattle and raffle tickets at the Durham Fair. I

8

have seen you at car shows, department stores, and at the fireworks. My first reaction when I see you is repulsion, but it is quickly followed by sorrow. I know what it is like for you, since you are all victims (yes, victims do exist), just as I was.

It is interesting what I am able to see now that I couldn't see then. For as long as I was there I knew that I was unhappy, but I was told that the problem was with my recovery, not my environment.

I remember making the decision to leave. It was like all of a sudden being struck with a bolt of sanity. I'm sure you all think it was because I had a boyfriend. Well, I made my decision a couple of months before I met him. After having been placed on probation, I remember standing in my room and thinking, "I can't do this anymore. I want to leave." It was not the first time I had ever had that thought, but this time it was different. This time it was followed by another thought, which was "I don't care what the consequences will be." As you all observed, I made no attempt to meet the terms of my probation.

When I first left, I was quite confused. Fortunately, I quickly got help from some professionals who have experience working with former members of RAI and other similarly destructive groups. They helped me see the insanity of the situation. The loss of freethinking. The emotional, sexual, and spiritual abuse we were all suffering. The psychopathology of Donald. I was also helped by some books—*Combatting Cult Mind Control* by Steve Hassan and *People of the Lie* by Scott Peck.

Well, the consequences of my leaving were *nothing* like I expected. What am I like today? I'm basically a happy person. I have a good job in my field with a Fortune 500 company. I have a nice apartment (yes, with off-street parking) and a decent car. I have a handful of close friends and many acquaintances. Most of my friends are in 12-step programs, but some aren't. I have good relationships with my family.

Most of all, I have **freedom**. I probably average three AA meetings a week—sometimes more, sometimes less. If I'm tired or just don't feel like going to a meeting, I stay home. Or I go somewhere else. I keep busy, but make time for myself too. I clean my apartment every week. I just finished reading a 1,000-page novel. On weekends I frequently get together with friends and go dancing, hiking, or on day trips. I have dated several guys in the last two years, and have had a couple of steady relationships, too.

How's my relationship with God? Fine. I worship the god of *my own* understanding.

I am not overweight, nor am I underweight. I eat two or three meals a day, and sometimes, if I feel like it, I have a snack in between.

I am able to express whatever is on my mind, and I don't have to follow any formula. I attend fairs and festivals as a participant, not as a vendor. I attend AA conventions as an AA member, not as a vendor—and not as a person of superior knowledge.

Not a Friday has gone by when I haven't come home from a long work week and said to myself, "Thank God I don't have to go to that awful meeting."

I feel sorry for other former members who haven't received the help they need. Many of them end up with tremendous guilt as a result of RAI's teachings. Some have joined other destructive groups. One has died. Fortunately, however, most of us have been helped by the proper professionals and have been able to live happy lives.

I wish you all the best, and hope that you will soon realize the amount of control and deception taking place in your surroundings.

Sincerely,
Holly

CULTS AND CULTIC
RELATIONSHIPS

If you are a former cult member coming to terms with what happened to you, it is important to understand what a cult is and what it means to have been involved in one. People whose lives have been deeply affected by cultic groups or relationships often describe the experience as one of being close to or overwhelmed by evil. Yet many former members confess that at first they felt a kind of wonder, as if they had drawn near something awesome. They experienced a sense of exhilaration, excitement, passion, or expectation that was almost overwhelming. For those who were in a close relationship with the leader, the cult's touch may have had an almost hypnotic quality. Members literally describe themselves as being "enthralled" with an ideal, a group, or a person—usually the leader.

Thrall is defined in the dictionary as "a servant slave: bondman; a person in moral or mental servitude; slavery; a state of complete absorption."(1) Thralldom can also express an almost mystical sense of rapture—an apt description of the passionate type of devotion to a cause, leader, or belief system typically found in a cultic group. In some cults, trance states and thralldom might be combined to create a heady, intoxicating brew. In Eastern-style cults, in fact, it is common to talk about "intoxication" with God, expressed through love and subjugation to the will of the guru. In aberrant Christian cults and shepherding groups, the lure is to become one with the body of Christ through belonging to a particular church and living in obedience to its strict guidelines.

It is important to remember that thralldom is bondage. When combined with deception, exploitation, and other abuse, thralldom becomes traumatic, painful, and utterly disillusioning—a spiritual rape, as many have called it.

Cult leaders and cult life can be likened to the societies described in

Hannah Arendt's seminal work, *The Origins of Totalitarianism*. In her examination of the goals of this century's totalitarian movements (Nazism and Bolshevism), Arendt states that their single goal was "the permanent domination of each single individual in each and every sphere of life."(2) Sound familiar?

For the person who has been in a cult, the traumatic effects of cult life must be confronted and explored in order to diminish their impact. To facilitate healing, cult survivors need to understand the issue of deliberate manipulation, the concepts of thought reform and undue influence, and the sophisticated variety of recruitment and control techniques that were used on them. Each former cult member must acquire an objective understanding of his or her own particular experience.

What Makes a Cult a Cult?

Since most people know very little about cults before joining one, part of the healing process involves education. Many former members read just about everything they can get their hands on about cults. For this reason we have included a recommended reading list and a list of resource organizations to contact for support or information (see Appendices B and C).

As a starting point for the educational process, here are some basic definitions and characteristics of cults and their techniques. Cult researchers have spent many years refining the definition of a cult and providing the general public with useful data about cults. The American Family Foundation (AFF), a nonprofit research and educational organization, has taken the lead in this work.(3) The following definition, adopted at a 1985 conference of scholars and policymakers, has been accepted by many cult researchers:

> **Cult:** A group or movement exhibiting great or excessive devotion or dedication to some person, idea, or thing, and employing unethical manipulative or coercive techniques of persuasion and control (e.g., isolation from former friends and family, debilitation, use of special methods to heighten suggestibility and subservience, powerful group pressures, information management, suspension of individuality or critical judgment, promotion of total dependency on the group and fear of leaving it), designed to advance the goals of the group's leaders, to the actual or possible detriment of members, their families, or the community.(4)

Three characteristics, which may be present to a greater or lesser degree, help to distinguish cults from other communities or groups. They are:

1. Members are expected to be excessively zealous and unquestioning in their commitment to the identity and leadership of the group. They must replace their own beliefs and values with those of the group.

2. Members are manipulated and exploited, and may give up their education, careers, and families to work excessively long hours at group-directed tasks such as selling a quota of candy or books, fund-raising, recruiting, and proselytizing.

3. Harm or the threat of harm may come to members, their families, and/or society due to inadequate medical care, poor nutrition, psychological and physical abuse, sleep deprivation, criminal activities, and so forth.(5)

Dr. Margaret Singer, a clinical psychologist who has been researching cults and thought-reform programs since the 1950s, provides us with several other characteristics relevant to cult identification, some of which highlight the role of the cult leader.

1. Cults are authoritarian in their power structure.

2. Cults tend to be totalitarian in their control of the behavior of their members.

3. Cults tend to have double sets of ethics [one for the leader and another for the members; one for those inside the group, another for dealing with outsiders].

4. Cult leaders are self-appointed and claim to have a special mission in life.

5. Cult leaders tend to be charismatic, determined, and domineering.

6. Cult leaders center the veneration of members upon themselves.

7. Cults appear to be innovative and exclusive.

8. Cults basically have only two purposes: recruiting new members and fund-raising.(6)

Cults can be chameleon-like, changing their character or modes of operating. They can be placed on a continuum of control and restriction, with their effects ranging from mildly damaging to dangerous. In *Cults in America: Programmed for Paradise* (an excellent book, unfortunately out of print but worth searching for), author Willa Appel offers some guidelines for assessing the degree of control.

> Cults can be categorized by the intensity of control they exert over their members, as well as by their ideological content. At one end of the intensity scale are the *totalistic* cults, which attempt to control the total environment of individual followers. Most totalistic cults advocate complete withdrawal from the world, condemning those outside . . . . These groups put tremendous pressure on members to conform completely to the group, to sever all ties with the past, and to give up any independent thoughts or actions . . . . Followers are strictly regimented—living together, working together . . . each day's activities dictated by the group.
>
> A key in determining the degree of control the group exercises over its members is the amount of time spent in mind-altering activities—prayer, chanting, meditation, group rituals, psychodrama, and confession, for these activities effectively isolate members from the outside world. A survey of 400 ex-cult members from 48 different groups revealed an average time of 55 hours per week spent in activities of this type . . . .
>
> Another important distinction must be made between groups that are live-in organizations and those that are not. Generally speaking, [the latter] have less control over their members. Some groups have two [or more] levels of membership . . . . Part-time members attend some functions, but their lives are not as dominated by the group . . . .
>
> Freedom of movement varies from cult to cult. Some cults . . . maintain security forces, which, along with protecting the group, prevent members from freely coming and going . . . . Moreover, the different branches of the same cult may vary in degree of control they exercise over members, and the structure and organization of any one cult may change over time.(7)

Although cults have existed throughout history, what concerns us today is the array of cults that emerged in the 1960s and continue to flourish. Most students of cults regard the sixties as the root era of this present-day phenomenon. Why the sixties?

"There were very few periods in American history in which the dominant sector—the white middle class—transformed itself as thoroughly as it did in the sixties and seventies, from the inside out, changing its costumes, its sexual mores, its family arrangements, and its religious patterns," wrote award-winning journalist and social critic Frances FitzGerald. "And of course a great deal did come of it: a host of new and imported religions, all the political and social movements, . . . literally hundreds of communes and other experiments in communal living, [and] a new psychotherapy and enthusiasm for a wild variety of pseudosciences and occult practices."(8)

From the turmoil and political upheaval of that era America witnessed the appearance of one cult after another, recruiting first the young, and now people of all ages and backgrounds.

Categories of Cults

Cults come in a variety of shapes and sizes. Categories of cults that are recruiting successfully today include:

Eastern meditation: characterized by belief in God-consciousness, becoming one with God. The leader usually distorts an Eastern-based philosophy or religion. Members sometimes learn to disregard worldly possessions and may take on an ascetic lifestyle. Techniques used: meditation, repeated mantras, altered states of consciousness, trance states.

Religious: marked by belief in salvation, afterlife, sometimes combined with an apocalyptic view. The leader reinterprets the Scriptures and often claims to be a prophet if not the messiah. Often the group is strict, sometimes using physical punishments such as paddling and birching, especially on children. Members are encouraged to spend a great deal of time proselytizing. (Note: included here are Bible-based neo-Christian and other religious cults, many considered syncretic since they combine beliefs and practices). Techniques used: speaking in tongues, chanting, praying, isolation, lengthy study sessions, many hours spent evangelizing, "struggle" (or criticism) and confession sessions.

Political, racist, terrorist: fueled by belief in changing society, revolution, overthrowing the "enemy" or getting rid of evil forces. The leader professes to be all-knowing and all-powerful. Often the group is armed and meets in secret with coded language, handshakes, and other ritualized practices. Members consider themselves an elite cadre ready to go to battle. Techniques used: paramilitary training, reporting on one another, guilt, fear, struggle sessions, instilled paranoia, long hours of indoctrination.

Psychotherapy/human potential (mass transformational): motivated by belief in striving for the goal of personal transformation, personal improvement. The leader is self-proclaimed, all-knowing, with unique insights, sometimes a "supertherapist." Sexual abuse is common in these groups. Techniques used: encounter sessions, altered states brought about by hypnosis and other trance-induction mechanisms, shame and intimidation, verbal abuse, struggle sessions.

Commercial: sustained by belief in attaining wealth and power, status, quick earnings. The leader, who is often overtly lavish, asserts that he has found the "way." Some commercial cults are crossovers to political and religious cults since they are based on family values, morals, good health, and patriotism. Members are encouraged to participate in costly and sometimes lengthy seminars, and to sell the group's "product" to others. Techniques used: deceptive sales techniques, guilt and shame, peer pressure, financial control.

New Age: founded upon belief in the "You are God" philosophy, in power through knowledge, wanting to know the future, find the quick fix. Often the leader presents himself as mystical, an ultraspiritual being, a channeler. Members rely on crystals, astrology, runes, shamanic devices, holistic medicine. Techniques used: magic tricks, altered states, peer pressure.

Occult, satanic, black magic: generated through belief in supernatural powers, sometimes worship of Satan. The leader professes to be evil incarnate. Animal sacrifice and physical and sexual abuse are common; some groups claim they perform human sacrifice. Techniques used: exotic rituals, secrecy, fear and intimidation, extreme violence.

One-on-one: based in belief in one's partner or teacher above all else. Generally an intimate relationship is used to manipulate and control the partner or student, who believes the dominant one to have special knowledge or special powers. Often there is severe and prolonged psychological, physical, and sexual abuse. Techniques used: pleasure/pain syndrome, promoting self-blame, and dependency, induced fear and insecurity, enforced isolation.

Miscellaneous, or cult of personality: rooted in a belief that reflects the usually charismatic personality of one who takes on the role of revered leader. Such groups revolve around a particular theme or interest, such as martial arts, opera, dance, a certain form of art, a type of medicine or healing. Techniques used: intense training sessions, rituals, elitism.(9)

Not every cult will fit neatly into one of the above categories, but this breakdown should provide some idea of the range of cultic groups and their reach into every walk of life.

The Cultic Relationship

Cults may be large or small. What defines them is not their size but their behavior. In addition to the larger, more publicized cults, there are small cults of less than a dozen members who follow a particular "guru"; "family cults," where the head of the family uses deceptive and excessive persuasion and control techniques; and probably the least acknowledged, the one-on-one cult.

The one-on-one cult is a deliberately manipulative and exploitative intimate relationship between two persons, often involving physical abuse of the subordinate partner. In the one-on-one cult, which we call a cultic relationship, there is a significant power imbalance between the two participants. The stronger uses his (or her) influence to control, manipulate, abuse, and exploit the other. In essence the cultic relationship is a one-on-one version of the larger group. It may even be more intense than participation in a group cult since all the attention and abuse is focused on one person, often with more damaging consequences.

Many marriages or domestic partnerships where there is spousal abuse may be characterized and explained in this way. Other one-on-one cults may be found in boss/employee situations, in pastor/worshipper milieus, in therapist/client relationships, in jailor/prisoner or interrogator/suspect situations, and in teacher/student environments (including academic, artistic, and spiritual situations—for example, a school professor, a yoga master, a martial arts instructor, or an art mentor).(10) It is our hope that those who have suffered such individualized abuse will find much in this book to identify with and use in healing their pain.

Since the upsurge of both public and professional interest in the issue of domestic violence, there has been some recognition of the link between mind control and battering. Men or women who batter their partners sometimes use manipulative techniques similar to those found in cults. The most common include "isolation and the provocation of fear; alternating kindness and threat to produce disequilibrium; the induction of guilt, self-blame, dependency, and learned helplessness."(11) The degree to which these features are present in a relationship affects the intensity of control and allows the relationship to be labeled cultic.

The similarities between cultic devotion and the traumatic bonding that occurs between battered individuals and their abusers are striking. "The repeated experience of terror and reprieve, especially within the isolated context of a love relationship, may result in a feeling of intense, almost worshipful dependence upon an all-powerful, godlike authority," writes psychiatrist Judith Lewis Herman. "The victim may live in terror of his wrath, but she may also view him as the source of strength, guidance, and life itself. The relationship may take on an extraordinary quality of specialness. Some battered women speak of entering a kind of exclusive, almost delusional world, embracing the grandiose belief system of their mates and voluntarily suppressing their own doubts as a proof of loyalty and submission."(12)

An abused partner is generally made to submit to the following types of behaviors:

- early verbal and/or physical dominance

- isolation/imprisonment

- fear arousal and maintenance

- guilt induction

- contingent expressions of "love"

- enforced loyalty to the aggressor and self-denunciation

- promotion of powerlessness and helplessness

- pathological expressions of jealousy

- hope-instilling behaviors

- required secrecy(13)

When psychological coercion and manipulative exploitation have been used in a one-on-one cultic relationship, the person leaving such a relationship faces issues similar to those encountered by someone leaving a cultic group. She feels a "paralyzing terror, constant anxiety, apprehension, vigilance, and feelings of impending doom . . . . [She feels] fatigued, passive, and unable to act, exhibiting . . . poor memory."(14)

Examples of the one-on-one cult

Tina Turner's autobiography recounts the horrific years she spent with her former husband, Ike, in an abusive relationship. Tina likened her torment to being "trapped in a sadistic little *cult*," where she was routinely beaten, humiliated, tortured, and—despite their fame and success—without her own financial resources. "He would *spend* money on me—when he felt like it but I could never *have* money. I mean, once I had asked him for five dollars a week, just as an allowance—*five* dollars—and he had said no."(15)

> Tina describes how Ike took control early on in the relationship: "I told him I didn't want to get involved any further with him. And that was the first time he beat me up. With a shoe stretcher—one of those men's shoe trees with the metal rods in the middle. Just grabbed one of those and started beating me with it. And after that he made me go to bed, and he had sex with me. My eye was all swollen—God, it was awful. And that was the beginning, the beginning of Ike instilling fear in me. He kept control of me with *fear*."(16)

From that point on Tina's life was a "horror movie, with no intermissions."(17) The incessant beatings and mental torture even drove her to a failed suicide attempt. But, after 16 years of the most brutal abuse and several unsuccessful efforts to escape, the tide turned. Tina wrote: "I looked at him for a second and thought, 'You just beat me for the last time, you sucker.' Then I got up, and I put a cape over my bloody clothes—didn't even change them. I had to leave my wig there because my head was too swollen to wear it, so I just tied one of those stretch wraps around my head. I figured he could get somebody else to wear that wig—he could wear it *himself*, for all I cared. I put on a pair of sunglasses, picked up one little piece of hand luggage with just some toiletry things in it, and I was gone."(18)

In the book's epilogue Tina writes about the period after she left Ike: "I had nothing, but I had my freedom."(19) We know the rest. Tina went on to unleash her talent, build her own musical career, and in 1984 won three Grammy Awards for Best Female Pop Vocal Performance, Best Female Rock Vocal Performance, and Record of the Year.

At a conference in 1989, Samuel Klagsbrun, executive director of the Four Winds Hospitals in New York, presented an extraordinary portrayal of his work with a patient who had been in a cultic relationship that included extreme battering. Through psychological manipulation and severe physical abuse, this woman had been "demeaned and diminished to slave level. She became an automaton, a robot." Klagsbrun's speech was entitled, "Is Submission Ever Voluntary?" By the end, listeners concluded that in cases such as these the answer is "No." The following is a summary of

Dr. Klagsbrun's presentation:

> After years of harsh verbal berating and a variety of punishments, which were meant to teach her how to behave, in the last two years with her partner, she was subjected to daily assaults and brutal beatings, sometimes with a 4x4 plank, "until torture and living in fear became normality." The couple's adopted daughter was manipulated by the father into "telling on her mother to improve her behavior," which intensified the woman's humiliation while pulling the young child into the father's sadistic rituals. Shortly, he began to beat the girl also, eventually murdering her, for which he is now imprisoned for life.
>
> In the beginning of her therapeutic treatment, Klagsbrun's patient was "almost mute and devoid of emotions . . . . One year later she was able to shed tears at the loss of her daughter." She knew her common-law husband was to blame, but she was still explaining how he loved her. The stages of working with her went from complete silence on her part, denial of the pain while she held onto the meaningful parts of their relationship, then slowly beginning to talk about the cycle of abuse, which included punishments, followed by reward, followed by further isolation, followed by another punishment, and so on.
>
> As she revealed the workings of their relationship, she began to see her partner's manipulativeness and premeditated behavior. In his role as her "teacher," he became the all-knowing omniscient figure who always soothed her after punishment and tended to her wounds, which led her to see him as a "healer." By occasionally rekindling the flame of their courtship and early years of living together, he was still also her lover. The enforced isolation (she was not allowed to leave the house or see her family) prevented her from receiving any outside validation. "He was the center of her universe from beginning to end. The goal of her existence became mere survival."(20)

One-on-one cults can evolve out of an abusive relationship that begins to resemble a cult in the methods used to dominate. Mind-control techniques begin to replace wholesome two-way communication between equals. Sometimes the abuser, or leader, intentionally seeks out a partner, or follower, whom he believes he can shape into submissiveness. In those cases the courtship phase is a type of cult recruitment: Prospective "members" are carefully screened and chosen. Once the "leader" makes a selection, usually based on knowledge of the individual's needs and vulnerabilities, courtship begins.

Another common characteristic of the one-on-one cult is that the victim's children (if any) are enmeshed in the cultic manipulation and abuse.

This was true in the example above and the one to follow.

In *"Rachel's"* narrative we learn that her lover and master, "Fred," not only had an abusive cultic relationship with her but also sexually abused her young daughter, "Jessica Kay" (who tells her side of the story in Chapter 22). At the same time, Fred was the charming and cunning leader of a group cult formed around his psychotherapy practice, where he also abused—emotionally, psychologically, and/or sexually—his associates and his clients.

Rachel's story

I was not feeling well that Thursday afternoon, so I took off work early. Obviously "Keith" was not expecting me home. Our marriage, already somewhat shaky, ended immediately when I arrived home to discover him with one of my friends. He confessed that they were having an affair. Devastated, I found myself alone with my children—Jon, three, and Jessica Kay, six. My confidence in myself as a woman was shattered. Keith was my childhood sweetheart, my first and only love. Now I doubted my desirability. But I was not without resources. Keith remained a devoted father to our children, and I was well-established in my career as a financial advisor in a successful investment firm.

I first met Fred on a consultation call less than a month after kicking my husband out of the house. Fred tried his best to impress me with his knowledge of the business world, the ins and outs of the stock market, retirement funds, and so forth, but I was too preoccupied with my own troubles to see him as anything other than a client. Since I was his investment advisor, he asked me to view some property with him. He was very flattering, interested in my personal life, solicitous of my welfare, and obviously interested in me as a woman. I felt my shattered ego beginning to flutter back to life. He pursued me with flowers, dinners, and presents. He even brought gifts for the kids and took a great interest in their behavior and schoolwork.

One evening at dinner I looked up at Fred and saw a great shimmering light, like a halo, around his head. We were talking about ESP, past lives, and the supernormal powers those who are enlightened are supposed to possess. I felt dizzy, giddy, and enrapt in his every word. I can't remember exactly what we talked about, but our conversation began to take on new significance. He was no longer a client turned boyfriend. I felt graced, humbled, and supremely fortunate to be the object of his attentions, respect, and affection. His appearance seemed to change as his ordinary features took on a glow and attractiveness that I was amazed I hadn't noticed before. His eyes especially became a focal point of my attention. Warmth and wisdom seemed to flow forth, bathing me in a comfort, love, and security I could only imagine I once felt as an infant in my mother's arms.

Thus began a three-year odyssey of adventure, possession, and hell for me and my children. Fred entered our lives and, in short order, took over. Once I accepted his apparent superiority over me and the supposed giftedness of his spiritual attainments, we were no longer equal. I became his handmaiden, lover, and partner in numerous investments and businesses. I didn't realize it at the time, but it was *my* expertise and experience that produced the successful outcomes, though Fred took all the credit.

At home, the children began to change immediately. Fred was a stern disciplinarian and insisted upon proper manners and instant obedience. Jessica Kay, however, turned sullen and resentful, which I interpreted as jealousy and laziness. (Only later did I learn of his sexual abuse of her.) At his insistence, I depended on Fred to turn around her misbehavior. As a therapist and expert on child behavior, he assured me there was no one better prepared to help her. I was grateful and relieved.

In the next few months, Fred began to change. Confidence and bravado turned to anxiety attacks and clinging dependency. I was no longer allowed to leave his sight. Our businesses and investments depended on my expertise and constant oversight, but his demands for my time and attention led to their ultimate downfall. His drinking increased and he had difficulty getting out of bed in the morning or going to the office. He wouldn't allow me to leave his side. Any resourcefulness, questioning, or attempts at independence on my part provoked his sudden and frightening rages. His ability to shatter me with his anger, cruelty, and cleverness with words incapacitated me. The children began spending more time with their birth father, who was kept in the dark about the true nature of our household. We were each sworn to secrecy, separately, by Fred.

We moved to Georgia in the third year of our relationship. My love for him was constantly tested in cruel and unusual ways. He would not tolerate anyone or anything that took me away from him or could be construed as any kind of threat. Before we moved, Fred made me give the children back to their father, Keith, as some sort of test—but then unexpectedly relented. I was so grateful! He could still be extremely generous, loving, and kind—especially after an episode of rage. I had gotten used to the wild roller-coaster rides of emotion. I was completely exhausted, numb, and dependent on his goodwill. I hoped the move would mean an improvement in our relationship.

We bought a house. Actually, I bought a house, with only a small contribution from him, which was the pattern in all our investments. I supplied the cash; he supplied the "brains" and inspiration. Our lives went downhill from there. I had given up a good career, many friends, and the trust of my children to follow this selfish, manipulative, and exploitative individual in the hopes of a better life and a loving relationship. My god had more than clay feet. His cruelty and pettiness increased daily. My children had become strangers to me, and I to them. Somehow I found the strength and courage to leave him after five months in Georgia. I bought my way out with money, giving him a huge sum for his share of the house.

The children and I entered therapy immediately as a first step in our recovery. We were shell-shocked, frightened, and confused, and the initial reaction of our therapist was that we looked like we had just come out of a cult. I hid from Fred for several months after leaving him, as he searched for us and begged me to take him back. When Jessica Kay felt safe enough to reveal Fred's sexual abuse of her, I was finally able to sever all emotional ties to him and see him for who he really was. I know him now as vengeful, spiteful, and sadistic. And I know that he is not superhuman. He cannot know my location by "thought waves," and he cannot hurt me. Rather, he is quite cowardly, is anxiety-ridden, and has deep feelings of inadequacy and fear. I don't hate or fear him anymore, but think of him as a pathetic and weak human being.

Five years after leaving Fred, I am successful in my career, involved in a healthy relationship with a truly kind and loving man, and my relationship with my children is slowly healing and growing stronger.(21)

CHAPTER TWO

SEDUCTION AND RECRUITMENT

Examining the techniques of persuasion and control used by your group is an important step in the healing process. Understanding the particulars of your situation—the seduction or recruitment process, specific thought-reform techniques, and methods of persuasion and control—will be key to undoing the aftereffects.

Janet Joyce's description of her recruitment and initiation into a psychotherapy/political cult provides a thoughtful depiction of how a person gets attracted to, deceived by, and drawn into a cult.

Janet's Story

The year was 1970. I had graduated from college the year before, a member of the Pioneer Class of the University of California at Santa Cruz. After spending a year working at various unchallenging jobs such as delivering newspapers and answering telephones, I decided it was time to get on with my life. I had majored in psychology and graduated with honors, based on my work organizing a volunteer program in which Santa Cruz students worked on the wards at Agnews State Hospital. I had also spent two summers working at a camp for state hospital patients in Connecticut. I decided to move back east to look for a job in activity or recreation therapy. I had contacts there and was looking forward to starting my career.

Soon after arriving in New Jersey, in an interview with the personnel director of a newly-funded community mental health center, I was able to create a position for myself as activity therapist on the psychiatric ward of the local city hospital. I started my job and began interviewing people to work with me in the new activities program. I hired several people and soon became friends with my coworkers. What I didn't know at the time was that the personnel director and most of the people I hired were part of a group known to outsiders as the Sullivanians.

My first real introduction to the group came several months later, in the summer of 1971. I mentioned to a friend at work that I thought I could use some counseling to help me do a better job. I was new at being a boss and wanted some help in how to be a friendly and compassionate boss while still providing structure and guidance to a developing program. My friend offered to give me her therapist's name, saying she was sure I would like her. I set up a consultation with this therapist in New York City and was soon seeing her three times a week. The cost per session was low, which meant I could afford to see her often; the philosophy of the therapy seemed sound to me. My therapist was well aware of problems I saw in American society and was supportive of my desires to make changes in the world—to make the world a better place for all to live, not just the rich.

Soon I was being invited to parties in New York—wild parties where people danced and talked a lot and seemed to have a lot of fun. I was asked for dates: dinner dates, play dates, bicycling dates, sleepovers. Suddenly I had a very active social life in New York. My therapist suggested I move into the city to be closer to my new friends. There was a bulletin board in the office waiting room with signs posted by people looking for roommates. Soon I had moved into a household connected to the group, although I was not fully aware of this or what it meant. I knew that it was a social scene—people to hang out with, people with similar political views (somewhat radical but not quite ready to be revolutionaries), people who wanted to make changes in the world and who were experimenting with new ways of living. I had long been interested in communal living and had read a lot about various utopian experiments. Several years earlier my brother had moved into a communal group in California, and he and his family seemed to be very happy in that situation. I was ready to try something new, and this seemed right.

Once I moved to New York, I was spending all my time with people who were in therapy either with my therapist or others belonging to the group. I would talk with my roommates and dates about my therapy sessions and would hear about theirs. My therapist often asked me about my childhood and encouraged me to talk about events that were painful. She said that it sounded like my parents didn't really want me or at best were simply unable to love me because their parents hadn't been able to love them. She said she thought it would be best for my therapy if I didn't see my parents for a while—just until I could understand my history better. She encouraged me to tell my personal history to my friends and to listen to theirs. My painful childhood memories were always validated, while the happy ones were disregarded. I became convinced that I had had a miserable childhood and it seemed like my new friends were the only ones who could understand since their family lives had been as miserable as mine.

I came to depend on my therapist for all major life decisions. After all, my friends always wanted to know "what my therapist thought" about any major change I was thinking about. Sometimes my therapist would tell me what she thought I should do even if I didn't ask. She seemed to know me so well and was interested in helping me make the best decisions so that I could be happy and productive. If I thought her advice was wrong for me I would be told by my friends and roommates that I should trust my therapist—that I wasn't far enough along in my therapy to understand what was best for me. It wasn't until many years later—after I left the group—that I understood that the decisions I was advised to make were dictated by the leader of the group, and were designed to keep members dependent on the group.

Saul, the leader and founder, trained and supervised all the therapists in the group. In that way he exercised great control over each person's life. Therapists who did not obey Saul's orders would be threatened with expulsion from the group and thus the instantaneous loss of their livelihood. Patients who did not obey would also be threatened with expulsion, which meant loss of friends, job, and emotional support. We were told that Saul had our best interests at heart, that we should be honored that he was thinking about us and advising us.

Over the years the group got much tighter. Saul considered himself not only a genius in the field of psychotherapy but also a brilliant political thinker. We started a political theater company to educate the public about the dangers of nuclear war, nuclear power, and the military-industrial complex. We monitored nuclear power plants in the area, listened to news reports constantly so that we could evacuate in case of any emergency, and maintained a fleet of buses for evacuation. When we became aware of the danger of AIDS we stopped eating in restaurants, and sterilized telephones, keyboards, even our dogs' paws after they had walked on city streets. The first line of a book written by Saul is "The world is a dangerous place," and the longer the group existed under his control the more we all acted like this was true. The only safe place seemed to be in the group.(1)

Janet remained a member of the Sullivanians for 17 years before a life-threatening illness shifted her perspective and caused her to question the quality of life the cult was providing. Her account of leaving the group and the period afterward can be found in Part Three.

Who Joins and Why?

Is there a certain type of person who is more likely to join a cult? No. Individual vulnerability factors matter much more than personality type. "Everyone is influenced and persuaded daily in various ways," writes Margaret Singer, "but the vulnerability to influence varies. The ability to fend off persuaders is reduced when one is rushed, stressed, uncertain, lonely, indifferent, uninformed, distracted, or fatigued.... Also affecting vulnerability are the status and power of the persuader.... No one type of person is prone to become involved with cults. About two-thirds of those studied have been normal young persons induced to join groups in periods of personal crisis, [such as] broken romance or failures to get the job or college of their choice. Vulnerable, the young person affiliates with a cult offering promises of unconditional love, new mental powers, and social utopia. Since modern cults are persistent and often deceptive in their recruiting, many prospective group members have no accurate knowledge of the cult and almost no understanding of what eventually will be expected of them as long-term members."(2)

With the flourishing of cults that has taken place in recent years, there have been some changes in the recruitment done by the cults that are active. In the 1970s and early 1980s, primarily young people, either in college or some other life transition, joined cults. At that time cults were extremely active—and they still are—on college campuses and in places where young people could be found. Today, however, increasing numbers of older persons also join cults. Still, no single personality profile characterizes cult members.(3)

Most experts agree, though, that whether the cult joiner is young or old, there are certain predisposing factors. These include:

- dependency (the desire to belong, lack of self-confidence)

- unassertiveness (inability to say no or express criticism or doubt)

- gullibility (impaired capacity to question critically what one is told, observes, thinks, etc.)

- low tolerance for ambiguity (need for absolute answers, impatience to obtain answers)

- cultural disillusionment (alienation, dissatisfaction with the status quo)

- naive idealism

- desire for spiritual meaning

- susceptibility to trancelike states (in some cases, perhaps, because of prior hallucinogenic drug experiences)

- ignorance of the how groups can manipulate individuals(4)

A rather wide range of human susceptibility emerges when we combine this list of predisposing factors with Dr. Singer's potential vulnerability points mentioned above. The stereotype is that it is the young person worried about leaving college or uncertain about "facing life" who is recruited. The reality is that anyone, at any age, who may be in a life crisis or transition can get sucked in. New in town, lost a job, recently divorced, someone close just died, need a career change, feel a little blue? The unstable feelings experienced at such times make a person vulnerable, whether that person is 20, 30, 40, or 70 years old. If the vulnerable person happens to cross paths with a cult recruiter who represents even a mildly interesting group or belief, then that recruiter stands a good chance of making his mark.

"Conversion to cults is not truly a matter of choice. Vulnerabilities do not merely 'lead' individuals to a particular group. The group manipulates these vulnerabilities and deceives prospects in order to persuade them to join and, ultimately, renounce their old lives," writes psychologist Michael Langone, one of the nation's leading cult researchers.(5)

While we are at it, let's shatter another myth: people who join cults are *not* stupid, weird, crazy, or neurotic. Most cult members are of above-average intelligence, well-adjusted, adaptable, and perhaps a bit idealistic. In relatively few cases does the person have a history of a preexisting mental disorder.(6)

So we see that anyone is capable of being recruited (or seduced) into a cult if the personal and situational circumstances are right. Currently there are so many cults formed around so many different types of beliefs that it is impossible for a person to truthfully claim that she or he would *never* be vulnerable to a cult's appeal. Cult recruitment is not mysterious. It is as simple and commonplace as the seduction process used by lovers and advertisers. However, depending on the degree of deception and manipulation used by the cult, the resultant attachments can be even more powerful.

Cult Recruitment

Social psychologist Robert Cialdini outlines six principles generally used in the process of influencing another person. If we consider cult recruitment an example of *undue* influence, then Cialdini's principles help us better understand the successful use of these techniques by cults.

Each of Cialdini's principles describes tendencies of human behavior that can be used to elicit compliance, as explained below:

Reciprocation, or the act of give and take, creates a sense of obligation. In cults, personal disclosure is often made reciprocal; that is, you are expected to reveal things about yourself and others to the group, just as others reveal to you. This exchange makes you feel beholden to the group; the reciprocity creates a social bond wherein you say yes to things you wouldn't ordinarily say yes to.

Consistency in actions brings about commitment. Once you give (or give in), you'll give (or give in) again. This sets the stage for greater compliance. Actions that are public—that is, performed in front of others, owned, and supposedly uncoerced—tend to reinforce the conditions necessary for lasting commitment. Hence, the value of "testifying" or group self-criticism sessions.

Authority more or less guarantees credibility. If an expert says it, it must be true. This logic causes people to stop thinking and simply react. In cults, the leader is all-knowing, speaking the Ultimate Truth.

Liking breeds friendship. Initially, cults make you feel wanted; in this way, you become a part of something. There is a strong sense of belonging.

Scarcity induces competition. You value what is rare, not easily available; its real worth is not necessarily an issue. Cults make themselves valuable by saying that their way is the *only* way. By saying they have exclusive information, cult leaders become all the more persuasive.

Consensus provides social validation, or social proof. In general, people follow the lead of others, especially similar others. "Look around you—a lot of people are doing what we are asking you to do," says the cult leadership. This is combined with systematically cutting you off from prior sources of information, so that your information only comes from similar others saying the same thing.(7)

Cialdini regards cults as a long-term influence situation. When these influence principles are applied in a controlled setting, he says, the consequences are extreme. In a keynote speech at the 1992 conference of the Cult Awareness Network, Cialdini stressed that we are all susceptible to these influence principles. "We can be fooled, but we are not fools. We can be duped, but we are not dupes," he said. These are good words to remember because they help get rid of the shame so many former cult members feel at having gotten involved in the first place.

Psychology professors Philip Zimbardo and Michael Leippe describe the unfolding of a typical recruitment as follows:

1. Cult recruitment builds an initially small commitment into pro-gressively bigger commitments (come to dinner, come for the weekend, stay for the week, give us your money).

2. Cults offer repeated persuasive arguments with straightforward solutions to vexing personal problems.

3. Cults sway opinions through the power of group dynamics—both the numbers and personal attractiveness of all those agreeing and agreeable members.

4. Cults deny recruits the opportunity to counterargue by keeping the recruit busily occupied with information and activities (and never alone).

5. Cults offer some positive reinforcements (such as smiles, good food, that special brand of attention that makes one feel good).(8)

The following description of an introductory training weekend illus-trates the more intense version of indoctrination:

On the surface it seems simple enough: come to a workshop, learn about some new ideas, try them out; if you don't like it, leave. But a lot more than that is happening. When a person is isolated, he is not in a good position to discover that he is being deceived. Deception and iso-lation reinforce each other. It begins with physical or geographic isola-tion. You can leave the camp in one of two ways. You can wait until the end of the weekend to take the bus home, or you can try to hitch a ride and hope that the right person will pick you up and drive you back to the city . . . .

Perhaps most important, you are isolated from your own mind. How can that happen? If your day starts at seven o'clock and ends at eleven-thirty or twelve, and is extremely active and filled with group events, it becomes difficult to turn inward and reflect. By the end of the day when your head hits the pillow, you just do not have the energy to stay awake . . . . In the workshops there is virtually no privacy. Some members actually accompany others to the bathroom and wait outside the stall. . . . You are intensely pressured to identify with the group. The whole is much more important than the individual. . . . You are put in the position of competing with the interests of the whole, which generates guilt. . . .

The workshop lectures are an emotional roller coaster and an intellectual barrage. To deal adequately with the concepts explored in a three-day workshop would take months and months, if not years and years. . . . By the end of the workshop, you have been through an intense period of no reflection, constant activity, no privacy, immense pressure toward identification with the group, suspicion of your desires to be separate from the group, roller-coaster emotions, and a barrage of ideas that have left you confused and unsure of yourself.(9)

These studies and examples show that certain accepted social interactions can be part of the bag of tricks used by con men and cult leaders to manipulate and control. For example, the cult recruiter knows that people will respond to certain buzzwords, such as *love, peace, brotherhood*. He or she explains to the recruit that these idealized goals can be attained if the recruit behaves "properly." The desired behavioral change is accomplished in small incremental steps.

Other studies show that recruitment and conversion techniques are similar to hypnotic techniques used in clinical situations. In the cult environment, however, this manipulation has a dual purpose: (a) to install deep hypnotic suggestions which are meant to change behavior and patterns of thinking, and (b) to maintain control of the individual. Clinical psychologist Jesse Miller believes that "using trance induction as a model for all behavioral influence helps to make the transformations effected by cultic groups seem less mysterious."(10) Miller's presentation, summarized here, highlights the similarities between the procedures used in cults and those used in hypnosis.

In trance induction the hypnotist serves as a "biofeedback machine," commenting on the subject's every action: your eyelids are getting heavy; you are seated in the chair; I am seated next to you; there is a noise in the hallway. Cult recruiters use similar tactics in their mirroring of the interests and attitudes of the recruit. By striking a responsive chord, the recruiter, like the hypnotist, paces the subject from a psychological beginning point, slowly and carefully leading the person to the next stage. If successful, the recruiter will now be able to define the recruit's reality.

The recruiter establishes an environment (at least initially) in which the recruit is made to feel special, loved, among newfound friends, belonging to something unique. While the recruit is in this susceptible state, verbal and nonverbal messages are indirectly conveyed about proper behavior and thinking patterns. "It cannot be stated strongly enough," writes Miller, "that the process of pacing and leading recruits is not only part of the initial indoctrination but is also—along with elaborate reinforcement schedules and the merciless manipulation of guilt and humiliation—an ongoing feature of cult membership."(11)

Beginning with the recruitment process and throughout the early stages of membership, cults keep careful watch over each individual's conversion, leading the person—sometimes painstakingly—to increasingly deeper levels of commitment. Using such techniques, cults can exert significant control over the individual, ultimately controlling a person's mental activities, even while she or he is physically away from the group.

Informed Consent

In the medical profession, there are contracts that assure "fully informed consent." That is, if a doctor fails to inform his patient about the risks and side effects of a treatment, the patient is entitled to legal recourse. Would that the same rules applied to cult members!

We have drawn up a "contract" for cult membership, based on one developed by psychotherapist Jennie Sharma for use with clients who are having relationship difficulties. Ask yourself whether you gave informed consent at the time of your recruitment, or whether you would have joined had you known all the terms of the contract below.

Contract for Membership in a Cultic Group or Relationship

I,_____, hereby agree to join _____.

I understand that my life will change in the following ways. I know what I am getting into and agree to all the following conditions:

1. My good feelings about who I am will stem from being liked by other group members and/or my leader, and from receiving approval from the group/leader.

2. My total mental attention will focus on solving the group's/leader's problems and making sure there are no conflicts.

3. My mental attention will be focused on pleasing and protecting the group/leader.

4. My self-esteem will be bolstered by solving group problems and relieving the leader's pain.

5. My own hobbies and interests will gladly be put aside. My time will be spent however the group/leader wants.

6. My clothing and personal appearance will be dictated by the desires of the group/leader.

7. I do not need to be sure of how I feel. I will only be focused on what the group/leader feels.

8. I will ignore my own needs and wants. The needs and wants of the group/leader are all that is important.

9. The dreams I have for the future will be linked to the group/leader.

10. My fear of rejection will determine what I say or do.

11. My fear of the group's/leader's anger will determine what I say or do.

12. I will use giving as a way of feeling safe with the group/leader.

13. My social circle will diminish or disappear as I involve myself with the group/leader.

14. I will give up my family as I involve myself with the group/leader.

15. The group's/leader's values will become my values.

16. I will cherish the group's/leader's opinions and ways of doing things more than my own.

17. The quality of my life will be in relation to the quality of group life, not the quality of life of the leader.

18. Everything that is right and good is due to the group's belief, the leader, or the teachings.

19. Everything that is or goes wrong is due to me.(12)

20. In addition, I waive the following rights:
   — to leave at any time
   — to maintain contact with the outside world
   — to have an education and career of my choice
   — to have reasonable health care
   — to have a say in my own and my family's discipline
   — to have control over my body, including choices related to sex, marriage, and procreation
   — to expect honesty in dealings with authority figures in the group
   — to have any complaints heard and dealt with fairly
   — to be supported and cared for in my old age in gratitude for my years of service(13)

CHAPTER THREE

UNDERSTANDING
THOUGHT REFORM

In this chapter we examine thought reform, the conversion process, and how cults change people. First, we should note that there are crucial differences between the systematic implementation of a cult thought-reform program and the kind of social conditioning used by parents and social institutions. As a rule, parents, schools, churches, and other reputable organizations do *not* use deception or unethically manipulative techniques in their teaching or training methods.

In most cases the purpose of social conditioning is to promote and encourage a child to become an autonomous adult, or to train and educate a person to function fully as a responsible adult in a particular organization or society such as the Marines or a monastic order. Cults, by contrast, use manipulation, deception, and exploitative persuasion and control to induce dependency, compliance, rigid obedience, stunted thinking, and childlike behavior in their members.

When we use the term *cult conversion*, we refer to the psychological and personality changes that a person undergoes as a result of being subjected to thought-reform and personality techniques, or a deliberate program of exploitative persuasion and behavior control. The effects of cult conversion are often disturbingly apparent to a cult member's family and friends, who may observe radical changes in the personality and behavior of their loved one. After recruitment into a cult or cultic relationship, people tend to withdraw, hold new beliefs and values, and behave in a manner quite different from, if not exactly the opposite of, their lifelong patterns.

Thought Reform, Mind Control, Brainwashing—Which Is It? What Is It?

Many former cult members selectively deny aspects of their cult experience. Some become angry and resistant at the mention of mind control, thought reform, or brainwashing, thinking that these things could not possibly have been done to them. It is very threatening to a person's sense of self to contemplate having been controlled or taken over. The terms themselves—mind control, thought reform—sound harsh and unreal. Yet only by confronting the reality of psychological manipulation can ex-cult members overcome its effects.

Deceptive psychological and social manipulation are part and parcel of the cult experience. Over the years various labels have been used to describe this systematic process. Robert Jay Lifton first used the term *thought reform* in the 1950s to describe the behavioral change processes he observed and studied in students at revolutionary universities in Communist China and in prisoners of war during the Korean War.(1) Like many others in this field we dislike the term *brainwashing* because it is a buzzword, often associated with Communism or torture. A prison cell or a torture chamber is a far cry from the subtlety and sophistication of the techniques of manipulation and control found in today's cults. Therefore, we prefer the terms *thought reform* and *mind control*, and use them interchangeably throughout this book.

Chapter 22 of Lifton's classic work, *Thought Reform and the Psychology of Totalism*, remains one of the most helpful resources for those coming out of a cult environment. Lifton outlines the psychological techniques used to impose what he calls a state of "ideological totalism." He describes this as a process of the coming together of the individual self and certain ideas, or the melding of the individual with a particular set of beliefs. Through his research Lifton came to the conclusion that within each person there is a tendency toward "all-or-nothing emotional alignment." The process of combining this tendency with an all-or-nothing ideology (usually about humankind and its relationship to the world) results in totalism. It is a rather surefire formula: immoderate individual character traits plus an immoderate ideology equals totalism—a world of extremes. And, writes Lifton, "where totalism exists, a religion, a political movement, or even a scientific organization becomes little more than an exclusive cult."(2)

Lifton identified eight "psychological themes" within a thought-reform environment which are now widely used as the criteria for evaluating whether or not a particular group meets the requirements. The more these psychological themes are present, the more restrictive the cult and the more effective the thought-reform program.

Each of Lifton's themes requires central control and sets off a predictable cycle: (a) the theme sets the stage, (b) the rationale for the theme is based on an absolute belief or philosophy, and (c) because of the extreme belief system, a person within this setting has a conflicting and polarized reaction, and is forced to make a choice. Enveloped in a totalistic environment, most individuals will make totalistic choices. The outcome of this psychological interplay is "thought reform"—that is, the person is changed.(3) Lifton's eight themes are set out below.

1. Milieu control, or the control of all communication and information, which includes the individual's communication with himself. This sets up what Lifton calls "personal closure," meaning that the person no longer has to carry on inner struggles about what is true or real. Essentially, this prevents any time being spent on doubts.

2. Mystical manipulation, or the claim of authority (divine, supernatural, or otherwise), which allows for the rationale that the ends justify the means since the "end" is directed by a higher purpose. Certain experiences are orchestrated to make it seem that they occur spontaneously. The person is required to subordinate himself to the group or cause and stops all questioning—for who can question "higher purpose"? Self-expression and independent action wither away.

3. Demand for purity, which is essentially a black-and-white worldview with the leader as the ultimate moral arbiter. This creates a world of guilt and shame, where punishment and humiliation are expected. It also sets up an environment of spying and reporting on one another. Through submission to the powerful lever of guilt, the individual loses his or her own moral sense.

4. The cult of confession, which is an act of surrender, of total exposure. The individual is now owned by the group. The person no longer has a sense of balance between worth and humility, and there is a loss of boundaries between what is secret (known only to the inner self) and what is known by the group.

5. The "sacred science," whereby the group's doctrine is seen as the Ultimate Truth. Here no questions are allowed. This reinforces personal closure and inhibits individual thought, creative self-expression, and personal development. Experience can only be perceived through the filter of the dogmatic belief.

6. Loading the language, or use of jargon internal to—and only understandable by—the group. Constricting language constricts the person. Capacities for thinking and feeling are significantly reduced. Imagination is no longer a part of one's actual life experiences; the mind atrophies from disuse.

7. Doctrine over person, which is denial of self and any perception other than the group's. There is no longer such a thing as personal reality. The past—society's and the individual's—is altered to fit the needs of the doctrine. Thus the individual is remolded, the cult persona emerges, and the person's sense of integrity is lost.

8. Dispensing of existence, whereby the group is the ultimate arbiter and all nonbelievers are considered "evil" or nonpeople. If nonpeople cannot be recruited they can be punished, even killed. This creates an "us-versus-them" mentality and breeds fear in the individual, who sees that one's own life depends on a willingness to obey. Here is found the merger of the individual with the belief.

Thought-reform techniques have been refined over the years, and this historical process was described in a seminal article by Margaret Singer and sociologist Richard Ofshe.(4) They stressed the important distinctions between changing a person's *central* versus *peripheral* elements of self. We summarize their notable contribution here, for it lends great insight into the success, impact, and aftereffects of today's thought-reform programs.

In present-day thought-reform programs, there is an attack on the core self, the person's central self-image. This is in contrast to the earlier versions (studied in the 1950s) which attacked a person's political and social views (or "peripheral" elements). Attacking the inner person, the self, makes the person feel defective at his or her very core. In these new groups, "Alter the self or perish" is the motto. The purpose of this attack is to get the person to identify with and merge with the group or leader. The effect is that members become extremely anxious about self-worth and, at times, about their very existence. In such an environment it is easy to bring on feelings of personal disintegration.

Threatened central elements are those that have developed over a person's lifetime—in other words, each person's "me," which has been shaped since childhood. In life, a person learns to react to and cope with a variety of emotions, relationships, and events. Through this process a person develops psychological defense mechanisms which she or he continues to use in perceiving and interpreting reality, and in dealing with life's interactions. A systematic attack on the person's central self, however, tears apart the inner equilibrium and perception of reality. For some, the "easiest way to reconstitute the self and obtain a new equilibrium is to 'identify with the aggressor' and accept the ideology of the authority figure who has reduced the person to a state of profound confusion. In effect, the new ideology (psychological theory, spiritual system, etc.) functions as a defense mechanism . . . and protects the individual from having to further directly inspect emotions from the past which are overwhelming."(5)

Recognizing this process of stripping a person's psychological stability and defense mechanisms becomes crucial to understanding why some cults are able to cause such a rapid and dramatic acceptance of their ideology, as well as why membership in cults may produce psychological difficulties and other adjustment problems. We see, then, that the goal of a thought-reform program is to change a human being at the very core so that she or he will believe in a certain ideology, doctrine, or leader—and behave in a certain way. Once that is accomplished, compliance or obedience on the part of the group member or intimate partner is usually guaranteed.

Conditions for a Thought-Reform Program

In what kind of environment can someone implement psychological manipulations such as those just described? The most concise and useful outline of the conditions necessary to carry out a thought-reform program come from Margaret Singer:

1. Controlling an individual's social and psychological environment, especially the person's time.

2. Placing an individual in a position of powerlessness within a high-control authoritarian system.

3. Relying usually on a closed system of logic, which permits no feedback and refuses to be modified except by executive order.

4. Relying on unsophistication of the person being manipulated [that is, the person is unaware of the process], and he or she is pressed to adapt to the environment in increments that are sufficiently minor so that the person does not notice changes.

5. Eroding the confidence of a person's perceptions.

6. Manipulating a system of rewards, punishments, and experiences to promote new learning or inhibit undesired previous behavior. Punishments usually are social ones, for example, shunning, social isolation, and humiliation (which are more effective in producing wanted behavior than beatings and death threats, although these do occur).(6)

There is an important distinction to be made between a thought-reform program and a cult. *Cult* refers to the particular power structure of a group (or one-on-one relationship). A cult is usually started by a self-appointed leader who claims to have some special insight or knowledge and who says he will share this special knowledge with you if you follow him and turn your decision-making powers over to him. A *thought-reform program* is what most cults use to achieve the desired behavioral changes in their followers. The use of a thought-reform program does not necessarily mean that the overall context is a cult, but almost all cults employ some type of thought-reform program to ensure control over their members.

Methods used by cults to create conditions conducive to thought reform include:

- induced dissociation and other altered states (through speaking in tongues, chanting, trance induction via repeated affirmations, extended periods of meditation, lengthy denunciation sessions, public trials, "hot seat" criticisms focusing on one individual, sexual abuse, torture, etc.)

- control of information going in and out of the group environment

- isolation from family and friends

- control of members' financial resources

- sleep and food deprivation

- peer and leadership pressure

- extensive indoctrination sessions (through Bible lessons, political training, sales training, self-awareness lessons)

- rigid security regulations and daily rules

Not all groups use all of these techniques. A psychotherapy cult, for example, may be quite efficient at thought reform using only a few of the above coupled with the charm of a manipulative therapist. Some cults may have no need to utilize isolation, inadequate diet, or fatigue to exert control over their members. The point is that most cult leaders have at their command, and consciously use, a selection of thought-reform techniques which they employ as needed to control their followers.

After exposure to the type of undue influence just described, "the person appears to be a mentally and emotionally constricted version of his former self."(7) Is it any wonder, then, that families and friends express concern when a loved one joins a cult and begins to exhibit striking personality and behavioral changes? Or is it a wonder that a person coming out of such an environment should require a period of healing?

A Word about Dissociation

The word *dissociation* appears frequently in this book because *induced dissociation* is such a commonly used cult technique and *involuntary dissociation* is a frequently experienced postcult aftereffect. Through induced dissociation cults are able to control their members' thoughts and behaviors. After leaving a cult many people may find that they involuntarily slip into or are "triggered" into a dissociated state because of cult-related memories or habits (more on this in Chapters 6 and 7).

Since the 1890s, beginning with work done by Pierre Janet and Sigmund Freud, it has been recognized that unbearable emotional reactions to traumatic events can produce an altered state or dissociation. Dissociation is an "abnormal state, set apart from ordinary consciousness," wherein the normal connections of memory, knowledge, and emotion are severed. "If overwhelmed by terror and helplessness, a person's perceptions become inaccurate and pervaded with terror, the coordinative functions of judgment and discrimination fail . . . the sense organs may even cease to function . . . . The aggressive impulses become disorganized and unrelated to the situation in hand."(8)

Lifton refers to dissociation as "psychic numbing," or a sequestering of a portion of the self. As a form of adaptation, this mental phenomenon can help explain, for example, how Nazi doctors were able to suppress feeling in relation to their participation in murder.(9) Dissociation, then, is a kind of fragmentation of the self, sometimes referred to as "splitting" and considered an "altered state of consciousness." These altered states may come about through purposeful trance induction, such as hypnosis, or be a response to trauma. This state can be brought about through techniques such as chanting or meditating or achieved through a combination of long hours of lecture or criticism sessions, fatigue, and fear.

In some cults, dissociation is the stated goal (for example, it may be likened to approaching the godhead). In others, dissociating is a means of survival, otherwise the cult world in which one lives would be impossible to bear. Whichever it is, a person in a dissociated state is not functioning at full capacity and is highly suggestible and compliant, thereby furthering the cult's ability to control.

Cult Conversion—
Deception, Dependency, and Dread

The researchers who first studied the use of thought reform by the Chinese Communists witnessed a drastic conversion of belief, which they determined to be the result of what they called the "DDD syndrome"—debility, dependency, and dread.(10) Robert Lifton and other researchers later demonstrated that debility, or actual physical coercion, was not a necessary ingredient for conversion. More recently Michael Langone proposed a modified DDD syndrome used in cult conversion: deception, dependency, dread.(11)

Deception

Modern-day cults rely on subtle means of persuasion. The hallmark of a cult is its use of deception in the recruitment process and throughout membership. Rarely are the true purpose, beliefs, and ultimate goals of the group spelled out. Cults use meditation classes, computer schools, health clinics, telemarketing programs, publishing enterprises, financial appeals, business seminars, real estate ventures, Bible study groups, political study groups, and campus activity groups as front organizations to lure potential new members into the recruitment web.

Because cults appeal to the normal desires of ordinary people, cult recruitment may be viewed as a kind of courtship. The prospective devotee is wooed with the promise of reward, be it personal fulfillment, special knowledge, spiritual growth, political satisfaction, religious salvation, lifelong companionship, riches, power—whatever is most dear to that person at the time. This connection to a person's innermost desire is the recruitment "hook." In a way, the cult leader becomes like a genie holding out the promise of wish fulfillment. Most often, the deception takes root during this initial phase of recruitment.

Dependency

The recruitment stage and the early days of membership are often called the "honeymoon phase." Frequently, as a teaser, one of the recruit's wishes may be granted. Once such a favor is granted, the potential recruit is made to feel even more indebted to the group, wishing to return the favor (an example of Cialdini's "reciprocity").

Meanwhile, recruits and new members are encouraged to share or confess their deepest secrets, weaknesses, and fears, opening themselves up as the cult leadership probes for further knowledge. Prospective disciples are carefully paced throughout the conversion process. They are fed just enough information to maintain their interest; they are tricked and psychologically coerced (usually via guilt or fear) into making further commitments to the group or relationship; they are never pushed so far as to cause undue discomfort or outright suspicion.

To cultivate dependency, long-term members model preferred group behavior that brings reward, status, and acceptance. This provides social proof of the efficacy, strengths, and advantages of the new belief system. The superiority of the group is firmly established through the combination of peer pressure and constant reminders of the new member's weaknesses and vulnerabilities. The new member begins to rely on the beliefs of the group or leader for his or her future well-being. Having been successful in capturing the interest of the recruit, the group can now lead the person into desired frames of thought and types of behavior that meet the cult's needs and goals.

At this point psychological coercion also increases, with the intensified use of meditation, chanting, long prayer sessions, hypnosis, sleep deprivation, and other mind-altering techniques of manipulation and control. At the same time indoctrination into the "sacred science" continues with long study sessions, lectures, and seminars. Encouraged to declare formal allegiance to the group or "path" while becoming increasingly isolated from former ways of thinking, the new member now accepts the group's definition of what is right and wrong, good and bad, and converts to the cause.

The cult now puts forth even higher expectations and demands. The new member's weaknesses and failures are emphasized and criticized more and more, with little focus on strengths. Nothing short of total dedication is accepted. The group or leader is presented as always right. Doubts and dissent are actively discouraged, if not punished.

To suppress the recruit's "evil" or precult personality, increased participation in group activities and even more practice of mind-altering techniques are actively promoted by the group. Either because it is forbidden by the group or because it is an act of self-protection, access to outside information is limited and the new member is discouraged from maintaining precult contacts, especially with family. Such contact might point up the conflicts between new and old beliefs and upset the still delicate underpinning necessary to secure adherence to the group.

Dread

Gradually the cult insinuates a feeling of dread in the recruit's mind, which further isolates the members and prevents defections from the group. This is accomplished by increasing dependency on the group through escalated demands, intensified criticism and humiliation, and, in some cults, subtle or overt threats of punishment which may be physical, spiritual, emotional, or sexual. Even infants and children may be held responsible for the smallest infractions, forced to conform to group demands despite their age. Threats of excommunication, shunning, and abandonment by the group become powerful forces of control once members become fully dependent on the group and alienated from their former support network. If a person is completely estranged from the rest of the world, staying put appears the only option. Members come to dread losing what they consider to be the group's psychological support, regardless of how controlling or debilitating that support may be in reality.

Another technique used to invoke dread is the induction of phobias. Cults convey phobic messages, for example: "If you leave, you are doomed to countless cycles of incarnation." "You will go crazy or die if you leave the group." "You will be ruined and never find a way to survive." "You are doomed to failure or terrible accidents if you do not obey." "If you leave this church, you are leaving God." Almost all groups use this sort of phobia induction as a means of control and domination.

The Double Bind

In addition to the techniques described above, the double bind may be used to enhance the effectiveness of the thought-reform program. This emotional cul-de-sac is defined as a "psychological dilemma in which a usually dependent person receives conflicting interpersonal communication from a single source or *faces disparagement no matter what his response to a situation*" [emphasis ours].(12) It imparts a message of hopelessness: you're damned if you do and damned if you don't.

Cult manipulations are typically designed to elicit compliance. They demand and have an answer. The double bind, however, has no answer. The person is criticized no matter what he or she does. *Jackson's* story provides an example:

Jackson was in a left-wing political cult that taught its members "to take initiative within the bounds of discipline," which was supposed to mean that members were to apply all their creativity and intelligence to whatever situation they were in without violating the group's strict norms and policies. This rule allowed the leadership to criticize members all the time because just about any independent behavior could be deemed "outside" the bounds of the discipline, while at the same time to not act in any given situation could be criticized as "wimpishness, cowardice, or passivity."

While at a demonstration in front of City Hall protesting a cut in city workers' wages, Jackson saw the mayor approaching. Thinking himself a brave militant ready to defend his organization's stand, Jackson walked directly up to the mayor and asked him what he was going to do about the wage cuts. When this action was reported to the cult leader, she blew up and ordered Jackson to be harshly criticized for breaking discipline, saying that Jackson was self-centered, only promoting himself and trying to grab power. One week later Jackson was sent to another picket line, where a union boss was expected to show up. The leader told Jackson that he better be prepared to confront the union boss. "What about?" Jackson asked, trembling. "You know damn well what about!" exclaimed his leader.

Double binds magnify dependence by injecting an additional element of unpredictability into cult members' relationships to their leadership. Consequently, members can never become too comfortable. Fear prevents them from challenging those on whom they have become dependent. When this tactic is successful, members are unable to move out of a state of dependence. The mere fact of living creates insecurity and induces fear and withdrawal.

When this type of manipulation (a blatant power trip) is used, cult members spend most of their time feeling as though they are walking on eggs, knowing that they must act—and yet to act may bring rebuke, punishment, or worse.

The Cult "Pseudopersonality"

Two leading cult experts, Margaret Singer and Louis Jolyon West, professor of psychiatry at the UCLA Neuropsychiatric Institute, developed the following list of elements that are most likely to be part of a successful cult indoctrination. Each element is a drastic technique used to control and exploit the individual.

1. Isolation of the recruit and manipulation of his environment

2. Control over channels of communication and information

3. Debilitation through inadequate diet and fatigue

4. Degradation or diminution of the self

5. Induction of uncertainty, fear, and confusion, with joy and certainty through surrender to the group as the goal

6. Alternation of harshness and leniency in a context of discipline

7. Peer pressure, often applied through ritualized struggle sessions, generating guilt and requiring open confessions

8. Insistence by seemingly all-powerful hosts that the recruit's survival—physical or spiritual—depends on identifying with the group

9. Assignment of monotonous tasks or repetitive activities, such as chanting or copying written materials

10. Acts of symbolic betrayal and renunciation of self, family, and previously held values, designed to increase the psychological distance between the recruit and his previous way of life(13)

The effects of such a program are that "as time passes, the member's psychological condition may deteriorate. He becomes incapable of complex, rational thought; his responses to questions become stereotyped; he finds it difficult to make even simple decisions unaided; his judgment about events in the outside world is impaired. At the same time, there may be such a reduction of insight that he fails to realize how much he has changed."(14)

Michael Langone summarizes the effects of the conversion process this way: "After converts commit themselves to a cult, the cult's way of thinking, feeling, and acting becomes second nature, while important aspects of their precult personalities are suppressed or, in a sense, decay through disuse . . . . If allowed to break into consciousness, suppressed memories or nagging doubts may generate anxiety which, in turn, may trigger a defensive trance-induction, such as speaking in tongues, to protect the cult-imposed system of thoughts, feelings, and behavior. Such persons may function adequately—at least on a superficial level. Nevertheless, their continued adjustment depends upon their keeping their old thinking styles, goals, values, and personal attachments in storage."(15)

Upon leaving a cult, ex-members are bequeathed an altered version of themselves. This is why recently exited cult members often appear confused, at a loss for what to say or do. Cult membership tends to reduce formerly well-adjusted and intelligent individuals to slow thinkers who must try to make their way back to what they vaguely remember being like before joining the group. Often they lack self-confidence and are riddled with shame, guilt, and fear. Many former members state that they weren't able to really laugh or cry for months after leaving the group. They felt unable to connect with people, afraid to say something "wrong" or "stupid." At the time, many didn't even realize how they were behaving or reacting.

A dramatic change of identity is required in order for the mind to adapt to a high level of coercive deception. This phenomenon has been identified by Robert Lifton as *doubling*. Doubling is the formation of a second self which lives side by side with the former one, often for a considerable time. According to Lifton, doubling is a universal phenomenon reflecting each person's capacity for the "divided self," or opposing tendencies in the self. "But," he writes, "that 'opposing self' can become dangerously unrestrained, as it did in the Nazi doctors . . . . That opposing self can become the usurper from within and replace the original self until it 'speaks' for the entire person."(16)

During cult recruitment and throughout membership, the devotee is encouraged to lose his or her personal identity and become absorbed in the persona of the group or leader. In some Eastern meditation cults this is linked to the metaphor of dyeing one's robes over and over again until they are the same color as the guru's: by emulating the guru, meditating, and copying his behavior, one eventually becomes one with the Master. In other cults this oneness or state of totalism is achieved through other types of training and conditioning. The mind-manipulating techniques used to induce altered states also serve to support the development and emergence of the cult personality.

Thus we see that under the stress of complying with the cult's demands, the individual member develops a secondary cult personality. This emergence of a "pseudopersonality," as it is called by Louis J. West, enables a person to carry out cult-imposed activities that would normally be against his or her value system, such as begging, sexual promiscuity, lying, forgoing needed medical attention, and participating in violence or criminal activity. This phenomenon helps to explain why there is no apparent internal disagreement between the competing value systems of a person's cult and precult personalities. The former smiles benignly because the latter is safely bound and gagged, locked up in a cage of fear. Simply put, it explains why decent and rational people can end up doing indecent and irrational things.

This capacity to adapt has also been recognized as integral to the human psyche. At times it can save lives, such as for a soldier in combat.(17) This life-saving aspect is relevant to our understanding of the cult member's situation, wherein personality adaptation is both a cult-imposed requirement and a person's means of survival.

As explained earlier, the goal of thought reform is for the subject to become one with the ideal. In cults, personal ego boundaries disappear as the member begins to live for the group or the ideology. This change in identification, often accompanied by such actions as leaving school, changing jobs, dropping old friends, interests, and hobbies, and avoiding family, is what so alarms people as they watch a family member or friend become totally consumed by cult life.

Many who come out of cultic situations may not even be aware that they have taken on a pseudopersonality and, along with their families and friends, are puzzled by their own inconsistent behaviors and feelings. This may cause some former members to feel even more isolated and frustrated, because they feel and know that something is awfully wrong but do not know what or how. Obviously, prospective cult members are not informed during recruitment that such deep, devastating changes might occur.

CHAPTER FOUR

INDIVIDUAL DIFFERENCES AFFECTING RECOVERY

Each person's experience with a cult is different. Some may dabble with a meditation technique but never get drawn into taking "advanced courses" or moving to the ashram. Others may quickly give up all they have, including college, career, possessions, home, and family, to do missionary work in a foreign country or move into cult lodgings.

After a cult involvement, some people carry on with their lives seemingly untouched; more typically, others may encounter a variety of emotional problems. People who leave cults may experience an array of troubling psychological difficulties ranging from inability to sleep, restlessness, and lack of direction to panic attacks, memory loss, and depression. To varying degrees they may feel guilty, ashamed, enraged, lost, confused, betrayed, paranoid, and in a sort of fog. Mental health professionals working with cult veterans note that it can take from one to two years for former cult members "to return to their former level of adaptation, while some may have psychological breakdowns or remain psychologically scarred for years."(1)

The following case examples highlight the range of response.

Cynthia B., age 38, had spent 12 years in a New Age group, where she achieved a high level of leadership. She listed her reasons for leaving as, "I didn't feel right staying there anymore. I knew something was terribly wrong with the group and thought I'd go crazy if I stayed." She moved in with her parents, resumed college, and had a good job when she entered therapy five years after her cult departure to address some of the residual issues. Cynthia started therapy for treatment of a mild depression, complaining that life seemed rather flat and uninteresting. She had difficulty making friends and trusting people; she felt she had missed out on life compared to others her age who were married, had children, owned their own homes, and were advanced in their careers.(2)

•

After three months of intensive course work and counseling in the same group as Cynthia, *Brian A.* was hospitalized because of a suicide attempt. An 18-year-old college freshman at the time of his recruitment, his class work deteriorated immediately after he got involved with the group. He began hallucinating, seeing and hearing his leader talk to him; he was afraid of being possessed by demons. Too distraught, Brian was told by the group to disaffiliate—he was becoming a hindrance. Since he wasn't allowed to stay, he believed that he had to kill himself in order to be reborn and start again in the group. He had no history of emotional difficulty prior to joining and had a good relationship with his family and peers. After hospitalization, medication, and outpatient psychotherapy, Brian is now doing well, is back in school, and has a part-time job.

Assessing the Damage

Why are some people so damaged by their cult experience while others walk away seemingly unscathed? Why do some have psychotic episodes or attempt suicide after leaving the group while others are able to put their lives in order quite easily? There is no simple answer to these questions; a number of variables determine postcult adjustment difficulties.

As discussed in Chapter 2, there are predisposing personality factors and levels of vulnerability that may enhance a person's susceptibility to cult recruitment and conversion. Still other factors affect the person's continued vulnerability and susceptibility while in the group. All these factors govern the impact of the cult experience on the individual and the potential for subsequent damage. In assessing this impact, three different stages of the cult experience—before, during, and after—need to be examined.

The material in this section is based on observations from our work, the experience of other counselors, and human development research.

Before involvement

Vulnerability factors before involvement include a person's age, prior history of emotional problems, and certain personality characteristics.

Age

Children born or raised within a cult grow up in a closed, controlled environment where bizarre, unorthodox, and harmful beliefs, values, and mores are accepted. When someone raised in a cult leaves it, that person may truly feel like a stranger in a strange land, and may have difficulty adapting to the dominant, noncult society. Cult life may have delayed emotional and educational development; it may have hampered medical needs. In addition, the child may have suffered physical, emotional, and sexual abuse—a common and serious problem for children in cults.(3)

Individuals recruited while in high school and college may also face postcult problems. In general, this age group has much to accomplish in life. There are developmental tasks to be completed, such as individuation and separation from the family. There are educational and career choices to be made. And there are issues about dating, sex, and marriage to explore. Cult members do not get the opportunity to pass through these normal developmental stages and experiences, and sometimes complain of being 30- or 40-year-old teenagers when they get out of the cult.

Certain life events or crises may enhance susceptibility to cult recruitment at any age. These include times of high stress like divorce, unemployment or a job change, entering or graduating from school, a significant loss (personal or monetary), relocation, marriage, a birth in the family, and death of a loved one. Cult membership, with its promise of relief from suffering, offers a substitute for personal mastery of these life events. The relief usually proves premature and temporary at best, detrimental to real personal growth at worst.

Usually the very issues that confronted the person before joining the cult are still there to be dealt with when she or he leaves. Their resurfacing may influence how the person handles cult-related issues as well as the conflicts and emotions attached to the original crisis.

Prior history of emotional problems

Prior emotional disorders or distress may increase vulnerability to cult recruitment and susceptibility to thought-reform programs. There are cults, for example, that focus their recruitment on individuals involved in drug rehabilitation programs or Alcoholics Anonymous and other 12-step programs, seeing this milieu as ripe hunting ground for potential members. Some Eastern meditation groups specifically promise relief from emotional problems, while others offer a mystical appeal to former users of psychedelic drugs. Similarly, there are psychotherapy, human potential, political, commercial, and New Age cults that prey on the enormous population of individuals seeking change—whether in themselves or society.

Individuals with a prior history of emotional problems are also more likely to experience emotional problems while *in* the group. Therefore, they more commonly require psychotherapeutic interventions following their cult departure.

Personality factors

Certain intrinsic factors in the psychological makeup of the individual may intensify or minimize postcult difficulties. We are all born with different degrees of intelligence, sensitivity, emotional resilience, and various other personality traits. These traits are not only inherited but are also strengthened or weakened by educational and social opportunities during early childhood and adolescence. Depending on inherited personality characteristics and related strengths or weaknesses, and the type of education and socialization received, each person responds differently to trauma and stress, including that brought on by participation in a cult. For example, someone who has access to resources and is aggressively able to pursue treatment is likely to alleviate the impact of the experience faster than someone who has been denied these things. In addition, how a person has handled and mastered prior life crises may affect how well cult-related trauma is dealt with.

During involvement

Length of time spent in the group

There is quite a difference in the impact a cult will have on a person if she or he is a member for only a few weeks, as compared to months or years. A related factor is the amount of exposure to the indoctrination process and the various levels of control that exist in the group. In some groups, it may take years of involvement before deleterious effects become apparent. In others, indoctrination into higher levels of cult activity may be open only to a select few. In still others, new members may be swept up into a full-time commitment within a matter of weeks.

Another factor related to time is the type of responsibility the person had while in the group. For example, someone who was in the leader's inner circle could have been privy to knowledge and decisions that later might exacerbate feelings of shame or guilt.

Intensity and severity of the thought-reform program

Each cult has its own methods for persuading the recruit to make a commitment. Although different at first glance, most cults' techniques are basically similar, and their purpose and outcome the same. For example, hours spent meditating or speaking in tongues to commune with one's god may initially appear different from hours of group criticism sessions. Yet all these techniques have a common goal: to get, change, and keep the member bound to the group, serving its goals and its leader.

Nevertheless, the *intensity* and *severity* of cults' efforts at conversion and control vary in different groups and in the same group at different times. And members who are in a peripheral, "associate" status may have very different experiences from those who are full-time, inner-core members.

Specific methods will also vary in their effect. An intense training workshop over a week or weekend that includes sleep deprivation, hypnosis, and self-exposure coupled with a high degree of supervision and lack of privacy is likely to produce faster changes in a participant than a group process using more subtle and long-term methods of change. Some cults use methods that affect members on an intimate level. For example, there might be mandated relationships—either with leaders or other members—which can be a source of great discomfort and abuse.

Physical harm and the threat of violence

Many groups use the threat of violence to control. Sometimes there is involvement with criminal activity, which can compound feelings of guilt and shame, and raise fears of legal retribution and blackmail by the cult. Physical and sexual abuses may also increase the risk of emotional trauma and damage. Fear is a very powerful weapon, and living in fear for any length of time may have a significant impact on a person's state of mind and well-being.

Poor or inadequate medical treatment

A former cult member's physical condition and attitude toward physical health may greatly impact postcult adjustments because stamina is required for the transition to mainstream society. In many cults, medical and dental care is unavailable or even forbidden. As with everything else, attention to personal physical health is always subordinate to the goals of the group or the leader's wishes.

Such everyday necessities as eyeglasses or hearing aids may not be available, which can have disastrous consequences. One cult member who was unable to care for his failing eyesight died after a fall into an elevator shaft.(4) In some groups, disease is interpreted as a lack of faith, the work of demons, shirking, or simply something to be overcome through prayer. In others, disease is just ignored. In still other groups, severe illness, either medical or psychological, is cause for ejection from the group, with ill members being deposited in the emergency rooms of local hospitals or, if lucky, shipped home.

To date there are no studies to indicate the morbidity or mortality rates in cultic groups. Many anecdotal reports in the media as well as in medical and psychological journals suggest that involvement in cultic groups and relationships has produced a number of preventable casualties.

Loss of outside support

The availability of a network of family and friends and the amount of outside support certainly will bear on a person's reintegration after a cult involvement. Many cults discourage members from continuing precult relationships. Some even forbid contact with certain family members or friends. Other cults encourage their members to maintain good relationships with family but keep them so busy with cult activities that meaningful contact with anyone outside the group becomes impossible. Some cults promote good family relations in the hopes of receiving money, substantial gifts, or inheritances.

Skewed or nonexistent contact with family and former friends tends to increase the members' isolation and susceptibility to the cult's worldview. The reestablishment of those contacts is important to help offset the loss and loneliness the person will quite naturally feel upon leaving such an intense environment.

After involvement

Various factors can hasten healing and lessen postcult difficulties at this stage. Many are related to the psychoeducational process. Former cult members often spend years after leaving a cult in relative isolation, not talking about or dealing with their cult experiences. Shame and silence may increase the harm done by the group and can prevent healing.

Understanding the dynamics of cult conversion is essential to healing and making a solid transition to an integrated postcult life. The following courses of action can help:

- Engage in a professionally led exit counseling session.

- Educate yourself about cults and thought-reform techniques.

- Go to a rehabilitation facility, especially one that specializes in postcult recovery issues.

- Involve family members and old and new friends, if that feels comfortable, in reviewing and evaluating your cult experience.

- See a psychotherapist or other type of counselor, such as a pastoral counselor, preferably someone who is familiar with or is willing to educate herself or himself about cults and common postcult problems.

- Attend a support group for former cult members.

In an article calling for a public-health response to the cult menace in our society, Dr. Louis J. West aptly wrote: "Existing data now suffice to convince any reasonable person that the claims of harm done by cults are bona fide. There are a good many people already dead or dying, ill or malfunctioning, crippled or developing improperly as a result of their involvement in cults. They are exploited; they are used and misused; their health suffers; they are made to commit improprieties ranging from lying ('heavenly deception') to murder. Their lives are being gobbled up by days, months, and years."(5)

Leaving the Cult

The way in which someone leaves a cult may also have an effect on the healing process. Emotional trauma may be minimized or increased by the manner of separation. The common ways to leave a cult are (a) to walk away (walkaways), (b) to be thrown out (castaways), (c) to lose the leader or find that the group has collapsed, and (d) to be counseled out. Each type of leaving can create specific reactions and aftereffects as the former member suddenly finds herself or himself in the real world again.

If you have left a cult, we hope that the information, case examples, personal stories, coping techniques, and suggestions for healing presented in this book will help you find a path to the future that works for you.

Walkaways

The majority of cult members walk away on their own. A 1991 survey of more than 500 former members revealed that 75 percent left their groups without any kind of intervention.(6) Oftentimes walkaways cannot pinpoint what made them leave. They simply could not tolerate being in the group or relationship any longer.

Initially, most walkaways have little or no idea what they have been involved in. The nature of the psychological manipulation and abuse in the cult is usually not apparent to people who are still influenced by the leadership's justifications and rationalizations. Some people leave the group or relationship knowing only instinctively that for their emotional or physical survival they must get out.

The decision to walk away is never easy and is often physically difficult to carry out. *Patricia R.* is an ex-member of The Work, led by Julius Schacknow, aka Brother Julius. The Work is a "messiah"-led group, combining Bible study and interpretation with real-estate and construction businesses.(7) Describing the process of making her decision to leave, Patricia said:

> It is as if there is a shelf where all your doubts and misgivings are placed while you are in the group. Over the months or years you observe so many things that may conflict with your original beliefs and values, or you see things done by the group or leader that are just not right. Because of the indoctrination and not being allowed to ask questions, you just put it on the shelf. Eventually, the shelf gets heavier and heavier and finally just breaks, and you are ready to leave.(8)

Some manage to escape from their group only with great difficulty, occasionally in danger. *Hana Eltringham Whitfield* described her departure from a large mass transformational group as follows:

> I saw several members of my family only once during my 20-year involvement. When I finally left the group, I was estranged from most of my relatives, all of whom lived several thousand miles away on another continent. They might as well have been on another planet. Alone, penniless, and unfamiliar with the society I had been living in but not a part of for almost two decades, I felt like a stranger both to myself and my country.(9)

Castaways

For those who are told to leave the group for whatever reason, the shame and guilt can be overwhelming. They rarely perceive this event as fortunate. Both walkaways and castaways may feel that they have failed God and lost all spiritual hope, or failed their political or philosophical commitments. Some may believe that they are condemned not only in this life but also in the hereafter and perhaps for countless incarnations to follow.

As exit counselor Steven Hassan wrote in his landmark book, *Combatting Cult Mind Control,* "The people who have been kicked out . . . are always in the worst shape of all former cult members . . . . Most of them devoted their entire lives to the group, turning over bank accounts and property when they joined. They were told that the group was their 'family,' which would take care of them for the rest of their lives. Then, years later, they were told that they were not living up to the group's standards and would have to leave. These people, phobic toward the world outside their cults, have been cast into what they view as utter darkness."(10)

Some groups deliberately use threats of expulsion as a means of controlling the membership. In one guru-oriented meditation group, for example, newcomers and older members are separated occasionally while the guru denounces those not present as being unspiritual, demon-controlled, and unworthy. He elevates those at the meeting, and at the same time lets them know they will have to shape up. Expulsions from the group are frequent and arbitrary, often forgiven, then threatened again for imaginary noncompliance. Similarly, in cultic relationships the threat of abandonment or rejection is a powerful means of manipulation.

Unless they receive counseling or at least some education about cults and thought reform, castaways are prone to suffer an extreme sense of loss and isolation, as portrayed here:

> *George T.,* a high-ranking member of a small political cult, was encouraged to sell drugs to raise money for the group. When arrested he found himself alone to shoulder the consequences, which included lack of financial support for legal expenses and a hefty jail term. Later when he returned to the group, he was ejected because he dared to voice disappointment with the group's lack of support. Shunned and on his own, George yearned for the political "highs" he felt while in the group, the warmth and solidarity of his comrades, and the sense of elitism.
>
> George went into a deep depression. He felt he was a total failure and politically useless. Finally allowed back after months of pleading and apologizing, he was placed on probation and given menial tasks. Shortly

afterward George was commanded by the group's leader to perform sexual acts on him. Totally demoralized, George was asked to leave again, with no explanation offered. Embittered and confused, he felt a combined sense of failure and loss, which led to an even deeper depression than before, pushing him to the brink of suicide.

While in the cult it had been impossible for George to question the behavior of his superiors or to disobey orders. Only after leaving could he begin to analyze and question. His despair eventually led him to seek answers and see the group in a more realistic light. With this insight, he was able to mourn his losses and rebuild his life.

Loss of the leader

The loss of the leader may cause a group to disband, unless there is a potential new leader in its midst with similar emotional characteristics and leadership qualities who is able to convince the others to follow him. Often there is a struggle for leadership, which may result in some groups becoming less authoritarian while others become even more restrictive and abusive.

Whether the leader "retires" to a warmer climate, gets arrested, is overthrown by his followers, or dies, the initial impact of his absence is disorienting for the group. Members usually react in certain ways: they may (1) rationalize the loss, (2) blame society, (3) wait for the return or rebirth of their leader, or for their promised salvation, (4) blame themselves, or (5) simply drift apart.

1. Rationalization, or making excuses, is an emotional defense against anxiety. It is typically used in cults to explain behaviors that contradict or violate the teachings. It stops analytical thinking and reinforces dependency. This dependency may continue long after the leader is gone. Rationalizing is common when the leader's personality and behavior are erratic. Thus, the leader's leaving may be regarded by the members as one more admirable action rather than a betrayal. The following is an illustration of such rationalization:

Dr. D., the leader of a psychotherapy cult, was highly admired by his followers for his unique style of therapy and his glamorized, adventurous lifestyle. A self-proclaimed millionaire and entrepreneur, he stated that success such as his was possible for all his clients who followed his teachings and example. When Dr. D. announced his retirement he claimed he was exhausted from his tireless work on his clients' behalf and needed to recover in a warmer climate. Turning his practice over to others, he made vague comments about returning someday. His clients, trained over the years to accept his lengthy vacations and unpredictability, accepted the news with ambivalent feelings. They rationalized their loss and looked forward to the day when they would be "healthy" enough to follow his example. They envied his apparent freedom, taking the announcement as new evidence of his highly evolved life instead of the desertion it really was. Fortunately, through sessions with an ethical therapist, most of the followers were eventually able to see Dr. D. for the con artist he was and consider his departure a blessing rather than a loss.

2. Blaming society is a result of the us-versus-them mentality. Many leaders and groups set themselves apart from society, sometimes provoking situations for which they then blame society. For example, this sometimes happens with cults that stockpile illegal weapons and then, when investigated, leaders and members act outraged and blame others.

3. Waiting for the return or rebirth of the leader or for the promised salvation can go on for long periods of time. Cult members may wait indefinitely for the leader to reincarnate or to inhabit the body of a living member. Groups that proclaim the coming of the Last Judgment may postpone that fateful day over and over again once their leader is gone.

4. Some members will **blame themselves,** no matter how the leader leaves. They will feel that they were not spiritual enough, did not honor the guru enough, were not worthy of the leader's efforts, caused the leader's illness or death by their bad karma, were selfish, and so on.

> *Ruth M.* was frequently told by her guru that in other lifetimes she had failed to become enlightened and this was the last time he would come back for her. When he left for South America without clarifying their relationship, initially she felt abandoned and that she had failed him. The reality, she later learned, was that he was bored with the responsibility of the group, which he also felt was not profitable enough, and was seeking an easier, more lucrative way to earn a living. This knowledge, although hurtful, helped Ruth put the experience in perspective.

5. Drifting apart may be members' final reaction to losing their leader. The death of a leader may leave a group in crisis, especially if it is unexpected and there are ensuing struggles for control of the group. Sometimes another powerful figure takes the former leader's place, pulling some of the followers around him. Sometimes the group splits into two or more factions. Sometimes cults drift apart while waiting for the leader to return or while members try to sort out what they should be doing.

Counseled out via planned interventions

A small percentage of cult members leave their group or relationship by means of an exit counseling, an intervention similar to that done with someone who has a drug or alcohol abuse problem. These are planned meetings of the member, the family or friends, and a team of professionals who use an educational model to enable the member to reach an informed decision about her or his allegiance to the group.(11)

In the 1970s increasing numbers of families became concerned with the role of cults in their children's new and disturbing behavior: dropping out of school, cutting ties to families and friends, and sometimes disappearing completely. In this context, efforts at "deprogramming" emerged, which were early attempts to deal with what appeared to be a type of brainwashing used by the groups on their members. The term *deprogramming* was used to identify a process originally seen as the polar opposite of the cults' "programming" of members.

Over time, as cults increasingly prevented outsiders, including families, from having access to members, deprogramming began to involve the actual abduction and forcible detention of the cult member in a locked room at home or in a motel or in whatever locale the deprogramming was taking place. Although initially not a coercive process, deprogramming is currently associated with the "snatching" and confinement of cult members by their families.

Although frequently successful in getting an individual out of the cult or cultic relationship, this type of *involuntary* intervention can produce problems. Kidnapping and detention have been found to be traumatizing in their own right. Ex-members who have been deprogrammed report being highly ambivalent about the experience. Though grateful to their parents or spouse for getting them out of the cult, they sometimes also feel deep anger over the manner of intervention. Posttraumatic symptoms such as nightmares, intrusive thoughts, and flashbacks of the deprogramming may also slow down their recovery from the cult experience.

We acknowledge the deep pain of families who feel there are no other alternatives to freeing their loved one from an abusive, restrictive cult or relationship, but we are opposed to deprogramming as a means of getting someone out of a cult. It may seem to be the only course of action, but there is danger of the family being misinformed and panicking. Many times, with patience, a way can be discovered and developed that will lead to a less traumatic exiting from the group.

As legal risks have increased and parents and most deprogrammers have become concerned over the ethical issues, new noncoercive means of helping cultists have developed. Deprogramming has been replaced by a more respectful approach, which is educational in nature, more professional in delivery, more effective in outcome and, because it is voluntary, generally nontraumatizing. This process, known as exit counseling, is described in Carol Giambalvo's book, *Exit Counseling: A Family Intervention,* important reading for anyone interested in learning more about this type of voluntary intervention. Professionals who help cult members make informed decisions about their group affiliations are known as "exit counselors" or "cult information specialists."

"Exit counselors are usually former cult members themselves," writes Giambalvo. "They have firsthand experience with mind control. They have knowledge of cult mind-sets, the dynamics of cult membership, and the history of the particular cult in question and its leader(s). They also have the ability to bypass the closed thinking brought about by mind control in order to reaccess the cultist's critical thinking abilities. These are vital areas of expertise."(12) The following examples highlight the possible positive outcome of an exit counseling. The first involves a planned intervention; the second, illustrates the merits of an exit counseling session for people who have already left the cult.

> *David O.* became increasingly concerned about his wife *Myra's* involvement in a New Age center that advocated bodywork combined with counseling by nonprofessionals, meditation, and channeling of discarnate entities. Communication became more and more strained as David and Myra began to disagree about child-rearing practices, sex, and household finances. When David heard rumors of sexual misconduct at the center he consulted a family therapist familiar with cults. He read all he could about thought-reform programs and New Age beliefs, then prepared for an exit counseling. He consulted and interviewed several professionals, finally choosing a team he felt was knowledgeable and with whom he felt comfortable.
>
> Both David and his in-laws, who were concerned about their daughter's increasingly strange behaviors, spent considerable time with the exit counseling team preparing for the intervention. The team researched the group's belief structure and its historical precedents, and interviewed the family extensively to become familiar with Myra as a person and gain an understanding of the roots of her vulnerability and interests.

The team and the family were well prepared, and the intervention went smoothly. Myra, surprised at first by her family's concern and the appearance of the team, agreed to listen to what they had to say. She could have ended the intervention at any time by asking them to leave or by leaving the house herself. At the end of three days [some interventions take longer], Myra was able to understand the techniques used by her group to manipulate and take advantage of her, and decided not to go back.

•

On a weekend in July 1992 two exit counselors met with 20 ex-members of an Eastern-style cult. Some had been members of the cult for 30 years. They had all left the group within a few months of learning of their guru's abusive sexual practices. The weekend was organized by two of the ex-members and was designed to be an educational experience, combining explanations of mind control with an overview of the philosophical beliefs of their system, its origins and fallacies of doctrine and leadership. In addition, a workshop was held for those women who had been sexually abused by the guru. This was a cathartic and healing weekend for those who attended. With an understanding of the dynamics of mind control and the effects of the guru's manipulations and lies, the former members began to deal with their sense of failure, shame, and guilt about their time in the cult. Many chose to continue this recovery process by entering therapy and attending support meetings for former members.(13)

One advantage of an exit counseling is that participants receive a short course on cults and thought reform along with the opportunity to learn how their particular group or leader deviates from accepted moral practices or belief structures. They learn the origin of the group's belief system, which may have been misinterpreted or kept hidden from them. This educational process provides them with an understanding of the true nature of their cult involvement. Armed with information and resources, and often backed up by an educated and supportive family environment, former cult members are more prepared to face the recovery process.

Evaluating Your Involvement

The following sets of questions have proven helpful to former cult members trying to make sense of their experience. Review these questions periodically as you travel on the road to recovery. They will lead to new insights and a deeper level of understanding of the cult experience.

Reviewing your recruitment

1. What was going on in your life at the time you joined the group or met the person who became your abusive partner?

2. How and where were you approached?

3. What was your initial reaction to or feeling about the leader or group?

4. What first interested you in the group or leader?

5. How were you misled during recruitment?

6. What did the group or leader promise you? Did you ever get it?

7. What didn't they tell you that might have influenced you not to join had you known?

8. Why did the group or leader want you?

Understanding the psychological manipulation used in your group

1. Which controlling techniques were used by your group or leader: chanting, meditation, sleep deprivation, isolation, drugs, hypnosis, criticism, fear? List each technique and how it served the group's purposes.

2. What was the most effective? the least effective?

3. What technique are you still using that is hard to give up? Are you able to see any effects on you when you practice these?

4. What are the group's beliefs and values? How did they come to be your beliefs and values?

It is useful here to review Lifton's eight criteria for thought reform, outlined in Chapter 3. They can be used as a measuring stick to evaluate your experience.

Examining your doubts

1. What are your doubts about the group or leader now?

2. Do you still believe the group or leader has all or some of the answers?

3. Are you still afraid to encounter your leader or group members on the street?

4. Do you ever think of going back? What is going on in your mind when that happens?

5. Do you believe your group or leader has any supernatural or spiritual power to harm you in any way, physically or spiritually, now that you have left?

6. Do you believe you are cursed by God for having left the group?

The answers to this last set of questions will help you to assess the degree to which the cult's destructive influence may still be operating within you.

CHAPTER
FIVE

CHARACTERISTICS
OF A CULT LEADER

People coming out of a cultic group or relationship often struggle with the question, "Why would anyone (my leader, my lover, my teacher) do this to me?" When the deception and exploitation become clear, the enormous unfairness of the victimization and abuse can be very difficult to accept. Those who have been part of such a nightmare often have difficulty placing the blame where it belongs—on the leader.

A cult cannot be truly explored or understood without understanding its leader. A cult's formation, proselytizing methods, and means of control "are determined by certain salient personality characteristics of [the] cult leader .... Such individuals are authoritarian personalities who attempt to compensate for their deep, intense feelings of inferiority, insecurity, and hostility by forming cultic groups primarily to attract those whom they can psychologically coerce into and keep in a passive-submissive state, and secondarily to use them to increase their income."(1)

In examining the motives and activities of these self-proclaimed leaders, it becomes painfully obvious that cult life is rarely pleasant for the disciple and breeds abuses of all sorts. As a defense against the high level of anxiety that accompanies being so acutely powerless, people in cults often assume a stance of self-blame. This is reinforced by the group's manipulative messages that the followers are never good enough and are to blame for everything that goes wrong.

Demystifying the guru's power is an important part of the psychoeducational process needed to fully recover.(2) It is critical to truly gaining freedom and independence from the leader's control. The process starts with some basic questions: Who was this person who encouraged you to view him as God, all-knowing, or all-powerful? What did he get out of this masquerade? What was the real purpose of the group (or relationship)?

In cults and abusive relationships, those in a subordinate position usually come to accept the abuse as *their* fault, believing that they deserve the foul treatment or that it is for their own good. They sometimes persist in believing that they are bad rather than considering that the person upon whom they are so dependent is cruel, untrustworthy, and unreliable. It is simply too frightening for them to do that: it threatens the balance of power and means risking total rejection, loss, and perhaps even death of self or loved ones. This explains why an abused cult follower may become disenchanted with the relationship or the group yet continue to believe in the teachings, goodness, and power of the leader.

Even after leaving the group or relationship, many former devotees carry a burden of guilt and shame while they continue to regard their former leader as paternal, all-good, and godlike. This is quite common in those who "walk away" from their groups, especially if they never seek the benefits of an exit counseling or therapy to deal with cult-related issues. This same phenomenon is found in battered women and in children who are abused by their parents or other adults they admire.

To heal from a traumatic experience of this type, it is important to understand who and what the perpetrator is. As long as there are illusions about the leader's motivation, powers, and abilities, those who have been in his grip deprive themselves of an important opportunity for growth: the chance to empower themselves, to become free of the tyranny of dependency on others for their well-being, spiritual growth, and happiness.

The Authoritarian Power Dynamic

The purpose of a cult (whether group or one-on-one) is to serve the emotional, financial, sexual, and power needs of the leader. The single most important word here is *power*. The dynamic around which cults are formed is similar to that of other power relationships and is essentially ultra-authoritarian, based on a power imbalance. The cult leader by definition must have an authoritarian personality in order to fulfill his half of the power dynamic. Traditional elements of authoritarian personalities include the following:

- the tendency to hierarchy

- the drive for power (and wealth)

- hostility, hatred, prejudice

- superficial judgments of people and events

- a one-sided scale of values favoring the one in power

- interpreting kindness as weakness

- the tendency to use people and see others as inferior

- a sadistic-masochistic tendency

- incapability of being ultimately satisfied

- paranoia(3)

In a study of twentieth-century dictators, one researcher wrote: "Since compliance depends on whether the leader is perceived as being both powerful and knowing, the ever-watchful and all-powerful leader (and his invisible but observant and powerful instruments, such as secret police) can be invoked in the same way as an unobservable but omniscient God . . . . Similarly, the pomp and ceremony surrounding such an individual make him more admirable and less like the common herd, increasing both his self-confidence and the confidence of his subjects. The phenomenon is found not only with individual leaders, but with entire movements."(4)

We will see, however, that an authoritarian personality is just one aspect of the nature of a cult leader.

Who Becomes a Cult Leader?

Frequently at gatherings of former cult members a lively exchange takes place in which those present compare their respective groups and leaders. As people begin to describe their special, enlightened, and unique "guru"—be he a pastor, therapist, political leader, teacher, lover, or swami—they are quickly surprised to find that their once-revered leaders are really quite similar in temperament and personality. It often seems as if these leaders come from a common mold, sometimes jokingly called the "Cookie-cutter Messiah School."

These similarities between cult leaders of all stripes are in fact character disorders commonly identified with the psychopathic personality. They have been studied by psychiatrists, medical doctors, clinical psychologists, and others for more than half a century. In this chapter we review some of this research and conclude with a psychopathological profile of traits commonly found in abusive leaders.

Cultic groups usually originate with a living leader who is believed to be "god" or godlike by a cadre of dedicated believers. Along with a dramatic and convincing talent for self-expression, these leaders have an intuitive ability to sense their followers' needs and draw them closer with promises of fulfillment. Gradually, the leader inculcates the group with his own private ideology (or craziness!), then creates conditions so that his victims cannot or dare not test his claims. How can you prove someone is *not* the Messiah? That the world *won't* end tomorrow? That humans are *not* possessed by aliens from another world or dimension? Through psychological manipulation and control, cult leaders trick their followers into believing in something, then prevent them from testing and disproving that mythology or belief system.

The Role of Charisma

In general, charismatic personalities are known for their inescapable magnetism, their winning style, the self-assurance with which they promote something—a cause, a belief, a product. A charismatic person who offers hope of new beginnings often attracts attention and a following. Over the years we have witnessed this in the likes of Dale Carnegie, Werner Erhard (founder of est, now The Forum), John Hanley (founder of Lifespring), Maharishi Mahesh Yogi, Shirley MacLaine, John Bradshaw, Marianne Williamson, Ramtha channeler J.Z. Knight, and a rash of Amway "executives," weight-loss program promoters and body-building gurus.

One dictionary definition of charisma is "a personal magic of leadership arousing special popular loyalty or enthusiasm for a public figure (as a political leader or military commander); a special magnetic charm or appeal."(5) Charisma was studied in depth by the German sociologist Max Weber, who defined it as "an exceptional quality in an individual who, through appearing to possess supernatural, providential, or extraordinary powers, succeeds in gathering disciples around him."(6)

Weber's charismatic leader was "a sorcerer with an innovative aura and a personal magnetic gift, [who] promoted a specific doctrine.... [and was] concerned with himself rather than involved with others.... [He] held an exceptional type of power: it set aside the usages of normal political life and assumed instead those of demagoguery, dictatorship, or revolution, [which induced] men's whole-hearted devotion to the charismatic individual through a blind and fanatical trust and an unrestrained and uncritical faith."(7)

In the case of cults, of course, we know that this induction of whole-hearted devotion does not happen spontaneously but is the result of the cult leader's skillful use of thought-reform techniques. Charisma on its own is not evil and does not necessarily breed a cult leader. Charisma is, however, a powerful and awesome attribute found in many cult leaders who use it in ways that are both self-serving and destructive to others. The combination of charisma and psychopathy is a lethal mixture—perhaps it is the very recipe used at the Cookie-cutter Messiah School!

For the cult leader, having charisma is perhaps most useful during the stage of cult formation. It takes a strong-willed and persuasive leader to convince people of a new belief, then gather the newly converted around him as devoted followers. A misinterpretation of the cult leader's personal charisma may also foster his followers' belief in his special or messianic qualities.

So we see that charisma is indeed a desirable trait for someone who wishes to attract a following. However, like beauty, charisma is in the eye of the beholder. Mary, for example, may be completely taken with a particular seminar leader, practically swooning at his every word, while her friend Susie doesn't feel the slightest tingle. Certainly at the time a person is under the sway of charisma the effect is very real. Yet, in reality, charisma does nothing more than create a certain worshipful reaction to an idealized figure in the mind of the one who is smitten.

In the long run, skills of persuasion (which may or may not be charismatic) are more important to the cult leader than charisma—for the power and hold of cults depend on the particular environment shaped by the thought-reform program and control mechanisms, all of which are usually conceptualized and put in place by the leader. Thus it is the psychopathology of the leader, not his charisma, that causes the systematic manipulative abuse and exploitation found in cults.

The Cult Leader as Psychopath

Cultic groups and relationships are formed primarily to meet specific emotional needs of the leader, many of whom suffer from one or another emotional or character disorder. Few, if any, cult leaders subject themselves to the psychological tests or prolonged clinical interviews that allow for an accurate diagnosis. However, researchers and clinicians who have observed these individuals describe them variously as neurotic, psychotic, on a spectrum exhibiting neurotic, sociopathic, and psychotic characteristics, or suffering from a diagnosed personality disorder.(8)

It is not our intent here to make an overarching diagnosis, nor do we intend to imply that all cult leaders or the leaders of any of the groups mentioned here are psychopaths. In reviewing the data, however, we can surmise that there is significant psychological dysfunctioning in some cult leaders and that their behavior demonstrates features rather consistent with the disorder known as psychopathy.

Dr. Robert Hare, one of the world's foremost experts in the field, estimates that there are at least two million psychopaths in North America. He writes, "Psychopaths are social predators who charm, manipulate, and ruthlessly plow their way through life, leaving a broad trail of broken hearts, shattered expectations, and empty wallets. Completely lacking in conscience and in feelings for others, they selfishly take what they want and do as they please, violating social norms and expectations without the slightest sense of guilt or regret."(9)

Psychopathy falls within the section on personality disorders in the *Diagnostic and Statistical Manual of Mental Disorders,* which is the standard source book used in making psychiatric evaluations and diagnoses.(10) In the draft version of the manual's 4th edition (to be released Spring 1994), this disorder is listed as "personality disorder not otherwise specified/ Cleckley-type psychopath," named after psychiatrist Hervey Cleckley who carried out the first major studies of psychopaths. The combination of personality and behavioral traits that allows for this diagnosis must be evident in the person's history, not simply apparent during a particular episode. That is, psychopathy is a long-term personality disorder. The term psychopath is often used interchangeably with sociopath, or sociopathic personality. Because it is more commonly recognized, we use the term *psychopath* here.

Personality disorders, as a diagnosis, relate to certain inflexible and maladaptive behaviors and traits that cause a person to have significantly impaired social or occupational functioning. Signs of this are often first manifested in childhood and adolescence, and are expressed through distorted patterns of perceiving, relating to, and thinking about the environment and oneself. In simple terms this means that something is amiss, awry, not quite right in the person, and this creates problems in how he or she relates to the rest of the world.

The psychopathic personality is sometimes confused with the "antisocial personality," another disorder; however, the psychopath exhibits more extreme behavior than the antisocial personality. The antisocial personality is identified by a mix of antisocial and criminal behaviors—he is the common criminal. The psychopath, on the other hand, is characterized by a mix of criminal and socially deviant behavior.

Psychopathy is not the same as *psychosis* either. The latter is characterized by an inability to differentiate what is real from what is imagined: boundaries between self and others are lost, and critical thinking is greatly impaired. While generally not psychotic, cult leaders may experience psychotic episodes, which may lead to the destruction of themselves or the group. An extreme example of this is the mass murder-suicide that occurred in November 1978 in Jonestown, Guyana, at the People's Temple led by Jim Jones. On his orders, over 900 men, women, and children perished as Jones deteriorated into what was probably a paranoid psychosis.

The psychopathic personality has been well described by Hervey Cleckley in his classic work, *The Mask of Sanity,* first published in 1941 and updated and reissued in 1982. Cleckley is perhaps best known for *The Three Faces of Eve,* a book and later a popular movie on multiple personality. Cleckley also gave the world a detailed study of the personality and behavior of the psychopath, listing 16 characteristics to be used in evaluating and treating psychopaths.(11)

Cleckley's work greatly influenced 20 years of research carried out by Robert Hare at the University of British Columbia in Vancouver. In his work developing reliable and valid procedures for assessing psychopathy, Hare made several revisions in Cleckley's list of traits and finally settled on a 20-item Psychopathy Checklist.(12) Later in this chapter we will use an adaptation of both the Cleckley and Hare checklists to examine the profile of a cult leader.

Neuropsychiatrist Richard M. Restak stated, "At the heart of the diagnosis of psychopathy was the recognition that a person could appear normal and yet close observation would reveal the personality to be irrational or even violent."(13) Indeed, initially most psychopaths appear quite normal. They present themselves to us as charming, interesting, even humble. The majority "don't suffer from delusions, hallucinations, or memory impairment, their contact with reality appears solid."(14)

Some, on the other hand, may demonstrate marked paranoia and megalomania. In one clinical study of psychopathic inpatients, the authors wrote: "We found that our psychopaths were similar to normals (in the reference group) with regard to their capacity to experience external events as real and with regard to their sense of bodily reality. They generally had good memory, concentration, attention, and language function. They had a high barrier against external, aversive stimulation . . . . In some ways they clearly resemble normal people and can thus 'pass' as reasonably normal or sane. Yet we found them to be extremely primitive in other ways, even more primitive than frankly schizophrenic patients. In some ways their thinking was sane and reasonable, but in others it was psychotically inefficient and/or convoluted."(15)

Another researcher described psychopaths in this way: "These people are impulsive, unable to tolerate frustration and delay, and have problems with trusting. They take a paranoid position or externalize their emotional experience. They have little ability to form a working alliance and a poor capacity for self-observation. Their anger is frightening. Frequently they take flight. Their relations with others are highly problematic. When close to another person they fear engulfment or fusion or loss of self. At the same time, paradoxically, they desire closeness; frustration of their entitled wishes to be nourished, cared for, and assisted often leads to rage. They are capable of a child's primitive fury enacted with an adult's physical capabilities, and action is always in the offing."(16)

Ultimately, "the psychopath must have what he wants, no matter what the cost to those in his way."(17)

The Master Manipulator

Let us look for a moment at how some of this manifests in the cult leader. Cult leaders have an outstanding ability to charm and win over followers. They beguile and seduce. They enter a room and garner all the attention. They command the utmost respect and obedience. These are "individuals whose narcissism is so extreme and grandiose that they exist in a kind of splendid isolation in which the creation of the grandiose self takes precedence over legal, moral or interpersonal commitments."(18)

Paranoia may be evident in simple or elaborate delusions of persecution. Highly suspicious, they may feel conspired against, spied upon or cheated, or maligned by a person, group, or governmental agency. Any real or suspected unfavorable reaction may be interpreted as a deliberate attack upon them or the group. (Considering the criminal nature of some groups and the antisocial behavior of others, some of these fears may have more of a basis in reality than delusion!)

Harder to evaluate, of course, is whether these leaders' belief in their magical powers, omnipotence, and connection to God (or whatever higher power or belief system they are espousing) is delusional or simply part of the con. Megalomania—the belief that one is able or entitled to rule the world—is equally hard to evaluate without psychological testing of the individual, although numerous cult leaders state quite readily that their goal is to rule the world. In any case, beneath the surface gloss of intelligence, charm, and professed humility seethes an inner world of rage, depression, and fear.

Two writers on the subject used the label "Trust Bandit" to describe the psychopathic personality.(19) Trust Bandit is indeed an apt description of this thief of our hearts, souls, minds, bodies, and pocketbooks. Since a significant percentage of current and former cult members have been in more than one cultic group or relationship, learning to recognize the personality style of the Trust Bandit can be a useful antidote to further abuse.

The Profile of a Psychopath

In reading the profile, bear in mind the three characteristics that Robert Lifton sees as common to a cultic situation:

1. A charismatic leader who . . . increasingly becomes the object of worship

2. A series of processes that can be associated with "coercive persuasion" or "thought reform"

3. The tendency toward manipulation from above . . . with exploitation—economic, sexual, or other—of often genuine seekers who bring idealism from below(20)

Based on the psychopathy checklists of Hervey Cleckley and Robert Hare, we now explore certain traits that are particularly pertinent to cult leaders. The 15 characteristics outlined below list features commonly found in those who become perpetrators of psychological and physical abuse. In the discussion we use the nomenclature "psychopath" and "cult leader" interchangeably. To illustrate these points, a case study of Branch Davidian cult leader David Koresh follows this section.

We are not suggesting that all cult leaders are psychopaths but rather that they may exhibit many of the behavioral characteristics of one. We are also not proposing that you use this checklist to make a diagnosis, which is something only a trained professional can do. We present the checklist as a tool to help you label and demystify traits you may have noticed in your leader.

1. Glibness/superficial charm

Glibness is a hallmark of psychopaths. They are able to use language effortlessly to beguile, confuse, and convince. They are captivating storytellers. They exude self-confidence and are able to spin a web that intrigues others and pulls them into the psychopath's life. Most of all, they are persuasive. Frequently they have the capacity to destroy their critics verbally or disarm them emotionally.

2. Manipulative and conning

Cult leaders do not recognize the individuality or rights of others, which makes all self-serving behaviors permissible. The hallmark of the psychopath is the *psychopathic maneuver,* which is essentially interpersonal manipulation "based on charm. The manipulator appears to be helpful, charming, even ingratiating or seductive, but is covertly hostile, domineering . . . . [The victim] is perceived as an aggressor, competitor, or merely as an instrument to be used . . . . The manipulation inevitably becomes the end-all and is no longer qualified by the reality principle."(21) In other words, there are no checks on the psychopath's behavior—anything goes.

The psychopath divides the world into suckers, sinners, and himself. He discharges powerful feelings of terror and rage by dominating and humiliating his victims. He is particularly successful when, through an overlay of charm, he makes an ally of his victim—a process sometimes described as emotional vampirism or emotional terrorism. Examples of this type of manipulation are plentiful in the literature of Jonestown and other cultic groups. It is especially prevalent in the one-on-one cultic relationship, where there is direct involvement with the manipulator.

3. Grandiose sense of self

The cult leader enjoys tremendous feelings of entitlement. He believes everything is owed to him as a right. Preoccupied with his own fantasies, he must always be the center of attention. He presents himself as the "Ultimate One": enlightened, a vehicle of god, a genius, the leader of humankind, and sometimes even the most humble of humble. He has an insatiable need for adulation and attendance. His grandiosity may also be a defense against inner emptiness, depression, and a sense of insignificance. Paranoia often accompanies the grandiosity, reinforcing the isolation of the group and the need for protection against a perceived hostile environment. In this way, he creates an us-versus-them mentality.

4. Pathological lying

Psychopaths lie coolly and easily, even when it is obvious they are being untruthful. It is almost impossible for them to be consistently truthful about either a major or minor issue. They lie for no apparent reason, even when it would seem easier and safer to tell the truth. This is sometimes called "crazy lying."(22) Confronting their lies may provoke an unpredictably intense rage or simply a Buddha-like smile.

Another form of lying common among cult leaders is known as *pseudologica fantastica,* an extension of pathological lying. Leaders tend to create a complex belief system, often about their own powers and abilities, in which they themselves sometimes get caught up. "It is often difficult to determine whether the lies are an actual delusional distortion of reality or are expressed with the conscious or unconscious intent to deceive."(23)

These manipulators are rarely original thinkers. Plagiarists and thieves, they seldom credit the true originators of ideas, often co-opting authorship. They are extremely convincing, forceful in the expression of their views, and talented at passing lie detector tests. For them, objective truth does not exist. The only "truth" is whatever will best achieve the outcome that meets their needs. This type of opportunism is very difficult to understand for those who are not psychopaths. For this reason, followers are more apt to invent or go along with all kinds of explanations and rationales for apparent inconsistencies in behavior: "I know my guru must have had a good reason for doing this." "He did it because he loves me—even though it hurts."

5. Lack of remorse, shame, or guilt

At the core of the psychopath is a deep-seated rage which is split off (i.e., psychologically separated from the rest of the self) and repressed. Some researchers theorize that this is caused by feeling abandoned in infancy or early childhood.(24) Whatever the emotional or psychological source, psychopaths see those around them as objects, targets, or opportunities, not as people. They do not have friends, they have victims and accomplices—and the latter frequently end as victims. For psychopaths, the ends always justify the means. Thus there is no place for feelings of remorse, shame, or guilt. Cult leaders feel justified in all their actions since they consider themselves the ultimate moral arbiter. Nothing gets in their way.

6. Shallow emotions

While they may display outbursts of emotion, more often than not they are putting on a calculated response to obtain a certain result. They rarely reveal a range of emotions, and what is seen is superficial at best, pretended at worst. Positive feelings of warmth, joy, love, and compassion are more feigned than experienced. They are unmoved by things that would upset the normal person, while outraged by insignificant matters. They are bystanders to the emotional life of others, perhaps envious and scornful of feelings they cannot have or understand. In the end, psychopaths are cold, with shallow emotions, living in a dark world of their own.

Hiding behind the "mask of sanity," the cult leader exposes feelings only insofar as they serve an ulterior motive. He can witness or order acts of utter brutality without experiencing a shred of emotion. He casts himself in a role of total control, which he plays to the hilt. What is most promised in cults—peace, joy, enlightenment, love, and security—are goals that are forever out of reach of the leader, and thus also the followers. Since the leader is not genuine, neither are his promises.

7. Incapacity for love

As the "living embodiment of God's love," the leader is tragically flawed in being unable to either give or receive love. Love substitutes are given instead. A typical example might be the guru's claim that his illness or misfortune (otherwise inconsistent with his enlightened state) is caused by the depth of his compassion for his followers, whereby he takes on their negative karma. Not only are devotees supposed to accept this as proof of his love but also are expected to feel guilt for their failings! It becomes impossible for members to disprove this claim once they have accepted the beliefs of the group.

The leader's tremendous need to be loved is accompanied by an equally strong disbelief in the love offered him by his followers; hence, the often unspeakably cruel and harsh testing of his devotees. Unconditional surrender is an absolute requirement. In one cult, for example, the mother of two small children was made to tell them nightly that she loved her leader more than them. Later, as a test of her devotion, she was asked to give up custody of her children in order to be allowed to stay with her leader. The guru's love is never tested; it must be accepted at face value.

8. Need for stimulation

Thrill-seeking behaviors, often skirting the letter or spirit of the law, are common among psychopaths. Such behavior is sometimes justified as preparation for martyrdom: "I know I don't have long to live; therefore my time on this earth must be lived to the fullest." "Surely even I am entitled to have fun or sin a little." This type of behavior becomes more frequent as the leader deteriorates emotionally and psychologically—a common occurrence.

Cult leaders live on the edge, constantly testing the beliefs of their followers, often with increasingly bizarre behaviors, punishments, and rules. Other mechanisms of stimulation come in the form of unexpected, seemingly spontaneous outbursts, which usually take the form of verbal abuse and sometimes physical punishment. The psychopath has a cool indifference to things around him, yet his icy coldness can quickly turn into rage, vented on those around him.

9. Callousness/lack of empathy

Psychopaths readily take advantage of others, expressing utter contempt for anyone else's feelings. Someone in distress is not important to them. Although intelligent, perceptive, and quite good at sizing people up, they make no real connections with others. They use their "people skills" to exploit, abuse, and wield power.

Psychopaths are unable to empathize with the pain of their victims. Meanwhile, part of the victims' denial system is the inability to believe that someone they love so much could consciously and callously hurt them. It therefore becomes easier to rationalize the leader's behavior as necessary for the general or individual "good." The alternative for the devotee would be to face the sudden and overwhelming awareness of being victimized, deceived, used. Such a realization would wound the person's deepest sense of self, so as a means of self-protection the person denies the abuse. When and if the devotee becomes aware of the exploitation, it feels as though a tremendous evil has been done, a spiritual rape.

10. Poor behavioral controls/impulsive nature

Like small children, many psychopaths have difficulty regulating their emotions. Adults who have temper tantrums are frightening to be around. Rage and abuse, alternating with token expressions of love and approval, produce an addictive cycle for both abuser and abused, as well as create a sense of hopelessness in the latter. This dynamic has also been recognized in relation to domestic abuse and the battering of women.

The cult leader acts out with some regularity—often privately, sometimes publicly—usually to the embarrassment and dismay of his followers and other observers. He may act out sexually, aggressively, or criminally, frequently with rage. Who could possibly control someone who believes himself to be all-powerful, all-knowing, and entitled to every wish, someone who has no sense of personal boundaries, no concern for the impact on those around him? Generally this aberrant behavior is a well-kept secret, known only to a few disciples. The others only see perfection.

These tendencies are related to the psychopath's need for stimulation and inability to tolerate frustration, anxiety, and depression. Often a leader's inconsistent behavior needs to be rationalized by either the leader or the follower in order to maintain internal consistency. It is often regarded as divinely inspired and further separates the empowered from the powerless.

11. Early behavior problems/juvenile delinquency

Psychopaths frequently have a history of behavioral and academic difficulties. They often "get by" academically, conning other students and teachers. Encounters with juvenile authorities are frequent. Equally prevalent are difficulties in peer relationships and developing and keeping friends, marked control problems, and other aberrant behaviors such as stealing, fire setting, and cruelty to others.

12. Irresponsibility/unreliability

Not concerned about the consequences of their behavior, psychopaths leave behind them the wreckage of others' lives and dreams. They may be totally oblivious or indifferent to the devastation they inflict on others, something which they regard as neither their problem nor their responsibility.

Psychopaths rarely accept blame for their failures or mistakes. Scapegoating is common, blaming followers, those outside the group, a member's family, the government, Satan—anyone and everyone but the leader. The blaming may follow a ritualized procedure such as a trial, "hot seat" denunciation, or public confession (either one-on-one or in front of the group). Blame is a powerful reinforcer of passivity and obedience, producing guilt, shame, terror, and conformity in the followers.

13. Promiscuous sexual behavior/infidelity

Promiscuity, child sexual abuse, polygamy, rape, and sexual acting out of all sorts are frequently practiced by cult leaders. Conversely, there is often stringent sexual control of the followers through such tactics as enforced celibacy, arranged marriages, forced breakups and divorces, removal of children from their parents, forced abortions or mandated births. For psychopaths, sex is primarily a control and power issue.

Along with this behavior comes vast irresponsibility not only for the followers' emotions but also for their lives. In one cult, for example, multiple sexual relations were encouraged even while one of the top leaders was known to be HIV positive. This kind of negligence toward others is not uncommon in the psychopath's world.

Marital fidelity is rare in the psychopath's life. There are usually countless reports of extramarital affairs and sexual predation upon adult and child members of both sexes. The sexual behavior of the leader may be kept hidden from all but the inner circle or may be part of accepted group sexual practices. In any case, due to the power imbalance between leader and followers, sexual contact is never truly consensual and is likely to have damaging consequences for the follower.

14. Lack of realistic life plan/parasitic lifestyle

The psychopath tends to move around a lot, making countless efforts at "starting over" while seeking out fertile new ground to exploit. One day may appear as a rock musician, the next a messiah; one day a used car salesman, the next the founder of a mass self-transformation program; one day a college professor, the next the new "Lenin" bringing revolution to America.

The flip side of this erratic life planning is the all-encompassing promise for the future that the cult leader makes to his followers. Many groups claim as their goal world domination or salvation at the Apocalypse. The leader is the first to proclaim the utopian nature of the group, which is usually simply another justification for irrational behavior and stringent controls.

The leader's sense of entitlement is often demonstrated by the contrast between his luxurious lifestyle and the impoverishment of his followers. Most cult leaders are supported by gifts and donations from their followers, who may be pressured to turn over much of their income and worldly possessions to the group. Slavery, enforced prostitution, and a variety of illegal acts for the benefit of the leader are common in a cult milieu. This type of exploitation aptly demonstrates Lifton's third point of idealization from below and exploitation from above.

Psychopaths also tend to be preoccupied with their own health while remaining totally indifferent to the suffering of others. They may complain of being "burned out" due to the burden of "caring for" their followers, sometimes stating they do not have long to live, instilling fear and guilt in their devotees and encouraging further servitude. They are highly sensitive to their own pain and tend to be hypochondriacs, which often conflicts with their public image of superhuman self-control and healing abilities.

According to them, the illnesses they *don't* get are due to their powers, while the ones they *do* get are caused by their "compassion" in taking on their disciples' karma or solving the group's problems. This of course is another guru trick.

15. *Criminal or entrepreneurial versatility*

Cult leaders change their image and that of the group as needed to avoid prosecution and litigation, to increase income, and to recruit a range of members. Cult leaders have an innate ability to attract followers who have the skills and connections that the leaders lack. The longevity of the group is dependent on the willingness of the leadership to adapt as needed and preserve the group. Frequently, when illegal or immoral activities are exposed to the public, the cult leader will relocate, sometimes taking followers with him. He will keep a low profile, only to resurface later with a new name, a new front group, and perhaps a new twist on the scam.

A Case Example—David Koresh

In Waco, Texas, on April 19, 1993, more than 80 men, women, and children died as fire swept through the Branch Davidian compound known as Ranch Apocalypse. These Davidians were an unaffiliated offshoot of the Seventh-Day Adventist Church. The members were followers of David Koresh, the "Sinful Messiah." Koresh's devotees believed until the very end that their life or death was his to give or take away.

Immediately after the dreadful televised conflagration there was much public controversy over the fire: was it set off by the FBI while using armored vehicles to inject tear gas into the building or was it deliberately set by followers at Koresh's order? On some level the answer is immaterial. Some of us who watched in horror as flames engulfed the buildings knew that this was no mass suicide, but perhaps an inevitable ending for a group of people under the spell of a psychopathic charismatic cult leader.

In the period of analysis following the tragedy, some mental health professionals classified Koresh as psychotic, others as a psychopath. Richard Restak, in an article in the *Washington Post,* bitterly attacked the government's mishandling of the affair. He believed that if Koresh had been treated as a psychotic and not "just another criminal" the tragedy could have been averted. He went on to describe the chief indicators of psychosis: "a delusional preoccupation with persecution, usually associated with grandiosity; more or less continuous erratic, disorganized excitement accompanied by irascibility; bizarre delusional ideas coupled with obvious indifference to social expectations; and pervasive convictions of evil or wickedness in self or others." According to Restak, "Koresh satisfied these criteria in spades."(25)

Another article questioned whether Koresh suffered from the "Jerusalem syndrome." According to Eli Witztum, a psychiatrist who treats and studies this disorder, some pilgrims to Jerusalem have become delusional and disoriented while visiting the city, requiring hospitalization before being stabilized and sent home. These religious and paranoid delusions have been experienced by pilgrims of all faiths and nationalities. Koresh visited Jerusalem in 1985. Though there is no record of Koresh's admission to a psychiatric hospital, Witztum speculates that Koresh's visit to the Holy City intensified his messianic self-image.(26)

Though we believe Koresh exhibited many of the psychotic traits outlined by Restak and others, it is our premise that primarily he was not psychotic but was a psychopath. This will become clearer as we compare his personality profile to the characteristics of a psychopath just outlined, and highlighted below in italic type.

David Koresh, born Vernon Wayne Howell, was the illegitimate child of his 15-year-old mother.(27) When he was two, his father left home; his mother eventually married another man. According to his grandmother, David and his stepfather did not get along; Koresh himself said he was abused at home. *Early behavior problems* were apparent. A poor student with a history of learning disabilities and poor attendance, Koresh dropped out of school in the ninth grade. In 1979, at about age 19, he was expelled from the Seventh-Day Adventist Church as a troublemaker, a bad influence on the young people of the church. He wanted power and would not adhere to the principles of the church. Yet it was also observed that from an early age he had a striking ability to memorize passages of the Bible. With *glibness and superficial charm* he exploited this skill as a teacher of the Scriptures and leader of his future flock.

In the early 1980s Koresh joined a Branch Davidian sect led by the Roden family. Through *manipulation* and a variety of power plays, Koresh was able to wrest control of the group by *conning* and outwitting the leader, George Roden. In 1987 Roden challenged Koresh to see who had more divine power by bringing a deceased member back to life. When Roden exhumed the body, Koresh had him arrested for "corpse abuse." An armed conflict followed between Koresh and Roden. Although Koresh was arrested and charged with attempted murder, his trial ended in a hung jury and the charges were dropped.

While Roden was incarcerated Koresh took over the group and began using classic thought-reform techniques, such as isolation, sleep deprivation, physical exhaustion through mindless activity and overwork, food deprivation, and phobia induction. He led long hours of indoctrination, sometimes subjecting his followers to 15-hour sessions of Bible study. Koresh built up a following of several hundred men, women, and children, including those recruited on trips to Israel, Australia, England, and other parts of the United States.

His *grandiose sense of self* was well-known. His business card was imprinted "Messiah," and he is quoted as having stated on countless occasions, "If the Bible is true, then I'm Christ." Some believed him. He was able to convince husbands to give up their wives to him, families to turn over their money and children. By April 19, 1993, there were almost one hundred people willing to die with him for the promise of a heavenly afterlife.

Koresh's *callousness and lack of empathy* were apparent in the treatment of his followers, especially the children, whom he abused physically, emotionally, and sexually, then held as hostages, pawns in his power play. In the end, there were probably 25 children among the followers who died. Koresh's *pathological lying* touched media, government forces, and his followers. For example, he repeatedly reneged on promises to surrender, and he assured his followers that they would be safe in underground bunkers. His *lack of remorse, shame, or guilt* was evident over the years as he frequently admitted that he was a sinner without equal. At no time is he known to have shown remorse for the harm inflicted on so many of his followers or for the suffering of their families outside the group.

Koresh clearly revealed his *incapacity for love* and *sexual instability* by bedding and "wedding" all the women in the group, including other men's wives, and girls as young as 12 years old. After demanding celibacy from all the men, it must have provided Koresh with sadistic enjoyment to be openly sexual with their wives, even though some of these men were his most loyal lieutenants. A restless *need for stimulation* was displayed in his stockpiling of weapons and ammunition, his irrational outbursts, and the frenzied activity within the compound. *Poor behavior controls* were evident in his raging and his physical abuse of the children and adults who worshiped him, and in his constantly changing rules about acceptable behavior. His *parasitic lifestyle* allowed him to live off the earnings of others while he regarded himself as a biblical king, Christ himself. His *impulsive nature* was apparent in the punishments that rained down on adults and children alike at any perceived disrespect or disobedience. He ruled by whim and fiat; he ruled by terror.

His *criminal versatility* was exhibited throughout his life. A known troublemaker since his teens, he had been arrested for attempted murder, had stockpiled illegal weapons, and had sexually abused children and others. Finally, his own death and that of his followers—whether the fires were accidentally ignited by FBI tanks or deliberately set by cult members—showed that Koresh was *irresponsible,* to say the least. For the psychopath, those who follow him are fools, suckers, dupes; they don't exist as people except to be used and abused. The idea of taking responsibility is as foreign as the ability to feel compassion, empathy, or sympathy—unless the psychopath has some ulterior motive in simulating such feelings.

Throughout his life David Koresh displayed a certain sense of purpose. He also had the psychopath's ruthless determination to reach his objectives no matter what the cost to others. It is likely that his behavior suffered a psychotic degeneration under the intense pressure of his last two months. Mental health professionals and cult researchers may continue for some time to question the labels that are put on Koresh, not so much as a matter of scientific debate as an issue of deep social concern.

Unmasking the Guru

As you read the 15-point checklist and David Koresh's profile, you may notice characteristics that match and explain some of the attributes and behaviors of your leader. Unmasking or demystifying the leader is an important part of postcult recovery. Becoming familiar with this personality type may help to prevent revictimization. Here are some questions to ask about your own experience:

- How well did you know your leader? Was it through firsthand knowledge or others' accounts?

- What did you feel when you met him or her?

- Did those feelings change during the time you spent in the group or relationship?

- Was your leader charismatic, charming, quick-witted, able to sway a crowd? How were those traits used by your leader to get his or her way?

- Did you believe your leader to have special powers, exalted spirituality, or special knowledge? Do you still believe that?

- Did you ever catch your leader lying or faking? Being inconsistent? How did you rationalize that what you saw and heard was okay when it was clearly aberrant, irrational, or abusive?

- How did your leader rationalize his or her behavior when it was aberrant, irrational, or abusive?

- How many of the 15 traits listed in the profile did you observe in your leader?

- Were there second-level leaders in your group? Did they psychologically resemble the leader or were they devoted disciples blindly following orders?

- What do you know of your leader's childhood, adolescence, and early adulthood? Does he or she fit the pattern?

- Were you sexually intimate with your leader? How did that relationship come about and how was it explained or justified?

THE HEALING PROCESS

*You know when healing's occurred when you can remember
when you want to and forget when you choose.*
—Bessel van der Kolk

THE UNMAKING OF A SPIRITUAL JUNKIE

JOSEPH F. KELLY

Joe Kelly spent 14 years in two different Eastern meditation cults, Transcendental Meditation and the Church of the International Society of Divine Love. He describes the difficulties he faced in making the final break from these groups, and then methods that worked to help him regain his life. Joe is now a cult education specialist helping others evaluate their cult membership.

I was between my freshman and sophomore years, contending with the transition from the fairly isolated world of my Catholic high school to the diversity of an urban community college. The year was 1974. Thanks to the tumultuous sixties and the self-reflective seventies, traditional answers to life's problems were no longer satisfactory to me. Through my studies I read about Transcendental Meditation (TM), and Maharishi Mahesh Yogi's message seemed so easy to embrace. He claimed that there was no need to change one's beliefs, philosophies, or lifestyle, and that TM was a scientifically verifiable meditation, a way "to solve the problems of individuals and society."

I signed up, going quickly from introductory lectures to preparatory courses to residence courses. As the months passed I devoted more and more time to the TM center; I attended 18 residence courses over the next few years. I associated less and less with my "stressed out" friends, whose lifestyles I considered to be less evolutionary. During this time I also began to manifest the first signs of meditation's side effects: the loss of short-term memory, a lessened ability to focus, and a chronic mild head pressure. These side effects were explained away by the TM movement as signs of stress release, or "unstressing."

As my commitment grew, I participated in the TM-Sidhi program, which purported to teach meditators how to fly, walk through walls, and find lost objects hidden from view, among other things. Considering the cost, $4,500, it was a high price to pay for finding my lost car keys. The increased meditation exacerbated my periods of "spacing out," again interpreted by the movement as signs of my expanded consciousness. I was also beginning to feel confusion over some other inconsistencies between theory and practice. TM officials told me that more meditation would cure my confusion—and I squelched my doubts. Until I met the Swami.

When I heard that a "genuine" Indian swami, Swami Prakashanand Saraswati, was going to be speaking at a local church, I jumped at the chance to hear him. During his talk he spoke of loving God, a topic played down in the TM movement. He also spoke of the danger of being involved in philosophies that promote Sidhi powers at the expense of devotion to God. I finally felt that someone was addressing my difficulties: Swami was able to describe the potential side effects of TM's practices. He seemed sincere. His orange robes and beard certainly looked the part. I was in conflict, but my loyalty to TM kept me from immediately jumping ship.

As luck would have it, the Swami moved in next door. After years of reading Eastern philosophy, which states "When the devotee is ready, the master comes," I thought that God must be telling me something. The Swami's pull was too strong to resist. Despite the loss of friends I loved dearly, I left the TM movement and became one of the Swami's disciples.

TM now seemed like kindergarten. Being involved with the Swami was like acceptance into a spiritual Ph.D. program. With TM the changes in my life had been gradual over the course of nine years. The Swami turned up the heat! Changes took place rapidly. His followers, most of them former TMers, were well conditioned. Years of TM processing and indoctrination made us prime adherents, ready to surrender. The Swami demanded regular attendance at meetings known as *satsangs*, and before too long I was encouraged to live in the Philadelphia ashram. We worked to build his mission headquarters, the Church of the International Society of Divine Love, Inc. (ISDL), and we spent from two to eight hours daily in meditation, depending on the whims of the master. There was a certain potency in the Swami's mix of myth (we were worshipers of Krishna), meditation technique, and strict environmental control.

The longer I was with the Swami, the more I began to reevaluate my time in TM. Like other former TMers I was feeling that I had been misled. A number of us requested refunds for the Sidhi levitation courses. TM challenged us to sue, so we did. Through the course of filing and preparing for the suit I met an attorney familiar with the negative effects of cultic groups, and I began reading material on thought reform and even attended a Cult Awareness Network (CAN) conference. The case histories of former members of various thought-reform systems (Hare Krishnas, Moonies, etc.) were strikingly similar to my experience. Yet I was still unable to examine my current involvement with the Swami and ISDL. It was easy to see how Maharishi, Swami Prabhupada, and Reverend Moon had duped and controlled their followers, but my Swami was different, I thought.

Nevertheless I left the conference shaken. Resolved to continue my involvement, I told myself that we were a legitimate alternative religion. I decided that the CAN people just didn't understand new religions, that the yardstick used to evaluate cults didn't apply to ISDL. My rationalizations were endless. But down deep I was scared.

The following year I attended my second CAN conference. Because I was learning more about mind control from various associates, it was becoming increasingly difficult for me to make excuses and ignore the swami's manipulations. My conviction that he was omniscient and omnipotent was being shaken: his lies were so commonplace. I found myself less willing to "just surrender." "Was this looking like other cults?" I asked myself.

Toward the end of the following summer I was put under extraordinary pressure. Swami wanted me to go to India for advanced training as an ISDL preacher. No longer would outside relationships be tolerated. I was afraid. I had seen the personality changes in those he had sent to India. One evening I sat with Swamiji and told him of my financial difficulties. My business was on the verge of bankruptcy. He listened, then requested another $2,000 donation. I had already given over $30,000. I was broke—and brokenhearted at his request. I knew this must be a test. I must get the money to pass. I still wanted God.

As the days passed I could no longer suppress the information I had on cults, thought reform, and hypnosis. It confronted me day and night. I felt I was going insane. I prayed to the only one who I knew could help— the Swami. No answers came. I was alone, scared, with my world crashing in on me. All I could think was that I needed to leave the Mission, the Swami, and my friends—again. I needed room to think. I had to leave, had to separate myself.

It was hot in New York City on August 13, 1988, the day I finally made my decision to leave the Swami. At age 33 I was confronted with the reality that I was without a career, financial stability, a home. I was in a spiritual crisis that sent my mind reeling. I felt a part of me die that hot summer day: the innocent part of myself that I reserved for my relationship with God was crushed. As I made my decision, I knew I would lose my devotee family, just as I had lost my TM family.

I made the decision. Then my recovery began.

The first night away from the Mission was one of the most difficult. Constant chanting played in my head involuntarily, a reminder of where I had been. Thoughts of the Swami, God, Hell, my mortality rushed through my head. It took months for these thoughts to pass. I constantly questioned myself: Was I making the right choice? Am I going to have to descend into lower animal forms? Will I spend many lifetimes searching for God before I am given another chance at a human birth? Over time I began to realize that these thoughts were phobias induced by the group.

I felt deeply depressed over the realization that I had lost many years devoting my energy to the whims of gurus. I was emotionally regressed and spiritually spent and knew I needed to get out of the quagmire of unhealthy spirituality. I wanted help, but whom could I trust? Both groups had discredited the value of therapy. Maharishi said therapy was "just stirring up the mud." The Swami taught that all problems were spiritual. I was confused about what I might gain in therapy, so I didn't do anything in that direction right away.

As I spoke with exit counselors I understood better the techniques of persuasion that I had been subjected to in the two cults. During the 14 years I had spent more than 10,000 hours doing hypnotic trance-inducing techniques. That leaves a legacy. The meditation practices left me with an inability to focus or concentrate. I had difficulty maintaining logical thought, reading, even carrying on a conversation. I was suffering from a dissociative disorder that had me feeling that I wasn't in my body, a sensation that undermined my sense of self. I spaced out easily, especially when confronted with stressful situations.

To regain my self-confidence, I worked with my brother-in-law at a fairly physical job. Physical work helped me get back my ability to focus. One of the strategies recommended to me to combat my tendency to dissociate was a regular exercise program. I find even today that regular exercise helps me clear my thinking and maintain a connection to my physical self. When I felt more confident I took my first step into the business world, working for a company that installed seasonal displays in retail stores. The job required me to develop management and decision-making skills. From it, I became more self-directed.

The depression continued sporadically for another eight months. Thoughts of finding a therapist resurfaced, but it took time to overcome my prejudice against therapy. I needed a therapist who would be willing to work with me as an equal, someone who would be a coach more than an authority figure. I interviewed therapists and carefully chose one, which in itself was empowering.

For a while I was bothered by triggers, things that reminded me of the group. The smell of incense, for example, would trigger me to feel as though I were chanting again. Music was also a stimulus that carried me back to feeling connected to the Swami. While a disciple, I had been encouraged to direct all my emotional feelings toward him. No emotion toward another person or thing could be tolerated. I had been conditioned to suppress any type of feeling that was not approved. The only good emotion was a "devotional" emotion. Now, while driving, love songs on the radio would send me into a crying jag. I would feel the loss, like someone who had just lost a lover. I would sometimes get confused that these floating experiences were signs from God directing me back to the path.

As I reflected on the experiences of others who had left similar groups, I was more able to understand what was happening to me. "Floating" is experienced by many former members, and learning to label and thus defuse the episodes was vital to my recovery. Seeing the origin of my reactions helped me to resist the group's conditioning, and my emotional compulsion to return to the group subsided. Not allowing the triggers to cause me to dissociate gave me control over my life, another step in taking back my autonomy.

I was desperately desirous of finding spiritual meaning in my life. I knew what I didn't want: a pseudospirituality that produced a dependent state, or an exclusive or secretive spirituality. I needed a mature spirituality that incorporated both mind and heart. I decided to reexplore the tradition of my family, Catholicism. I was fortunate to find a a priest who responded with sensitivity and with whom I could talk intelligently about my concerns.

Fourteen years of immersion in groups living apart from the world had taken their toll. When I thought back to my precult days, my hopes for the future, my original goals, it became glaringly apparent that what I had wanted for myself was quite different from where I ended up. To help sort out what happened, I carefully examined how I had been led on a divergent path. Going through that process in therapy was very helpful.

The world, while formidable at first, was also clearly a beautiful and exciting place to be. Both the TM movement and the Swami's Mission had stressed how uncaring the outside world was: "It's a pool of mud," they said. Yet back in the world now, I found it to be so very different from what they had taught. I learned how caring and helpful my true friends and family could be. They accepted me as I was. They didn't require absolute belief or use pressure.

Most of my friendships over the years were in some way cult connected. Friendships in the group were often quickly made, superficial, offering a false sense of intimacy. Making new friends was an important part of my healing but also a struggle since the cults had taught me that all worldly relationships were mundane and ultimately meaningless, self-centered, and based on what others could take from you. Where should I go to meet people? What would we talk about? Where would we find a common ground? The first step was learning to accept people as they are and to not be spiritually judgmental.

During this time I met others who had made the postcult transition effectively. They gave me support and I, in turn, began to give others my support as they left their groups. I was now strong in my decision and no longer felt the pull to go back. I gained this clarity through the process of sharing my experience while continuing to study group influence, hypnosis, behavior modification techniques, and thought reform. Groups tend to dictate how to learn, what to study, who is a valid source, and what to avoid. It was important for me to understand for myself what had happened and how not to make the same mistake again. The CAN and AFF [American Family Foundation] conferences continue to be important resources for me, but I also feel the need to use sources outside those circles.

Looking back on the goals and expectations I had as a young man, I recognized that like many others I came from an idealistic period in history. I have now found a way to realize my goals and satisfy my idealistic nature. My background with Eastern groups coupled with my academic training in comparative religion has provided me with the opportunity and the skills to help others. This has become the basis of a new career in the field of influence education, where I help others reevaluate their own group involvement. This is a rewarding experience, allowing me to turn my past to a positive use.

I also find it necessary to have a balanced life. Helping others is important, but equally vital is having a life separate from my cult past. Travel, relationships, literature, film, politics, human rights, and family are interests that enrich my life with the diversity I once so repressed. Life is difficult yet exhilarating—and a refreshing change from a life that at one time was so singularly focused.

Reflecting on my experience, I realize that I attempted to escape into a "bondage" that was called "ultimate freedom." The only thing that allowed me to escape the bondage of cultic involvement was an inner sense of integrity. There was a part of me that I never gave over. It was repressed and covered by layers of doctrine, hidden and hard to access; but it was never lost. In the words of Erich Fromm in *Escape from Freedom*: "Escape only helps to forget [the] self as a separate entity. [Man] finds new and fragile security at the expense of sacrificing the integrity of his individual self. He chooses to lose his self since he cannot bear to be alone. Thus freedom—as freedom from—leads into new bondage."

CHAPTER SIX

TAKING BACK YOUR MIND

The simple realization that you were in a cult is often a shock. No one knowingly joins a cult, or believes that she or he is in one. Accepting the truth may take months or even years. Acknowledging that you were duped and abused can be painful to absorb. It can injure a person's mental and emotional integrity and be both frightening and enraging. Cult exploitation is an attack on a person's very sense of self. Because of this, many former cult members do not want to recognize that they were in such a group or relationship.

This denial is common among former members who do not seek exit counseling or some measure of education about cults. Knowledge of cults gives you the language to explain to yourself what happened. Unless you accept the experience as a cultic one, time for education, introspection, and insight might not be considered a priority.

If you question whether or not you were in a cultic group or relationship, there are several things you might do to settle your mind:

- Review the "Checklist of Cult Characteristics" (see Appendix A).

- Make a list of Robert Lifton's eight thought-reform themes (see Chapter 3), and determine whether any of these apply to your situation.

- Review Margaret Singer and Louis J. West's list of typical cult indoctrination techniques (see Chapter 3) and determine whether any were used in your situation.

The first step to recovery is leaving the cultic situation. Admitting to yourself that you were in a cult is the second step. Now, at your own pace, you will begin to recognize what was done to you and the unfairness of being exploited. The feelings that may follow are normal responses to trauma, including shock and denial, then grief responses: hurt, guilt, shame, fear, and anger.

There is no magic wand to make these feelings go away quickly. Healing cannot be rushed, but it will take place. Attempts at self-soothing through alcohol and other substance abuse, sexual promiscuity, cult hopping (seeking a quick fix by joining another cult), and suicide attempts are actions that delay healing, compound the problems, and prolong the period of denial.

Cognitive difficulties are those involving a person's awareness and judgment, and are common among people who have left cult life. In this chapter we describe some of the major cognitive difficulties encountered by former members, and in the next chapter we outline some useful exercises and aids in combatting them. As you identify the mind-control techniques that were used in your situation, you can learn to disarm their psychological effects. You may know the legend of the Russian officer Potemkin, who tried to impress Empress Catherine by erecting rows of fake houses for her to see as she passed through the desolate Ukraine. As with those long-ago facades, so will it be with the wounds of your cult experience. One by one, the houses in "Potemkin's village" will fall.

The Cloud of Indecisiveness

Ex-members may experience problems making decisions. Deciding something as significant as "what to do with the rest of your life" may seem impossible. By dictating the rules to live by and eliminating choice, cults create a childlike dependency in their members. This level of control is often true for one-on-one cultic relationships.

In some groups, dependence is increased by monitoring the members' behavior through the use of "disciplers," "one-helps," or "control officers" who oversee and approve or disapprove of all aspects of daily living. Other groups use self-monitoring techniques: keeping diaries or writing reports (or self-criticisms) of all negative thoughts, behaviors, and actions that broke rules. These diaries and reports are turned over to the group.

Small mistakes and any attempt at autonomy are punished in most cults. This may result in reprimand, or "rebuking" as some call it; sleep or food deprivation; physical punishment or hard labor; group denunciation and humiliation; threats of expulsion, damnation, or possession by demons; death threats; and even, in some instances, death. Whether overt or covert, these controls promote dependence on the group and become barriers to personal decision making and autonomy. This ingrained behavior often becomes a cult residue, to be dealt with after the person leaves. The following example illustrates how one ex-member coped with her inability to make decisions.

> *Sharon G.* left a Bible-based group after four years of intense speaking in tongues and devotion to her pastor, who guided her in all facets of her life. She described herself as a fish out of water, flip-flopping on dry land, unable to make a decision and stick to it. Thoughts felt slippery. As soon as she decided on a course of action she either forgot why she chose it or proceeded to talk herself out of it. This was exasperating for her and for family and friends. Sharon had difficulty with major decisions: whether or not to move out of her parents' house, change her employment, go back to school. Almost as difficult were minor choices: what to wear, eat, or do at any given time.
>
> Sharon found list making an important first step. When confronted with a choice or decision, small or large, she would reduce it to its smallest pieces. For example, she made a list of the pros and cons of moving. After deciding that moving out was important, she made another list of what she would need to move out successfully.
>
> Sharon had been taught that her mind was the enemy. Thinking was a habit she had to relearn. She found that trusting herself could only come from thinking, first making small decisions, then enjoying the feelings of confidence and self-esteem that success brought. She had to learn to be patient with herself, allow herself to make mistakes, forgive herself, learn from her mistakes, and take credit for her successes.

The Barrier of "Loaded" Language

"Loading the language," one of Lifton's characteristics of a totalistic environment (see Chapter 3), is a mechanism of indoctrination and control used in practically every cult. Group slogans and terminology serve as shortcuts for communication; they also stop creative, inquisitive, critical thinking. After leaving, ex-members commonly discover that they are still using group jargon without being aware of it. This "loaded" language interferes with the ability to think independently and critically and creates barriers to communication with others. Sometimes when a former member unexpectedly encounters the cult's language, she or he may dissociate or experience a variety of feelings: confusion, anxiety, terror, guilt, shame, or rage.

Most of us have an inner dialogue (called thoughts) that is so automatic we take it for granted. Our thoughts automatically interpret what we experience and feel. If you started to think in German without knowing the language, you would probably be frightened and confused. Similarly, changing the meanings of words produces anxiety and self-doubt, and can be truly thought-stopping and isolating. Because of the cult's "loaded" language, some ex-members find that they need to make a special effort to relearn their native language.

Cults change the meanings of many common, everyday words and expressions, making communication outside the group painful and confusing. You may find that you no longer have a meaningful vocabulary to understand your own inner world, much less the world around you. *Carol B.*, an ex-member of a mass transformational group, writes:

> My vocabulary was mostly made up of what I call cultese, or cult terminology, basically the group's own language. It was difficult to verbalize what I was feeling inside because the words were the group's. All that would come up was the group's policy on leaving. It was hard enough being confused about what I really believed, but not having the words to explain myself in plain English was worse. The words at my disposal all had cult meanings attached to them and that would start my inner conflict over again. When I get excited or tired, I still have trouble with vocabulary. I'll start talking or thinking in cultese, and it can be a shock, and frustrating.
>
> Sometimes my thoughts would be circular, to the point of making me confused. It helped to just write them down. Then I didn't have to think about them or resolve anything—they were written down and could be resolved later. I'd write until I had nothing more to say. Sometimes I would reread the journals and could see I wasn't having as much trouble as before. That helped.
>
> I forced myself to read, and visited the library frequently. At first I really didn't understand much that I read, but I'd read each book as much as I was able. Especially helpful was Orwell's *Nineteen Eighty-Four*—I compared the characters' lives to my own.(1)

Hana Whitfield, who had been in a similar group for 20 years, had extreme difficulty speaking "normal" English, even though it is her native language. "I spent time every day for the first few weeks out of the group relearning English, until I had every cult word replaced with an English word."

Television, magazines, crossword puzzles, and books of all kinds can reacquaint a person with the language and help rebuild vocabulary. Reading the newspaper and listening to the news are also highly recommended for retraining the mind, learning vocabulary, and keeping up with world events. Another proven technique is to list all specific words and phrases connected to the cult, then look them up in a dictionary. Seeing the generally accepted definitions and usages can help reorient a person's thinking and reestablish the capacity for self-expression.

Difficulty concentrating is a typical aftereffect of cultic involvement. Many former cult members report that immediately after leaving their group they were unable to read more than a page or two of a book in one sitting, were incapable of reading a newspaper straight through, or forgot things a minute after reading or hearing them. This is due partially to the loss of critical thinking abilities caused by the cult's thought-reform program and controlled environment, and partially to the loss of familiarity with the person's native language. Although overwhelming at times, the inability to concentrate is generally temporary.

"Floating" and Other Altered States

Another common postcult difficulty is learning how to deal with the disconcerting phenomenon of "floating," also called trancing out, spacing out, and dissociation. Sometimes people float back and forth between their precult and cult personalities. Families will report relief at seeing the return of their loved one's spontaneity, sense of humor, and lively personality, only to experience confusion and anxiety when the veiled, flat, or suspicious cult persona reemerges.

Former members of groups that use chanting, speaking in tongues, intense group criticism, hypnotic and guided-imagery sessions, and meditation techniques frequently experience floating episodes. Floating occurs because the mind has been trained and conditioned to dissociate during those practices, and under certain conditions a person may involuntarily slip into a dissociated state. Depending on the cult's practices, dissociative episodes can include unpleasant or bizarre hallucinations and may cause considerable anxiety.

Dissociation can and does occur within the general population and can range from mild daydreaming to the extreme of multiple personality disorder. Postcult dissociative symptoms manifest in a variety of ways. When floating, the person feels disconnected (dissociated) from her environment or body. Concentration becomes difficult, attention spans shorten, and simple activities become major tasks. The need to make even minor decisions may produce confusion and panic. There is loss of a grasp on reality. Like other difficulties, these too will pass. In the next chapter we offer some exercises to help combat this uncomfortable and disorienting experience.

Moderate to severe cases of floating, known as *depersonalization* or depersonalization disorder, involve a sense of separation or detachment from one's body.(2) It feels as though you leave your body and float above yourself, watching yourself think, behave, and interact with others. In some groups, depersonalization is the goal, regarded as the highest state of consciousness; it is what members strive for. In reality, depersonalization is not a useful state of being, having no advantages for functioning in the world.

Derealization is another form of dissociation. In depersonalization the self seems unreal; in derealization the world seems unreal. The surroundings may seem lifeless, foggy, distant, or flat. Vibrant "auras" may be seen around inanimate objects, which may appear larger or smaller than they really are.

Occasionally both derealization and depersonalization happen at the same time. Either may be accompanied by visual or auditory hallucinations, often related to the cult's belief system. For example, former devotees may see or hear gods and demigods long after they have left the cult and stopped meditating.

One group, Transcendental Meditation, teaches that thoughts do not leave an impression on the mind, "like drawing a line on water." This is a direct posthypnotic suggestion for amnesia. Members are taught to attain a state of nonattachment: do not become attached to your thoughts; let your thoughts flow over you; a thought comes, a thought goes, it is not something to be concerned with. Because of this training many former members come away with only spotty recall of their time in the group, and are easily "triggered" into dissociating and flipping back into cult-learned behavior. Without proper counseling they may continue to have little awareness of the cause of their bizarre postcult behaviors. This impaired recall is known as *source amnesia* and is common to those who have experienced altered states in their cult.(3)

Giving a meditator instructions about exactly what to look for while in a trance state can be equivalent to posthypnotic suggestion. It is said among therapists that Freudian patients dream in Freudian symbolism while Jungian patients dream in Jungian symbolism. In cult-led meditation, the appearance of certain desired images or phenomena is interpreted by the leadership or trainers, and also thus by the cult members, as a sign of progress. Since constant dissociation through meditation can increase a person's vulnerability to suggestion and direction, indoctrination by direct or indirect suggestion can occur at those vulnerable times immediately before and after meditation. Suggestion and dissociation prevent followers from questioning or judging some of these tactics. Such sweeping statements as "Master always has a good reason" or "Master teaches on many levels" can then be accepted as an explanation for all behavior.

Such meditation practices can be found in the Transcendental Meditation (TM), Nichiren Shoshu of America (NSA), and the International Society of Krishna Consciousness (ISKCON), to name a few. In non-Eastern groups, chanting, speaking in tongues, guided visualization, decreeing, and repetitive physical movements such as spinning may also lead to trance states. Most political cults and some self-improvement, New Age, shepherding, and psychotherapy cults carry out intensive personal criticism sessions that can produce dissociation and floating effects. Dissociative symptoms are also a frequent aftereffect of witnessing or participating in a traumatic event, such as physical or sexual abuse within a cult.

The dissociative episodes caused by these experiences are usually temporary (heartening news for the person who is suffering from them), but may last as long as several months, eventually diminishing in frequency and duration.

The Distress of Memory Loss

There are many factors responsible for memory difficulties during cult membership and after departure. Short-term memory, also known as working memory, is the retention and recall of limited amounts of material before it is forgotten or placed in long-term storage. Long-term memory refers to what most of us think of as memory, that is, recalling significant events and information gathered in our lives.

While in the group the use of drugs and alcohol, the impact of emotional or physical trauma, the long-term practice of dissociative techniques, and intense levels of stress may interfere with both short-term and long-term memory. Elements of reality may be selectively tuned out or simply may not be stored by the brain in long-term memory.

In conjunction with memory loss, ex-members frequently complain of concentration difficulties, short attention spans, obsessional thinking, and dissociative episodes for some period of time after their cult departure. The following example shows how one former cult member dealt with the confusion in her life caused by temporary memory loss.

Marsha C. had such difficulty with even small tasks after exiting from her group that she often thought she was losing her mind. When she put something down, she would immediately forget where she had left it; when shopping, she would often forget why she had come to the store in the first place. Her forgetfulness increased when she was stressed, overtired, or hungry. Once a person who had prided herself on her memory, she now had difficulty remembering facts and figures; she even had trouble following conversations.

To deal with this problem Marsha made a list each night of what she wanted to accomplish the next day. She kept the list simple and broke down all the tasks into their smallest components so that she could feel a sense of accomplishment at both remembering and doing what she set out to do. She would also review what she had done at the end of the day. Keeping a journal became a way to connect her thoughts and watch her daily progress. If she read or heard important concepts she wanted to remember, she wrote them down, then personalized them with her own experiences. All this reassured Marsha that she wasn't crazy at all—and with time and practice her memory became stronger.

Other useful techniques for memory recovery include reminiscing with former friends and relatives about shared experiences, reviewing photo albums and journals, watching movies or reading books from precult days, writing a chronology of events before and during the cult, and visiting people and places from precult life.

The Disruption of Obsessional Thoughts

An obsession is defined in Campbell's *Psychiatric Dictionary* as "an idea, emotion, or impulse that repetitively and insistently forces itself into consciousness even though it is unwelcome. An obsession may be regarded as essentially normal when it does not interfere substantially with thinking or other mental functions; such an obsession is short-lived and can usually be minimized or nullified by diverting attention onto other topics . . . . Most commonly, obsessions appear as *ideas*, or sensory images, which are strongly charged with emotions . . . . Less commonly, obsessions appear as feelings unaccompanied by clear-cut ideas, such as anxiety or panic, feelings of unreality or depersonalization."(4)

Already prone to much self-doubt, former cult members easily fall prey to obsessional thoughts about the nature of reality, the truth about the leader or group, and especially about whether or not they did the right thing by leaving. The case example below illustrates this.

Clara R. was a devotee of an Eastern guru for five years. She observed him perform "miracles," produce items out of thin air, heal the sick, and go without sleep for days on end. As she assumed leadership duties at the ashram, she had a rude awakening as she saw a procession of women come and go to the chamber of her supposedly celibate guru. She could no longer deny her inner doubts or the rumors when she herself was invited to engage in sexual activities with her Master in the name of Tantra (achieving spiritual growth through sexual techniques). Depressed and disappointed, she left the group.

For many months afterward Clara was obsessed with questions about whether her guru was good or evil, whether she was now in some kind of spiritual danger, and so on. It wasn't until she consulted with an exit counselor knowledgeable about Eastern cults and mysticism that she got the information that enabled her to evaluate her experience. Debunking the miracles, seeing them as magic tricks commonly used by stage magicians, was enormously sobering and helped to free her mind of his grip.

The Poverty of Black-and-White Thinking

After a long time spent viewing the world in the rigid, dogmatic, black-and-white, good-and-evil, right-and-wrong light of the cult's training, it takes time to begin to sort through precult, cult, and postcult values and worldviews. As an independent person out in the world once again, the former cult member must choose her or his own morals and values. It is not enough to just leave the group—a new life must be put in place.

Seeing the world in black and white is one outcome of exposure to cult ideology. Cults create a world in which all the answers are known—and the cult supposedly has them. This type of thinking also serves a protective function, saving members from the anxiety of thinking for themselves. It keeps members functioning and cooperative.

Sometimes when people first leave a cult they temporarily reverse their values so that everything that was bad is now good and vice versa. This thinking is still limiting, simply a different version of the black-and-white formula. In fact, truth is made up of many shades of grey, a realization that can be frightening for it forces people to accept that there are not easy answers. Eventually, however, there is joy in discovering the vast array of colors as the mind opens to the richness of life.

One former member described her technique for dealing with the problem:

To help dismantle this all-or-nothing thinking, I began to ask myself, "Where is this on the gray scale?" This question became a favorite one of mine and was very helpful as I struggled to undo 7 years in a black-and-white world and 17 years in a dysfunctional family. I found that life is full of shades of gray. To reinforce the point to myself, I wandered into a redecorating store one day and looked at the number of paint samples from white to gray to black. There were dozens of shades. I saw so clearly that, indeed, there is more to life than black or white.(5)

The Role of Cognitive Distortion

Proponents of cognitive therapy, based on the work of Aaron Beck and others, believe that by changing the way we think we can have a profound effect on the way we feel.(6) In *Feeling Good: The New Mood Therapy,* David Burns outlines 10 common mistakes in thinking, which he calls *cognitive distortions.*(7) These distortions are explained here in the context of postcult recovery.

1. **All-or-nothing thinking:** Cults teach black-and-white thinking, such as "Everyone outside the group is controlled by Satan or is evil," "The leader is God and cannot make mistakes," "You must always strive for perfection in order to reach the group's goal." Such thinking stifles personal growth and keeps a person pitted against the rest of the world.

2. **Overgeneralization:** Simply making one mistake can cause a person to leap to the conclusion that the group's predictions about dire consequences for those who leave are indeed coming true. Former members often have difficulty allowing themselves to make mistakes without hearing criticisms in their head. Reviewing actions at the end of the day, no matter how simple, can help counterbalance the internal cult "chatter."

3. **Mental filter:** Cults teach people to dwell on their mistakes and weaknesses. In many cults each day's activities are reviewed, with concentration placed on any "sins" or wrongdoing. All thoughts, feelings, and behaviors are cause for criticism, prayer, and repenting. After such training, a person may obsess about a small mistake and lose sight of the positive things that are happening. Anything negative becomes a focus that filters out everything else.

4. **Disqualifying the positive:** One means of cult control is to not allow members to take pride in their achievements. All that is good comes from the Master, while members are made to feel stupid and inadequate. Making lists of personal strengths and accomplishments may counteract this reaction.

5. Jumping to conclusions: There are two forms of coming to a negative conclusion, which are probably familiar to ex-members:

(a) *Mind reading:* Those who were in New Age or Eastern cults may have been led to believe that mind reading is real. This belief is used to make assumptions about others. Doing the same now may be counterproductive. Don't jump to conclusions about another person's actions or attitudes. Don't substitute assumptions for real communication.

b) *Fortune telling:* Cults predict the failure of their critics, dissenters, and those who leave. Former members sometimes believe that depression, worry, or illness is sure to hound them (and their family) forever. Remember, such phobias and distortions have nothing to do with reality but have been instilled by the cult.

6. Magnification (catastrophizing) and minimization: Magnifying the members' faults and weaknesses while minimizing strengths, assets, and talents is common. The opposite holds true for the leader. This trend has to be reversed in order to rebuild self-esteem, although reaching a balanced perspective may take time. Feedback from trustworthy, nonjudgmental friends may be helpful here.

7. Emotional reasoning: In groups that place emphasis on feeling over thinking, members learn to make choices and judge reality solely based on what they feel. This is true of all New Age groups and many transformational and psychology cults. Interpreting reality through feelings is a form of wishful thinking. If it really worked, we would all be wealthy and the world would be a safe and happy place. When this type of thinking turns negative, it can be a shortcut to depression and withdrawal: "I *feel* bad, worthless, and so on, therefore I *am* bad, worthless, and so on."

8. "Should" statements: Cult beliefs and standards often continue to influence behavior in the form of shoulds, musts, have tos, and oughts. These words may be directed at others or at oneself—for example, thinking, "I should get out of bed." The result is feeling pressured and resentful. Try to identify the source of these internal commands. Do they come from the former cult leader? Do you really want to obey him anymore?

9. Labeling and mislabeling: Ex-members put all kinds of negative labels on themselves for having been involved in a cult: stupid, jerk, sinner, crazy, bad, whore, no good, fool. Labeling oneself a failure for making a mistake (in this case, joining the cult) is mental horsewhipping. It is an overgeneralization, inaccurate, cruel, and, like the other cognitive distortions, untrue and self-defeating. Labeling others in this way is equally inaccurate and judgmental. If there must be labels, how about some positive ones?

10. Personalization: Burns calls this distortion "the mother of guilt." A primary weapon of cult mind control is training members to believe that everything bad that happens is their fault. The guilt that accompanies this sort of personalizing is crippling and controlling. You are out of the cult now, so it is important only to take responsibility for what is yours.

These 10 cognitive errors are all habits of thinking that are deeply ingrained by the thought-reform processes and cult indoctrination. Tendencies toward these distortions may have been in place even before a person's cult involvement, which may have enhanced vulnerability to recruitment and increased susceptibility to the cult's practices. Given the habit of these kinds of destructive thinking patterns, is it any wonder that former cult members sometimes feel depressed? The good news is, like any habit, these patterns of thinking can be broken and discarded through awareness and practice.

CHAPTER SEVEN

UNDOING THE DAMAGE

The decision to leave a cultic group or relationship is the first step in the recovery process. The actual act of leaving may have been planned for months, or it may happen spontaneously. It may be the result of an outside intervention orchestrated by family and friends, or of circumstances beyond the person's control—for example, being expelled or learning that the leader has abandoned the group.

Suddenly finding yourself on your own after being in an intensely restrictive situation invariably releases a flood of emotions: joy, doubt, relief, regret, a feeling of liberation, a fear of the unknown. Carroll Stoner and Cynthia Kisser, authors of *Touchstones,* a book based on interviews with dozens of former cult members, describe departure this way:

> When cult members leave their movements and organizations, they manage to escape the hold of tyrannical leaders and true-believer fellow members, some of whom they count as close friends. They find themselves questioning doctrines and practices that have kept them in thrall for months, years, or, even in some cases, decades.
>
> Some have lost an idealism which propelled them into believing their groups could, in fact, save the world. Even if they manage to salvage that idealism, they have to face the harsh reality that their dreams did not work, that they were taken advantage of, and that they sacrificed and suffered more than is right.(1)

Postcult Symptoms of Trauma

In 1979 Margaret Singer wrote the first popular article describing the emotional and psychological problems faced by those coming out of cults. She outlined the major areas as depression, loneliness, indecisiveness, slipping into altered states, blurring of mental acuity, uncritical passivity, fear of the cult, the "fishbowl effect" (feeling as though everyone is watching you), the agonies of explaining, and perplexities about altruism, money, and no longer being able to feel like a "chosen" person.(2)

"Not all the former cultists have all of these problems," Singer wrote, "nor do most have them in severe or extended form. But almost all . . . report that it takes them anywhere from 6 to 18 months to get their lives functioning again at a level commensurate with their histories and talents."(3) Singer's early and highly significant work, "Coming Out of the Cults," remains a cornerstone for all further work done in the field, a vital source of information and comfort to former cult members.

Indecisiveness

One frustrating and debilitating postcult condition is indecisiveness. It is difficult watching those around you filling their days with decisions and actions when you sometimes feel stymied by the simplest things. Continued indecisiveness may lower your self-esteem and lead to depression, so it is important not to be too hard on yourself. Take it one step at a time. You are not the first person who had trouble deciding, for example, which bank to use to open up an account. The inability to make decisions is *not* caused by stupidity or laziness but by the shock of having to take responsibility for things again. In the cult you didn't have to make many personal decisions. Now it is time to retrain yourself.

Practice making small decisions first, such as what to wear or what to eat for breakfast. Making lists may make life more manageable. The night before, start a list of what you want to do the next day. Break it down into its smallest parts, beginning with getting up. Then list everything you need to do related to that activity: brush teeth, take shower, get dressed, make the bed, and so on.

A possible danger is becoming dependent on family, friends, or another group. Sometimes it requires great effort and willpower to remain independent. Well-meaning family and friends need to step back now, encouraging and allowing you to take responsibility for yourself and your decisions.

Decisions get easier as you learn to make them. Give yourself permission to make mistakes. Fears of making a mistake, of criticism, of the leader's unpredictability no longer need guide your actions. If you choose incorrectly, you can forgive yourself and take steps to remedy the situation. By relying on yourself for your choices, you become autonomous again. Your self-esteem will increase and so will your capacity for exercising control over your life. Your dependency on others will lessen.

"Loaded" language

Since language in the cult is "loaded," words and their meanings must be recaptured and relearned once you leave. Spending time with words facilitates this process. Start slowly and build up. Work at a reasonable pace, but try to do something related to words, language, or reading every day.

If the newspaper looks too dense or intimidating, try magazines or even comic books. Reread books you liked in the past. Listen to books on tape. Get to know your local library. Do crossword puzzles. Play Scrabble with yourself. Watch or listen to educational television or radio programs. Bookstores that sell used books are a good source of low-cost material.

If any of these activities makes you feel uneasy or causes you to dissociate (for example, if listening to a book on audiotape induces a trance state), trust your feelings and discontinue the activity until you have gained control over the source of discomfort.

Over time, and with some effort on your part, the world will become a familiar place again and you will be able to communicate clearly with those around you.

Black-and-white thinking

Because cults consider themselves superior to everything and everyone not part of the group, they bring out the worst judgmental features of each member. This thoughtless and enforced judgmentalism, which is narrow, prejudicial, and damaging to others, becomes deeply ingrained in the cult member's mind. Embedded and rote, this type of thinking sometimes persists after the person leaves the cult. If you continue to see things in the cult's black-and-white terms, you are still under the influence of your cult training. This us-versus-them mentality will hinder your recovery and keep you isolated from others.

Look back and review your precult beliefs and values as well as those instilled by the cult, then decide how you want to reshape them and work toward what you want to be like now. Remember, you are no longer in an environment where just because someone expresses an opinion it means you have to agree and conform. Nor are you wrong to have a differing opinion.

Most of all, have patience with yourself and others. Learn to tolerate differences of opinion and belief. Gradually, the ability to see others' viewpoints without feeling threatened or needing to change your own will develop. In the cult, isolation and the sense of being uniquely right hold the group together. Undoing this false bond is what recovery from a cult experience is all about.

Floating

A sense of disconnection, lack of concentration, and the feeling of dissociation from others and the environment are all symptoms of floating, a
common postcult difficulty discussed in the last chapter. According to
Margaret Singer, "When they leave the cult, many members find that a
variety of conditions—stress and conflict, a depressive low, certain significant words or ideas—can trigger a return to the trancelike state they knew
in cult days. They report that they fall into the familiar, unshakable lethargy, and seem to hear bits of exhortations from cult speakers."(4)

If you are having such experiences, it may be helpful to remind yourself regularly that floating is a natural by-product of the thought-reform
program and that it will decrease over time. Here are two techniques that
can be used to control it.

The first technique is the simpler:

1. Wear a rubber band around your wrist.

2. As soon as you notice difficulty in concentrating, snap the rubber
   band. Not too hard! This is to bring you back from a numbed
   state, not punish you.

3. Simply but firmly remind yourself that the experience was triggered by some stimulus and that it will pass. This small act is
   often enough to bring you back to ordinary awareness.

Remember, floating is a conditioned, automatic response. Once you
become aware of it and act upon your awareness, you are breaking the
response pattern.

If the first method proves insufficient, here is another. (For some of
you, this technique may be similar to ones used in your group during
visualization exercises. If so, skip this to avoid unpleasant suggestions or
memories.)

As often as possible, stop and take a moment to look around you.
Then, do the following:

1. *See* where you are, look at shapes, sizes, and colors. Take your
   time.

2. Pay attention to your body. What do you *feel?* Touch your face,
   the chair you are sitting in, the fabric of your clothes. Are they
   rough, smooth, hot, cold? Feel your feet on the floor. If you are

standing, walk around, notice the surface of the floor, the comfort or discomfort of your shoes.

3. Listen. What do you *hear* outside your head? Listen to the sounds in the room, the clock ticking, traffic, people talking.

4. Use your nose. Any interesting *smells?*

5. How about taste? Can you distinguish between different *tastes?* What does the inside of your mouth taste like?

The first three—seeing, feeling, and hearing—are the most important. If you are attending to what you see, feel (physically, not emotionally), and hear, you will be in an ordinary waking state.

Triggers

If floating persists and there seems to be some kind of pattern to it, then it is important to discover the *trigger* that is providing the stimulus to float. Obvious triggers could include music that was sung or heard in the cult, mantras, prayers, chants, group jargon, or even a certain tone or rhythm of voice.

Triggers are reminders. They are unique to each person and depend upon specific experiences. Some bring back the ambience of the cult experience. Others may be an event or ritual associated with the cult which becomes uncomfortable to experience after leaving.

A sudden trigger can induce a dissociated state accompanied by a flood of cult-related memories. According to Dr. Singer, there are three kinds of flooding memories: feeling states, content associations, and physical sensations.(5) Triggers may be found in a variety of daily situations, including at work or in an interpersonal relationship. For example, work you did while in the cult may be similar to work you do now that you are out. The following is an example of a work-related trigger.

Tess K. was in a political cult for more than 10 years. She was always given what were considered to be menial or low-level assignments. Often she was ordered to work for hours at the same repetitive task. Once she was assigned to photocopy a massive document for distribution at training meetings that evening. The machine jammed; neither Tess nor any of the other staff could get it working. Since it was after hours, they couldn't call the repair service. Even though the jam was no fault of hers, Tess was viciously criticized for "screwing up the job and preventing the leader from getting her new political line out to the members." That night Tess was made to appear at each local meeting of her cult, seven groups in all, with 10 to 15 comrades in each, in order to be publicly criticized by her peers. It was a draining and devastating experience for her.

Now out of the group and five years later, Tess was working at a law firm. While copying a document at the copier, she suddenly felt a rush of shivers, her whole body flushed. The company's copy room transformed into the cult's staff headquarters and Tess could hear voices screaming at her. She stood at the machine paralyzed and in a trance state—until a coworker nudged her several times to ask her what was wrong. Tess burst into tears and ran out.

Interactions with other people can also set off cult memories. Certain interchanges with friends, family members, or colleagues, or the kind of working relationship you have with your boss or coworkers may remind you of relationships in the cult. There might be individuals with whom you have to maintain an ongoing relationship after your cult departure, such as a former spouse or business associate, who are a constant trigger for cult-related memories and emotions.

Sensory triggers are probably the most common kind. Typical ones are listed here:

- Sights: special colors, flags, pictures of the leader, facial expressions, hand signals, symbols of the group, items used in group activities or rituals, a certain building or location

- Physical sensations: hunger, fatigue, touches, handshakes, a kiss or caress

- Sounds: songs, slogans, clicks in the throat, special laughter, mantras, prayers, speaking in tongues, curses, cue words and phrases, a certain rhythm or tone of voice

- Smells: incense, perfume or cologne of the leader, certain food aromas, room odors, body odors

- Tastes: certain foods, blood

Becoming aware of your triggers begins the process of becoming immune to them. If you have any souvenirs or reminders of your cult's rituals and observances, put them away—don't use them to keep testing yourself. The following example illustrates how one former cult member defused her triggers.

> *Julie B.*, an ex-member of a psychotherapy cult whose leader claimed special powers and abilities, believed that each time she saw her leader's first name it meant he was thinking of her, watching her. Since his name, though unusual, was also the name of a coffee and a bank, she saw it often enough to remind her of him and the power she still believed he had over her. Intellectually, she knew it was ridiculous, but on an emotional level she couldn't shrug off the feelings that he still knew all about her.
>
> Julie's new therapist continued to remind her that her former leader's mind-reading tricks were just that—tricks. He would get information from another client, then present it in a group session as though he were psychic or extremely intuitive. He had been able to convince Julie that she was thinking things that were not even in her mind or imagination, teaching her to distrust her own thoughts while trusting him to know her better than she knew herself. By focusing on all those times the leader had misinterpreted her and had been wrong, the anxiety of the name trigger was reduced.

One antidote to triggers is to be aware when they are likely to occur. Research indicates that triggering happens most frequently when the person is anxious or stressed, fatigued, and ill; and secondarily, when she or he is distracted, lonely, or uncertain.

Patrick Ryan and Joseph Kelly (whose story opens this section) are two exit counselors with personal as well as professional experience with Eastern cults. They have given many workshops on coping with trance states and suggest the following coping strategies:

Maintain a routine

1. Make change slowly—whether physical, emotional, nutritional, or geographical.

2. Monitor your health, including nutrition and medical checkups. Avoid drugs and alcohol.

3. Reduce dissociation, anxiety, and insomnia through daily exercise.

4. Avoid sensory overload. Avoid crowds or large spaces without boundaries (shopping malls, video arcades, etc.).

5. Drive consciously, without music.

Reality orientation

1. Establish time and place landmarks, such as calendars and clocks.

2. Make lists of activities in advance; update the lists daily or weekly. Difficult tasks and large projects should be kept on separate lists.

3. Before going on errands, review the list of planned activities, purchases, and projects. Check off items as they are completed.

4. Keep current on the news. Headline news and other news shows (such as those on CNN, talk radio, and PBS stations) are helpful, especially if you have memory/concentration difficulties, because they repeat.

Reading

1. Try to read one complete news article daily to increase comprehension.

2. Develop reading stamina with the aid of a timer, progressively increasing your reading periods.

Sleep interruptions

1. Leave talk radio or television news stations (not music) on all night.

Most of all, don't push yourself. Dissociation is a habit that takes time to break.(6)

Another useful tool is the Disarming Triggers Worksheet.(7) The worksheet, reproduced on the following page, can be used to help reorient reactions to cult-induced triggers. Make as many copies of this worksheet as you need and have it around you at all times. With it you will be able to confront your triggers head on and defuse them.

First, name the specific *Trigger*. Next, write down your *Immediate Response* to it, both intellectual and emotional? Ask yourself, what does it mean to me now? As an example, let's take Julie's reaction to her former leader's name. Every time she saw the name she believed, even if for a moment, that he was watching her. She felt sudden anxiety and shame.

The *Short-Term Consequences* for Julie were emotions of guilt, shame, and fear. She thought (the message) that she must be doing something "bad" and that he was laughing at her stupidity and ineptness, which had been a common occurrence in the cult.

For the *Challenge* section do some research if necessary. What are the facts? Does the rest of society believe this to be true? In examining the old message, "The leader can read minds," Julie remembered how often he

Disarming Triggers Worksheet

Trigger:

Immediate Response:

   Emotion:

   Message:

Short-Term Consequences:

   Emotion:

   Message:

Challenge:

   Old message:

   Is this message based on fact?

   What facts refute this message?

   What facts, if any, support it?

Results:

   What is the worst that could happen?

   What favorable things, if any, might happen?

New Message:

   What alternative thought could I try to replace the old message?

   How might I defuse my negative emotions?

   What things can I do to replace them with positive emotions?

had been wrong about her. And on those occasions when he had actually been right, she was now able to see that her own body language could have revealed her feelings. Also, she remembered that she had a friend in the cult who could easily have given the information to their leader.

Use your imagination in the *Results* section; see if you can picture and change the things that may happen. Remember those times when your cult or leader was wrong about something. Remember your doubts! Julie can now laugh at the thought of her leader spending 24 hours a day keeping track of all his clients' activities, past and present.

The *New Message* section allows you to try out messages that can replace the old ones. Examine your feelings about these ideas. Julie had to acknowledge that in some ways it was nice to believe someone "on high" was watching over her, able to correct her faults and lead her to a happier, healthier life—a common wish. But it was also okay now to put the group in the past, acknowledge that she was actually quite good at her job, and accept credit for her achievements. She could admit her negative thoughts and feelings about her leader. She had mourned over her losses and expressed anger at having been used—now she could put all that in the past.

Be patient with yourself. When you make the effort to disarm your triggers, you can make huge strides in regaining freedom from the cult's mind control.

Here is another example of disarming a trigger:

Monica R. was born into a cult that used flowers as a symbol for silence and death. A gift of flowers, even a greeting card with flowers, especially roses, represented a dire warning. After leaving the cult, Monica avoided anything depicting flowers. Her apartment even lacked green plants. As she began working through her beliefs in therapy, she remembered an old medicine woman who had befriended her in time of need who used plants, especially aloe leaves, for healing. A piece of the leaf could be torn off and the sap used to reduce the pain of minor burns and insect bites. Monica bought an aloe plant.

Next, she tried tomato plants. The meaning of flowers was changed as the tomato flowers led to tomatoes, her favorite vegetable. Not long after, she was able to bring nonflowering plants into her home and, finally, flowering ones. This change took place over a period of several months. Now, years later, Monica has a garden with roses, annuals, and perennials and she is able to enjoy their beauty without being constantly afraid.

Monica's case demonstrates the power that thought-reform programs are able to invest in normal, everyday objects.

With some modification, the Disarming Triggers Worksheet, particularly the Challenge section, can also be used to examine the cult's beliefs. If obsessional thinking is something that is troubling you, try using an adapted version of the worksheet to lessen the impact of the thoughts. Awareness and practice are key to combating obsessional thinking and specific questions may help demystify the thoughts. Ask yourself the following questions:

- Does the same thought come up repeatedly under similar circumstances?

- What was happening immediately prior to the thought's coming up?

- What meaning does it have for you?

- Is it attached to trauma in the group?

- Does it feel like a compulsion to obey or do something the group wanted?

- What are the feelings attached to the thought? Are you numb? Angry? Frightened?

Some of the cult's control techniques may lie outside your conscious awareness or may be difficult to grasp. It may help to consult an exit counselor familiar with your group or type of group. She or he should be able to explain and demystify the techniques used, which may be causing certain aftereffects. The aftereffects usually lessen when the manipulative technique is brought into your awareness.

Coming out of a cult means rebuilding almost every aspect of your life. Take your time making major decisions and changes, except of course for those that ensure your health and safety. Don't expect healing to happen overnight; at the same time, do not prolong it unnecessarily.

COPING WITH EMOTIONS

The rewards are few in cultic situations, the pain plentiful. Keeping the pain hidden becomes a means of survival. Once you separate from the group or your abusive partner, you may still find yourself hiding your emotions or unable to feel them. You may also be confused by what you actually feel and what you think you should feel. For so long, feelings were defined for you by the group: good or bad, acceptable or unacceptable, pure or evil.

In many groups, particularly Bible-based ones, members are taught that certain thoughts and feelings are sinful. For example, finding someone attractive may be defined as lust. After leaving such a group you need to recognize that having human thoughts and feelings is okay. Instead of continually confessing or suppressing feelings, you discover how to evaluate them and choose the ones you want to act upon.

Learning to feel again, distinguishing between different emotions and reacting appropriately, is vital to healthy functioning. For some former cult members, rediscovering the world of feelings is a big bortion of the healing process. If this is not addressed, they may lead a narrow, unsatisfying existence.

The Role of Emotions in Our Lives

Having feelings is neither good nor bad but a necessary part of our humanity, vital to survival. Without feelings there would be no enjoyment, no sense of accomplishment. We would be unable to proceed with the business of living and would be in danger of perishing as a species.

Feelings can be divided into four basic groups, perhaps oversimplified but handy for our discussion. They are sad, bad, glad, and mad. These are primary feelings, like the primary colors red, blue, and yellow.

All other colors are combinations of these primary colors, and most feelings are combinations of the primary feelings. Each primary feeling can be further differentiated or can be combined with other feelings. For example, when we feel bad, that may include feelings of guilt, rejection, or abandonment. Gladness can encompass joy, happiness, love, gratefulness, and a whole spectrum of pleasurable feelings. It is also possible—and normal—for individuals to have conflicting feelings. This is known as ambivalence. An ex-member's graduation from college provides an illustration: tears of happiness and sadness flow as she relishes her achievements and the pleasure of her family around her. But she also feels sadness at not accomplishing this until her thirties, after having spent 10 years in a cult.

Feelings not only combine and recombine, they also come and go. Anyone who has tried to "hold onto happiness" knows that emotional states are as elusive as the breeze. Forcing oneself to feel something, whether good or bad, is hard work. It can be achieved temporarily by thinking about things that are connected to desired emotions. Remembering a moment where you felt moved to tears may revive those feelings. Recalling a time of great rage or fear may bring up intense feelings again. The memory of pain can enhance survival: you only have to place your hand on a hot stove once to remember not to do it again!

The Role of Emotions in Cults

Feelings are central to our being. They are how we experience and evaluate our experiences; they influence the decisions and choices we make. Working in concert with intelligence and free will, they serve as signals that point us toward goodness, safety, pleasure, and survival.

Considering how powerful emotions are, how basic they are to survival and happiness, it is not surprising that they are used by cults to control members' feelings. Controlling someone's emotions means controlling the person, as illustrated in the following case example.

> *Adeline's* lover, Elliot, was an intelligent, persuasive, and charming English professor at the university she attended. In class he showed great interest in her and in her potential as a writer. Soon they became friends, by the end of the semester they were lovers. Admiring him greatly, Adeline put Elliot on a pedestal. She read and reread his poetry, acted as his secretary, and typed his manuscripts. She constantly attended to Elliot's needs and neglected her own writing, which started to deteriorate. When she did produce new works, she presented them to

him for approval and feedback. He became increasingly critical of her work, poking fun at her grammar and sentence constructions. Shamed, embarrassed, and discouraged, she stopped writing. Respect for her own talent diminished, then disappeared. Being Elliot's indispensable assistant gradually replaced being creative and independent. She reminded herself repeatedly how lucky she was to have such a wonderful mentor and lover.

Adeline's friends noted this transformation. When Elliot entered the room a subtle change came over her. Her mood switched at the slightest sign of his approval or disapproval. She no longer owned her emotions; they were controlled by Elliot, subject to his interpretation and approval. Adeline no longer was able to trust her feelings or herself. She attributed Elliot's rages and moodiness to his genius and artistic temperament. She did not then fully acknowledge her fear of him or the power he had over her.

Several years later, now a successful writer in her own field, Adeline can only look back in wonder at how much control Elliot had over all facets of her life. After Elliot left her for a younger admirer, Adeline began to get her life back. Hesitant and insecure at first, she began to write again and was surprised to find her work well received. Today, her success continues to grow and provide satisfaction. The anger she occasionally feels at the wasted years as Elliot's protégé has simply become fuel for her talents and work.

Emotions are manipulated in cultic groups and relationships in order to control the followers and further the group's or leader's goals. Cult members are taught to distrust this vital part of their being, to suppress certain emotions and encourage others. Guilt, shame, and fear are all used to foster compliance and control. Most other feelings are punished, suppressed, or forbidden.

What happens to these bottled-up emotions? By dividing members and outsiders into an us/them polarity, the cult reinforces the displacement of anger and fear onto nonmembers, family, or the government—a ploy that also helps justify isolationism and antisocial behavior. This was seen in David Koresh's Branch Davidians. Koresh was harshly punitive even to small children who provoked his displeasure. Punishment was meted out to young and old alike. (Paddling and birching are common in many neo-Christian religious groups.) Koresh controlled by fear, yet was successful in diverting the members' fear and anger toward the outside world.

Carefully planned activities that seem spontaneous, such as group singing, chanting, and honoring the leader, manipulate the participants' mystical and devotional feelings. Positive feelings are reserved for the group (or leader) and are manipulated to offset physical, emotional, and/or sexual abuse; food, sleep, or money deprivation; and overwork and isolation. Most cults function on a pleasure/pain principle, dangling the occasional carrot (perhaps a day off, a private interview with the Master, a promotion in duties, sometimes even permission for a holiday) to ensure the member's acceptance of the everyday abuses. What always rules, however, is the stick, which generally far outweighs whatever perks or pleasures the member may think she or he is receiving.

Emotions You May Feel
When You Come Out of a Cult

While in the cult, members learn to survive by denying and suppressing their feelings. Once they leave, they may be flooded with emotions that are difficult to identify and deal with. Having spontaneous feelings is both good and bad news.

You can begin to make sense of your emotions by sorting them, using the basic classification of bad, sad, mad, and glad. Start by asking yourself how you feel. Describe it. If you can't name it, write about it or draw it. Keep a journal—it is one of the best techniques for healing. Gradually you will find that your feelings, which at first seemed chaotic and indecipherable, will begin to make sense. You don't have to *do* anything with them; just observe, feel, and perhaps write about them. You don't have to judge them or get rid of them, even if they don't feel good.

Some people believe that freedom of thought, the ability to choose one's attitude or feelings about anything, is the last of the human freedoms. For example, Viktor Frankl, a Holocaust survivor and renowned psychiatrist, believed that a person's freedom to choose a way of thinking and feeling was something even the Nazis couldn't take away.(1) Unfortunately, for those living within today's thought-reform environments, that most basic freedom *can* be taken away.

Regaining freedom of thought can be liberating, disorienting, and even frightening. But before you can regain it, you have to acknowledge that you have lost it.

Grief and Mourning

Grief is a common reaction among trauma sufferers. After the initial shock and period of denial, feelings of grief surface as the full impact of the loss sets in. In fact, leaving a cultic group or relationship often means experiencing and confronting various losses, which may include the following:

- loss of the group, of a sense of belonging, of commitment; loss of goals

- loss of time; for some, loss of their youth

- loss of innocence, naïveté, idealism

- loss of spirituality, belief system, or meaning in life

- loss of family and loved ones

- loss of pride, self-esteem, and a sense of excitement about life

We will look at each of these losses in order to understand its potential impact on a person's emotional life. Being able to accept your losses is an important step in moving forward.

Loss of the group

While in the cult you probably experienced camaraderie, support, a sharing of ideals and goals. You felt a sense of purpose in life. And you probably also experienced fear and pain, hardship and misery. All of these create a strong bond. No doubt friendships were formed that were hard to leave. Those who spend more than a year or two in a cult there may not have old friends or family to go back to. Those bridges may have burned long ago. The cult may be the only link to the world.

However certain you may have been about your decision, it is natural to feel alone and lonely once you leave, and to mourn the loss of a group environment. It is also natural to feel sadness and confusion. Humans are social animals, drifting toward the pack. You are not "regressing" if you find that you miss what you just left behind. Try not to deny the feeling or berate yourself for having it.

The tendency toward black-and-white thinking may prevent some former members from acknowledging whatever good may have resulted from the cult experience—specific skills, certain types of knowledge, particular relationships with others in the group. The apparent contradiction in being positive about their cult experience may throw them into despair or confusion.

Being part of an intense group dynamic (even a bad one) or an intimate relationship (even an abusive one) is a unique experience. However exploitative or manipulative the encounter may have been, there was *something* good there or you probably you would not have been attracted to the group or person in the first place. Sometimes the something good may have kept you in the situation longer than you would have stayed otherwise. It will help your healing process if you examine this aspect as fully as possible—when you're ready. By looking for the good parts of the cult experience you can stabilize your sense of loss and not allow it to overcome you or, worse yet, drive you back to the group or abusive relationship or another one just like it. In the following chapters, there is more discussion on how to evaluate your experience and use what you learned to build for the future.

Loss of time

Mourning the loss of one's youth because of time spent in a cult is an unhappy but common experience. Trading a college education or career for menial work, fund-raising, or begging for a cult can be a source of bitter regret for many.

Any time spent in a cult—whether months or years—is time lost from loving, living, and growing. People who come out of cults or completely closed, isolating relationships often need to learn about technological advances, career possibilities, cultural differences, political changes, current slang expressions, trends, and fashion. For those born or raised in a cult, the culture gap may be dramatic. They may feel they have just come out of a time warp or landed from another planet.

Because former cult members often feel out of step, they must learn how to integrate their cult experience while dealing with the present and building for the future in a "new" world. They may feel disjointed and out of sync with others in their age group. Related to this, there may be a need to sort out identity issues.

Loss of innocence, naïveté, idealism

A cult experience tends to shake basic assumptions about people and the way the world works. Before the cult involvement you may have learned and believed such things as: the world is a safe place; be nice to people and they will be nice to you; life is fair. A cult experience can be a rude awakening.

Depending on the type of group, your proximity to the leader, and the types of abuses and/or illegal activity that went on, you may have witnessed or participated in an array of regrettable—sometimes perverse—

acts. Prior to your life in the cult you may not have realized that human beings could behave so destructively toward one another. It is helpful to come to terms with this new knowledge and balance it with a healthy skepticism.

The world is neither all good nor all bad, and most people are a mixture of each as well. When you next encounter someone you need to trust or rely on, what you learned from evaluating your cult experience will provide you with some tools to examine your options and make mature decisions about your life.

Loss of meaning in life

In cults, a love of God, the desire for self-improvement, and wishes to help humankind and society are twisted and used to control and exploit devoted believers. Followers are skillfully manipulated into believing that they have had genuine spiritual or psychic experiences, or that they have found the truth, the one path to freedom. It is frequently difficult to determine which experiences are real and which are manufactured by the cult. Later, when followers learn that their experiences were based on deception and cultic manipulations, they begin to doubt their very core. When they learn that they have devoted their time, money, and lives to support a corrupt leader, they often feel burned, betrayed, and unwilling to believe in anything anymore.

For many, the capacity to trust that special part of themselves—the altruistic, loving, and optimistic core—is shattered, sometimes forever. This part is often the last to heal. Redefining beliefs, values, and spirituality is a process that takes time and personal determination. Some former members resume their precult beliefs or return to the religion of their upbringing, while others develop a deep cynicism and distrust for any spiritual philosophy or belief system. Those who do not take the time to educate themselves about cults and mind control remain vulnerable to ever-present cult recruiters and wander from cult to cult, looking for the "right path" to fulfill their spiritual or belief needs. In fact, the belief issue is central to cult involvement and to postcult recovery, and is discussed further in Chapter 10.

Loss of family and loved ones

For former cult members, this loss can be a double whammy. They may lose their precult family and friends, *and* the family and friendships developed during cult membership. Reconnecting with family and friends is not always possible, although most former members make efforts to do so. Sometimes there has been too much water under the bridge and the other person has no desire to reestablish the relationship. Old friends may have relocated, certain important persons may have died. For long-term cult members estranged from their families, the loss of the opportunity to reconcile or say goodbye to a loved one can be especially painful.

Cult members who stay in a group for any length of time generally come to regard other members as family. The isolation inherent in cultic situations engenders this kind of bonding. The forced sharing of private thoughts and the mutual suffering establish illusions of intimacy that reinforce this feeling. For those who were born in a cult or married another cult member, various relatives may still be devoted members. For them, leaving the group can mean losing relatives, friends, and all relational ties. Chapters 9 and 10 address interpersonal issues further.

Loss of pride and self-esteem

Cult members are taught to regard the group and themselves as special, an elite, the chosen few: on the "jet plane to enlightenment" (Transcendental Meditation), on the "fastest path" (Sant Mat), on the "most direct path" to God (Eckankar), being in "the Kingdom" (Boston Church of Christ). The idea of being One with the Truth gives believers a sense of security and a feeling of superiority over others of "lesser" beliefs. Feeling you have found the Ultimate Answer—whether political, therapeutic, financial, spiritual, personal, or even extraterrestrial—can be a potent high.

A sense of elitism, the feelings of security, the friendships, the emotional highs, the fringe benefits if you were near the leader, all create powerful reasons to stay attached to the group. When you leave, you may feel as though the rug was ripped out from under you—no more magic carpet. The thrill is gone. As you confront the challenge of rebuilding your life, this emptiness will fade as you develop renewed purpose and meaning.

In cults and cultic relationships, one often feels a sense of satisfaction in giving love, serving a master, or dedicating oneself to a higher cause or ideal. In groups that emphasize self-improvement, suffering is often endured in service to the self. After all that sacrifice, it can be devastating to find that you were duped.

"One of the more painful of the small emotions is the feeling of being used," writes psychoanalyst Willard Gaylin. To better understand the significance of this emotion, he suggests comparing the *humiliation* of feeling used and the *pleasure* of feeling useful.

The feeling of usefulness provides a great joy and pleasure. To feel of use is one of the fundamental ingredients of pride. We pride ourselves by our uses. We even sense or acknowledge ourselves through our uses. We exist in our own mind's eye through the exploitation and expenditure of all of our personal resources. When we use ourselves, in almost any sense of the word, we are building a sense of our own worth....

How, then, do we explain the almost universal feelings of outrage, shame, hurt, and resentment that combine in that most humiliating feeling of "being used"? ... To feel used is to feel that our services have been separated from ourselves. It is a sense of the violation of our central worth, as though we ourselves are important to the other individual only because we are a vehicle for supplying the stuff that he desires. It may be most graphic and evident when what he desires is a material or physical thing—our money or our possessions—but we are equally offended when what is taken or used is our intelligence, our creativity, our companionship, or our love.(2)

While Gaylin may describe feeling used as a "small emotion," the enormity of the exploitation in cults gives that feeling greater prominence. Perhaps not wanting to feel duped keeps many people involved in the cult or cultic relationship longer than they would like. Pride, shame, guilt, fear, and love work in concert to prevent cult members from acting sooner. Once they do leave, they have to deal with the awful realization that they were tricked, fooled, and exploited by the very group or leader they idealized. Admitting this is very hard to do—but it can also be a great release.

Allowing yourself to grieve

After you lose the group environment, the sense of belonging, innocence, your belief system, family and friends, and feelings of pride, it is no wonder that you may feel a deep sadness. Unsettling questions might surface: "If I'm so glad to be out of the group, why do I miss it?" or "How can I weep for the loss of something so horrid?" The worst thing to do in the face of this enormous loss is to deny it or push it aside.

Remember this: there was nothing wrong with your commitment. What was wrong was that your commitment was turned against you and exploited. The mourning is for you as much as for the group. Your grief is justified and righteous, and your healing will be swifter if you allow yourself to feel the grief. There must have been good moments, good people, and good feelings, and it is normal to mourn their loss.

Do not let your sense of grief push you back into the group, or into another situation where you will be similarly abused. Remember, whatever good there may have been is most certainly outweighed by the lack of freedom, the exploitation, and the abuse you experienced. Let yourself grieve—then, move on to integrate the experience and rebuild your life . . . your *own* life.

The Specter of Boredom

More than one ex-member commenting about life in a cult has said, "At least it wasn't boring!" Indeed, the highs and lows of cult life produce memories that are often savored surreptitiously by ex-members. As cruel as a leader was or as challenging as the tasks were, they provided excitement, pleasure, and a sense of accomplishment. The emotional manipulations, mystical journeys, and exotic pilgrimages may have created some unforgettable experiences. Cult hardships and challenges catapulted life out of the ordinary.

Leaving a cult and coming into the mundane world, especially with the emotional baggage of the experience, may produce a strong letdown, a feeling of boredom or its cousin, ennui. Dissatisfaction, hopelessness, helplessness, fatigue and lethargy, vague longings, and a pinch of anger are the ingredients of those emotions.

The antidote is to acknowledge those things in daily life that give you pleasure—for example, being able to sleep late occasionally, to choose your own foods, to not have to take orders. As you recover from your losses, new discoveries will gradually add meaning to your life: new pleasures, new friends, new experiences, new realizations. When you can begin to enjoy the small wonders of living daily in freedom, then you will slowly be able to look forward to larger pleasures. Reawakening your sense of curiosity and your ability to fantasize and dream about the future requires exercising the imaginative muscles of the mind which were put to sleep in the cult.

Make time for enjoyment. In the cult, fun may have been denied as frivolous and self-indulgent or made into work, learning, or spiritual growth. Either way, to have fun or enjoy oneself lost its meaning. The best remedy for boredom is education. Whether it is returning to school or exercising the mind through reading, lectures, or challenging experiences, reawakening the ability to think and create encourages and enhances the return of self-confidence and self-esteem.

Start slowly—perhaps with a wish list of all the things that you would like to do, have, or be. Then make another list of things that are actually possible in the coming year, month, or week. Choose one item at a time that you can reasonably achieve. Boredom ends with the realization that life—your life—has value. That is a wonderful discovery to make.

Feeling Like a Failure

People leaving cultic situations frequently feel that they are failures for not having stayed in the group or relationship. Since cults typically blame the members for everything bad that happens, former members have a tendency to continue this practice of self-blame, as illustrated in the example below.

> *"Janis," "Martin,"* and their children were asked to leave the "Community" (a large Christian commune) three times due to "improper" attitude, although they were very hardworking. Each time the family was ejected, virtually penniless, they worked to reestablish themselves in the good graces of the leadership. Having spent more than 20 years in the cult, the family of 10 found it hard to adjust to regular society. They lacked marketable trades and skills and missed the group, which was like an extended family. Feelings of failure and hopelessness always led them back to the Community. The last time they were cast out, however, they did something different. They sought out others who had experienced a similar fate. Together with other excommunicated families, Janis and Martin found the support they needed to recover their independence—and not go back.(3)

As a former cult member you may be experiencing very low self-esteem, or lack of self-confidence, and excessively self-critical and blaming attitudes. These are characteristic of many people who have been in a cult and, if left unexamined, they may cause you to have difficulty getting your life in order after you leave.

It is helpful to keep a journal, perhaps at the end of the day, and record in it everything you did, the new feelings you felt, the people you talked to, and what you read or learned about the world and yourself. Each new experience presents an opportunity and a lesson for you: What did you do right? What would you do differently next time? How could you have avoided a problem or turned it around?

In the cult, you may have become so accustomed to being criticized that now you may feel your group, leader, or abusive partner is in your head, still berating you or giving orders. Silence that voice by literally saying "No! Go away!" Acknowledge something you achieved and take full credit for it, even if it was simply getting out of bed. Write it down in your journal. These small daily accomplishments will grow, especially once you take written notice of them. Soon you will see actual progress as you review your diary.

The flip side of feeling like a failure because you left the cult is feeling like a failure for having been there at all. When ex-members realize and accept the fact that they have been in a cult, sometimes they blame themselves for not having left sooner. Self-education is the key to getting rid of such thoughts. As you begin to recognize the thought-reform techniques used in the cult, you will understand why it was difficult to leave.

Other people will ask you why you didn't leave sooner or right away. It may be helpful to write an essay answering that question. Limit it to two or three pages, and focus on the precise mechanisms and emotional dynamics that kept you in the group. Being able to explain this to yourself and others will bring much relief.

Guilt and Shame

We experience guilt and shame when our thoughts and behaviors run counter to society's or our own feelings about what is right and wrong. While in the cult your prior beliefs and ethical system may have been dismissed, discounted, distorted, or reversed, which was all part of the cult's system of control. Now, as you begin to get in touch with your moral code, you may feel guilt and shame. Some of the reasons for feeling this way might be that you

- hurt and disappointed family, caused them worry, pain, and anger

- recruited friends, relatives, and other members

- participated in cult-related activities that went against your previous values, such as begging, lying, spying on friends and other members, or violent and criminal acts including drug usage or trafficking, stealing, assault, murder, and prostitution.

- attained a position of power and authority in the group and used it to support the leader and control or abuse others, thereby perpetuating the "victim chain"

We generally feel guilt when we do something we believe to be bad.

Only the psychopath feels no guilt at his own behavior, yet he is often skilled at using that emotion in order to control others. As a former cult member you are probably expert at feeling guilty! In all fairness to this emotion, however, guilt can serve uniquely noble purposes. It causes us to rise above our pettiness and selfishness as we extend ourselves. Occasional twinges of guilt (also known as conscience) encourage us to be better, more caring human beings. Cult leaders or abusive partners, who lack this capacity, are truly inadequate beings, worthy only of pity.

We generally feel shame when we perceive ourselves as bad in the eyes of others. According to Gaylin, "Shame is the sister of guilt and is often confused in usage with guilt. They serve the same purposes: both facilitate the socially acceptable behavior required for group living; both deal with transgression and wrongdoing against codes of conduct and are supporting pillars of the social structure. But whereas guilt is the most inner-directed of emotions, shame incorporates the community, the group, the other . . . . Shame requires an audience, if not realistically, then symbolically. Shame is a public exhibition of wrongdoing or the fear of being exposed in front of the group."(4)

The following exemplify how guilt and shame operate and are exploited in cults.

> In a rapidly growing commercial cult, members were encouraged to work in high-paying fields. During monthly meetings, each person was to state publicly what he or she was earning. Members were exhorted to earn as much as they could, their income the measure of dedication to the leader. Naturally, the more a person earned, the more money she or he was expected to pay for instruction. Those deemed to be poor earners were shamed before the group and made to feel morally inferior and unworthy of further instruction.

•

> In a Bible-based group, *Ann* was given fund-raising goals each day which were to be met through the sale of raffle tickets on the street. Underfed and working 12 to 18 hours a day, Ann always met her quotas but felt terribly guilty about sometimes withholding money for an occasional candy bar. Judging herself evil, selfish, and weak, she now heaped shame upon guilt, because of her fear that her holding out for herself be discovered.

Psychiatrist Judith Herman has written about the guilt and shame experienced by rape victims. Her insights are equally applicable to those who have been in a cult environment: "Beyond the issues of shame and doubt, traumatized people struggle to arrive at a fair and reasonable assessment of their conduct, finding a balance between unrealistic guilt and denial of all moral responsibility. In coming to terms with issues of guilt, the survivor needs the help of others who are willing to recognize that a traumatic event has occurred, to suspend their preconceived judgments, and simply to bear witness to her tale."(5)

The cultic system produces a continuous cycle of guilt, shame, and fear. The challenge now is to identify those actions you would regret given your precult ethical systems, or one you've developed that is not skewed by the cult's values. At the same time, you need to identify the factors within the group that diminished your capacity to make voluntary, informed choices. You must sort out the actions you should take responsibility for from those that are the responsibility of the group and leader.

Depression

Grief and mourning—especially when combined with despair, ennui, anxiety, inward anger, and shame—can produce an incapacitating depression. You may find yourself dealing with deep feelings of depression for some time after leaving the group. Commitment to an ideal, group, or leader fills life with purpose and direction. Once you are no longer part of the group or relationship, you must deal with the meaning of this loss. The broken promises and disillusionment coupled with life's new challenges and difficulties may be overwhelming.

The key to dealing with depression and other intense emotions is to express them somehow, sometime, to someone. Keeping a journal is one way to do this. Writing an account of the cult experience is an excellent way to make sense of it. It gets the feelings out of your head and body and onto paper. Use your imagination to express yourself—write, draw, paint, sculpt, knit, or crochet how you feel.

Finding someone to listen to your experiences and your feelings is a vital part of healing. The person you choose must be able to listen to you nonjudgmentally and sympathetically, must be interested in learning about cults and mind control, and must be objective and supportive of your efforts to heal.

One exercise that can prove especially useful is to recall what your former group believed or said about leaving. Many ex-members can remember their leaders telling the group that those who leave will become emotionally ill, even die. Did your group attempt to keep you under its control through the threat of insanity or death? By taking a look at your group's beliefs about emotions or emotional difficulties, you may find a way to defuse any hold those beliefs still have over you.

Hana Whitfield listed the following activities that helped her get through her bouts of depression after she left her group:

1. I put my attention on things I had to deal with every day.

2. I frequently told myself that the depression too would pass, as the cult experience had passed. That helped.

3. Doing physical tasks helped take my mind off the depression: scrubbing the floor, cleaning and waxing the car (whether it needed it or not), doing some hard digging in the yard, taking a very physical walk or jogging, and so on.

4. I kept a *daily* list of actions to accomplish that would better my life, my living situation, my salary, and so on, no matter how small they were. Things like seeing the landlady at the apartment house, buying a newspaper to look for part-time jobs, making a certain phone call, filing my nails, washing some clothes. I did this religiously and gave myself a pat on the back every single time one thing got done. This definitely gave me a sense of *real* accomplishment. Each evening I would make out the list for the following day.

5. I encouraged myself to trust myself; I did this consciously. Every day I would look at what I had accomplished that day and give myself strokes for it. I would tell myself that I *could* handle things, that I was getting ahead, even if slowly, that I *was* in control.

She adds:

1. Know that the depression will not last forever.

2. Underlying it are feelings of anger, sorrow, hurt, and betrayal.

3. It's all right and healthy to start experiencing those feelings and to let them surface.

4. It helps to write down whatever is surfacing, to let it come out.

5. It's all right and healthy to *feel,* to feel feelings of sorrow or hate or indecision or revenge or even to feel like killing someone in the group.

6. It isn't unhealthy or bad to need therapy or help or counseling. Sometimes a therapist is the best qualified to help you let those feelings surface and help you through them.

7. Look for and find some information that will help you understand your cultic experience, whether through books, an exit counselor, or a therapist.

Remember that depression, especially if accompanied by suicidal thoughts and self-destructive behaviors, may require the care of a mental health practitioner. Depression *is* treatable. Many ex-members have been helped by therapy and occasionally by medication with antidepressants.

Fear

Fear is the backbone of mind control. Cults control by fear: fear of those outside the group; fear of failure, ridicule, and violence within the group; fear of spiritual failure or the disintegration of your belief system. Comparing notes with other ex-members is the best antidote to fear. It is easier to recognize that your fear may be the result of psychological manipulation when you talk about it with others who have had similar experiences.

One resource for mutual support is FOCUS, a support network for former cult members. There are numerous FOCUS groups throughout the United States (see Appendix B).

Fear often comes in the form of plaguing questions:

- What if I was wrong and the leader really is the messiah or all-knowing one?

- What if harmful events actually do befall defectors?

- What if the group follows through on its threats?

People outside cults sometimes ask, "Why don't members leave cults if they want to? They aren't physically restrained." One answer to that question lies in the phenomenon known as phobia induction. A phobia is an intense reaction of fear to someone or something that, in effect, can immobilize a person from doing something. Sometimes the phobia causes physical responses such as heart palpitations, dry mouth, sweating, and other manifestations of tension.

"In some cults, *members are systematically made to be phobic about ever leaving the group*," wrote Steve Hassan. "Today's cults know how to effectively implant vivid negative images deep within the members' unconscious minds, making it impossible for the member to even conceive of ever being happy and successful outside of the group....Members are programmed either overtly or subtly (depending on the organization) to believe that if they ever leave, they will die of some horrible disease, be hit by a car, be killed in a plane crash, or perhaps even cause the death of loved ones."(6)

Phobia induction is a powerful means of control because it makes testing reality a frightening prospect, and because it can cause a kind of paralysis, an inability to act. In some groups, members are told that they will be possessed by the devil, die, or become psychotic if they leave the group. Since some cult members believe their leader has supernormal powers, they take such predictions seriously. In other groups, members are told that the outside world is cruel, unbearable, unsympathetic, and they will never survive out there.

Review in your mind the training that went on in your group. Think about the kinds of things that were said or taught. Remember the power of triggers. If you are fearful and having panic attacks, review the Disarming Triggers Worksheet and some of the other techniques mentioned in Chapter 7.

Because you have been warned about the dangers of leaving the group, you may still be blaming yourself for everything bad that happens. Do some reality checking. If the cult is responsible for the bad things that have happened to you since leaving, then who is responsible for the good? Be realistic about your former leader's powers and the cult's actual ability to follow through on threats. If harm from the cult is a real possibility, then take necessary precautions, some of which are outlined below.

Protecting Yourself

You may be convinced when you leave the cult that the leader or the group will pursue, kidnap, or punish you physically, emotionally, or spiritually. Usually, this is an empty threat. But even if your group is not known to be violent toward ex-members, you should protect yourself.

The following suggestions come from Kevin Garvey, an experienced exit counselor.(7)

Stage one: reality testing

Ask yourself the following:

1. Has your group ever hurt, sued, libeled, slandered, kidnapped, or actually killed someone?

2. Have you ever met anyone who was so harmed?

3. Has your group admitted to hurting or harassing others?

4. How important were you to the group? Does the group have any reason to fear you or the knowledge you have now that you are out?

5. How emotionally stable are the leader and the remaining group members?

Garvey says that 80 percent of his cases do not generate safety concerns. The remaining 20 percent involve aggressive efforts to contact the person, harassment, and legal threats. He calls this the "hollow threat" category, as the cult rarely follows through. "It usually reflects a leader's need to impress the followers," states Garvey.

Stage two: putting the cult on notice

Consider doing the following:

1. Write your cult leader and state emphatically that you have left the group and do not wish to be contacted. Send the letter by certified mail and ask the post office for a "Proof of Mailing" only. Do not ask for acknowledgment of receipt by the group, as many groups routinely refuse certified and registered mail.(8)

2. Hang up on all calls from the cult. Get an unlisted number if you get repeated calls. If they still persist, call the telephone company and complain.(9)

3. Go to the police and make a complaint. You may be able to get a restraining order if you are being seriously harassed.

4. Get professional legal help if you are subject to legal harassment from the cult.

Stage three: taking precautions

If there are direct threats of violence, consider the following:

- Try to assess the extent of the threat.
- Notify law enforcement and arrange for their help.
- Intensify normal safety precautions.
- Be aware of being watched or followed.
- Never travel alone.
- Keep track of any unusual telephone calls.
- Keep family cars protected.
- Carefully monitor family members, especially small children.
- Alter familiar daily patterns.
- Keep exterior house lights on at night.
- Install a home security system.
- Buy, borrow, or adopt a big or loud dog.
- Move to another locale.

Other safety issues

The safety protocols above can help to determine the potential for danger from the cult or leader. But there are also "small" everyday terrors that must be disarmed and dealt with. Ex-members need to feel safe in their homes and with others. Stability is important for recovery.

Registered nurse and counselor Anna Bowen's thoughts on safety issues and support networks are especially helpful for those coming out of a one-on-one cultic relationship or a particularly abusive group cult. She writes:

> In identifying safety, it is important to clarify what safety means by asking the person to be as specific in her answer as she is able. Some women have said to me that they don't feel safe at home. Yet, they spend most of their time there. When this occurs, I have them describe each room. I listen for hints that may convey a message of comfort, security or safety. Usually the person will identify at least one area

where she is able to feel comfortable. It may be a couch on which she sits with an afghan wrapped around her, or at the kitchen table where she likes to have a cup of tea. Recognizing that she can prepare for her own comfort and safety is validating and reassuring.

Making a list of the people in her support network is important. Sometimes assumptions are made as to who will be supportive and how each one will lend support. Writing down each person, place, and supportive thing and identifying how each lends support will provide a more accurate picture of the support system and can prevent misunderstandings.(10)

Ex-members who were in extremely violent or threatening cults may experience feelings of terror and have thoughts of suicide. If you have such thoughts and they become overwhelming, seek assistance. Ask a trusted friend to sit and talk with you until you are calm. Or, call a therapist or counselor with whom you are working or the Suicide Prevention Hot Line (you can get this number by calling your local information). The important thing is to confront your fears, not let them take over.

Anger

The emergence of anger is one of the first signs of recovery. Anger is a normal and healthy reaction to the hurts and assaults that you experienced. Anger is the most appropriate response to the abuse and manipulations of the cult. It is also the hardest emotion for some ex-members to get in touch with and deal with. If you feel angry, it means you are now ready to acknowledge that you were victimized, which can be incredibly painful. What was done was heinous—and you are entitled to your rage.

Just as fear is the backbone of mind control, anger is the fuel of recovery. Anger is an extremely valuable tool in healing. It fortifies your sense of what is right by condemning the wrong that was done to you. It gives you the energy and will to get through the ordeal of getting your life back together. Suppression of anger while in the cult contributed to depression and a sense of helplessness. Now the reverse is possible.

Anger can be a double-edged sword, however. It can motivate healing or be turned inward, against the self. Some people may find it easier to blame themselves than to use their anger to make necessary life changes. This can result in alcohol or drug use, physical illness, or emotional disorders including depression and suicidal thoughts and behaviors. Anger can also be directed at innocent others. If expressed inappropriately or unconsciously, anger can further a person's isolation. To be used effectively, anger must be focused on its source—primarily the cult leader.

Remember that your anger may be hard for family, friends, and sometimes even therapists to accept. You may be urged to forgive and forget. Ex-members who have been brought up to hide or deny negative feelings may not have the tools or experience to know how to express this potentially healing emotion.

Former cult members "need to realize that what was done to them was *wrong*," writes Michael Langone. "[They] must be allowed—encouraged even—to express appropriate moral outrage. The outrage will not magically eliminate the abuse and its effects. Nor will it necessarily bring the victimizer to justice. But it will enable victims to assert their inner worth and their sense of right and wrong by condemning the evil done to them. Moral outrage fortifies good against formidable evil. Even implicitly denying victims' need to express moral outrage shifts blame from victimizers to victims. Perhaps that is why so many victims are disturbed by 'detached' therapists, or 'objective' scientific researchers. They interpret the detachment or 'objectivity' as implicit blaming of themselves."(11)

People who have experienced a particularly traumatic cult involvement or childhood physical and sexual abuse share certain experiences. Both have been victimized by those they depended on and trusted. Many cult members have also been sexually and/or physically abused. All have been emotionally and spiritually victimized. Anger at such abuse can be expressed and transformed through the use of the techniques given below. Initially, it is important not to do these exercises alone. When repressed anger is first released, the intensity can be overwhelming, even frightening. Therefore, some of the activities listed here are best done with a trusted and stable friend or therapist.

1. Keep a diary and write about your anger and other strong feelings. Former cult members have consistently said that writing about their experience has been one of the most helpful vehicles for working through their feelings of betrayal and abuse.

2. Write a letter to your cult leader. Tell him or her off. It is not necessary to send it, especially if doing so would put you in danger. You don't have to mail the letter to feel the positive effects of having written it.

3. Talk to someone about your feelings. Make sure it is someone who can understand and empathize.

4. Turn on the shower, get in, and scream.

5. Get in your car, turn the radio on loud and scream—but not while driving.

6. Do something physically expressive: pound pillows with a whiffle bat or tennis racket. Go into the woods and pound boulders with a sledgehammer (wear protective goggles). Direct your anger into the activity.

7. Fantasize taking revenge; imagine it. People spontaneously imagine scenarios in which their injured pride is restored. Don't, however, act out by doing something illegal or dangerous to another.

8. Speak out publicly about your cult experience. Get involved in an anticult group. This has been therapeutic for many ex-members.

9. Get the law on your side. If your group has been involved in criminal activity, consult a lawyer for your own protection before going to the police.

10. Consider a civil suit for damages against the cult. Again, seek legal advice about this first.

11. Take an assertiveness training course.

The following story illustrates one ex-member's struggle with anger:

Divorced and alone, *Jill C.* joined Pastor John's church after the accidental death of her small daughter. At first she felt comforted by the loving solicitousness of the group and its leader. Besides full Sunday service, Jill spent three to four evenings a week attending Bible study and prayer meetings. This enabled her to avoid lonely evenings at home missing her daughter. Six months after she joined the church Pastor John's counseling turned affectionate, then sexual. Though she was not particularly attracted to him, Jill had difficulty saying no to her pastor and found herself passively submitting to his sexual attentions.

As the shame and guilt from the relationship became untenable, she withdrew and finally left the church and Pastor John. With time and distance, Jill felt her anger mount. At odd times during the day she would become preoccupied with hatred and rage toward her former spiritual leader. She found herself snapping at others, impatient, irritable over mistakes. Through counseling, Jill learned some techniques for dealing with her anger. If she started to become preoccupied and angry while at work, she would fantasize Pastor John coming into the room and herself picking him up and throwing him out the window of the skyscraper. When she could do something physical but safe with her anger she did; when it was impossible to take some action she gave herself permission to fantasize his destruction, embarrassment, or public humiliation. It took time for the rage to turn to anger, then to irritation and resentment. Finally, that too was all but gone.

In the cult or with your abusive partner, it may have been dangerous or forbidden to express anger or rage. You learned to turn your anger inward, or to deny and suppress it. Now, give yourself permission to feel this emotion! There is a big difference between thinking, feeling, and acting out. Some former cult members are afraid that their rage is so powerful it will overwhelm them, which is why it is important to channel it constructively. When you do, you will start to feel relief and reinforce your freedom from domination.

Going Crazy before You Go Sane

When one looks at the variety of intellectual (cognitive) and emotional difficulties that many ex-members experience, it is easy to understand why some feel they are going crazy. With cults telling their followers that only psychotic or evil people leave, or that they will go crazy (or die or go to hell) if they give up the group, problems such as dissociation, obsessive thoughts, memory loss, anxiety, and depression may cause ex-members to fear for their sanity. Fortunately, these problems, although often intense, are usually short-lived. Occasionally, however, ex-members *do* suffer brief psychotic episodes after leaving the cult and need immediate psychiatric attention.

Feeling crazy isn't the same as *going* crazy. Dissociation accompanied by anxiety or panic as discussed in previously, is a common aftereffect of cult conditioning. Be patient with yourself. If you find that such thoughts and feelings persist, get help from mental health professionals who are knowledgeable about cults and thought reform. Your symptoms may also be relieved through the temporary use of tranquilizers or antidepressants administered under the care of a licensed practitioner.

Forgiveness as a Means to Recovery

Forgiving yourself is essential to eliminating shame and guilt. Shame is toxic. It cripples self-esteem and retards emotional healing. Although guilt may help a person avoid the same mistakes again, excessive guilt prevents growth and learning from those mistakes.

The first step toward forgiveness is to bring into clear focus where you were when you were recruited. Your own vulnerability and the cult's recruitment tactics need to be understood. Separating what the cult recruiters did and said from your needs at the time of recruitment will help put the process in perspective. Remember, being vulnerable is not the same as being to blame. Knowing your vulnerabilities can help you to identify deceptive recruitment and indoctrination techniques.

Once a person is recruited, his or her personality changes, as the secondary or "cult" personality develops. Few persons can resist the systematic manipulation that occurs in a cult environment. Those practiced in thought-reform techniques can sense just how far and fast a person can be deceived and exploited. Pressure to conform and the promise of reward, along with induced feelings of guilt and fear, are powerful agents of change. Take all this into consideration when evaluating your situation. Above all, have compassion for yourself.

The following technique, adapted from 12-step programs, is a useful exercise for working through guilt and shame:

1. First make a list of everything you did in the group that now produces feelings of shame, guilt, and regret.

2. Share this with someone you trust, someone who will not judge you. Talk it over with a therapist, exit counselor, clergyperson, or another ex-member. You need someone else's perspective and objectivity. You need to get it out of you.

3. Look at the list and see if you can make amends to any of the people involved. This should not be done if it causes further pain to another or puts you at risk of reinvolvement with the group.

4. If you can, and if you find it helpful, ask for forgiveness from God or your spiritual source.

5. Don't forget to forgive yourself. This is both the hardest and the most important part. As long as you are operating on guilt or shame, you are emotionally handicapped.

We can seek forgiveness from those we hurt, from God, and from ourselves, but forgiving those who so deliberately hurt us is a different matter and a highly personal one. As more than one ex-member has said, "As a fellow member, I can forgive those in the group who hurt me. They were as much under the influence of our leader as I was. As for the leader, since he shows absolutely no remorse for what he has done to me, what he continues to do to others, and what he would still do to me if he could, I do not forgive him."

It has been said that success is the best revenge. Becoming functional and happy outside of the cult, rather than getting sick and dying or becoming a complete loser as the cult may have predicted, is the best manifesto of your success and the best exposure of the cult's lies about life outside of the group.

CHAPTER NINE

REBUILDING A LIFE

Two main topics are explored in this chapter. Each addresses a major aspect of life that may have been neglected or corrupted during time spent in a cult or cultic relationship: (1) physical and health issues, and (2) interpersonal issues, including old and new relationships with family, friends, spouses, and children.

The following cases exemplify contrasting emotional responses by two people after leaving their cults.

Steve P. was an attractive, bright 18-year-old college freshman when he was recruited into a Bible-based shepherding group. While others in his dorm were experimenting with partying and dating, Steve attended Bible study sessions and did volunteer work. A discipler appointed by the group monitored all of Steve's behaviors, thoughts, and feelings; all major and minor decisions were made under the discipler's guidance. Steve dropped out of school in his third semester to attend the cult's bible school full-time, preparing for missionary duties.

After eight years overseas Steve decided to leave the group after an exit counseling arranged by his family while he was home for a brief visit. Reunited with family and friends, Steve was alarmed, resentful, envious, and angry when he compared his life to that of his former friends, most of whom were absorbed in careers, marriage, and family. Overwhelmed by how much he had missed, he felt out of sync, like a middle-aged teenager. In a rush to make up for lost time and free from the group's rigid control, he overreacted, becoming quite sexually active, usually with much younger women, rarely dating anyone more than two or three times. Uncomfortable with himself, mildly depressed, and anxious, he was abusing alcohol and marijuana when he entered therapy.

•

After 10 years of devoted practice and meditation *Ron C.* left an Eastern meditation group's ashram where he had been celibate and a strict vegetarian. He had enjoyed the discipline and spiritual practices, which included four to six hours daily of meditation and yoga as well as service to the poor in the community. Successfully emulating his guru, Ron eventually became his secretary, a high honor. In such close proximity to his Master, he began to observe behaviors that bothered him. Finally confronted with direct evidence of his beloved guru's sexual involvement with a child disciple, Ron was devastated and disillusioned. Abruptly packing up his few belongings, he left the ashram for good.

Five years after his departure Ron is in a support group for ex-members. He is still a vegetarian, rarely dates or socializes, and only now is able to begin to evaluate his cult experience. Reintegration has been difficult for him. New experiences, friendships, and lifestyles have been hard to adjust to. Extremely disillusioned, feeling that his trust in himself and others has been shattered, he no longer meditates and describes himself as a turtle, peeking warily out of his shell. Slowly he is able to talk about his experience, finding comfort and understanding in a support group.

Steve and Ron each had individual ways of reacting to his cult experience. We hope that the information in this book will help you to find a reasoned and rewarding path to healing that is useful for you.

Taking Care of Your Body

In most cults the last thing members are permitted to care for is their own health. If you were in a situation that didn't allow for proper nutrition or exercise, medical care when you were ill or pregnant, or adequate dental hygiene and care, you might have special health problems. At the least, you should now have a general medical checkup, including eye, ear, and dental examinations. All children and adolescents who were in a cult need a complete physical and may need to be updated on vaccinations against serious childhood illnesses such as polio, measles, and whooping cough.

A medical checkup is essential if the following conditions exist:

1. You are presently suffering from a chronic (long-term) or acute (recent and severe) medical ailment—whether it developed before, during, or after your cult involvement.

2. You were pregnant at any time while in the group.

3. You were physically and/or sexually abused while in the group.

4. You were exposed to serious infectious diseases such as AIDS, hepatitis, tuberculosis, venereal diseases, and tropical diseases.

5. You have a prior history of a chronic illness such as diabetes, asthma, epilepsy, high blood pressure, or heart disease.

Most people coming out of a cult have no medical insurance or savings of any kind. In such cases it may be necessary to register as an outpatient at a community health center or public hospital. If you are fortunate enough to have a job with medical coverage, take advantage of what it offers.

Poor eating habits are typical in many cults, even those that profess "healthy" regimens. Often, inadequate nutrition is used by cults to further control of their members. Many groups enforce a vegetarian diet, which may or may not be healthy. Vegetarianism or any special diet must be well thought out and conscientiously practiced. Books such as *Diet for a Small Planet* by Frances Moore Lappé (Ballantine Books) and *Sundays at Moosewood Restaurant* by the Moosewood Collective (Simon and Schuster/Fireside) provide excellent advice and delicious recipes for those who wish to continue with vegetarian practices or simply eat well-balanced meals.

Nutritious food will probably be needed after any cult involvement longer than three or four months. Besides the long hours and unhealthy conditions, the stress and anxiety inherent in cult situations often have a negative impact. It is a good idea to reexamine your eating habits and evaluate your vitamin and mineral intake by doing some basic research on nutrition. If you feel incapable of figuring out the best diet for yourself or if you feel confused by the seemingly constant changes in advice about what to eat or not eat, discuss your situation with a medical doctor or a dietary and nutrition counselor. Many local hospitals offer public programs on this topic.

Some useful books that address health and nutrition issues are *The Johns Hopkins Medical Handbook* (Rebus), *Growing Older, Feeling Better in Body, Mind, and Spirit* by Mary Dale Scheller (Bull Publishing), *The New Our Bodies, Ourselves* by the Boston Women's Health Book Collective (Simon and Schuster), *The New A-to-Z of Women's Health* by Christine Ammer (Hunter House), *The Nutrition Challenge for Women* by Louise Lambert-Lagace (Bull Publishing), and *The Complete and Up-to-Date Fat Book* by Karen J. Bellerson (Avery Publishing). There are also several popular health-related newsletters: the *UC-Berkeley Wellness Letter*, *Mayo Clinic Health Letter*, and *Health Confidential*.

For older women there are several other highly recommended books on health issues and nutrition including *Ourselves, Growing Older* by the Boston Women's Health Book Collective (Simon and Schuster/Touchstone), *Menopause Without Medicine* by Linda Ojeda (Hunter House), and *Menopause Naturally* by Sadja Greenwood (Volcano Press).

Local libraries and stores that sell used books are two good sources of reading material. Many health agencies and medical offices also have free literature on health and other topics that may be of interest. One handy number is The American Dietetic Association's Consumer Nutrition Hot Line: 1-800-366-1655. By calling, you may listen to nutrition messages by registered dieticians, recorded in English or Spanish, Monday through Friday from 8 A.M. to 8 P.M. Central time; speak directly with a registered dietician, Monday through Friday from 9 A.M. to 4 P.M. Central time; and get a referral to a registered dietician in your area.

Some basic dietary guidelines for most Americans who do not require a special diet are:

- Eat a variety of foods.

- Maintain healthy weight.

- Choose a diet low in fat, saturated fat, and cholesterol.

- Choose a diet with plenty of vegetables, fruits, and grain products.

- Use sugars only in moderation.

- Use salt and sodium only in moderation.

- If you drink alcoholic beverages, do so in moderation.(1)

Besides having medical checkups and reevaluating your diet, get into an exercise routine. This will help you restore your physical and emotional health after leaving the cult. Regular exercise—whether it is walking, running, dancing, swimming, biking, or a fitness-center schedule—can have an extremely positive impact on your state of mind. According to the Federal Centers for Disease Control and Prevention and the American College of Sports Medicine, "every adult American should engage in 30 minutes or more of moderate activity—the equivalent of brisk walking at three to four miles an hour—at least five days a week."(2)

Exercise can help to get rid of negative emotions and arouse positive ones. It will almost certainly make you feel good about yourself again, a feeling you probably lost while under the cult's influence. Whatever exercise you choose should be done in consultation with medical professionals if you have any concerns about what might be right for you, or any health risks at all.

Trusting Yourself Again

Most cult members come to rely on the group or leader to tell them what is best. They believe that the cult is providing comfort, safety, and a sense of security. Instead, a cult environment is inhibiting and emotionally debilitating. After leaving this controlled environment, many people find it difficult to trust themselves to take care of themselves, make decisions, and know what is in their best interests.

It is quite common, especially for those who were in very restrictive cults, to have difficulty with new freedoms. Enforced celibacy, separation of the sexes, severe dietary restrictions, prohibitions about types of work and leisure activities, dress codes, monitoring of every thought, word, and deed—all these cult rules create proscribed thought patterns and an unhealthy dependency on the group. Coming out of such environments, where every minute may have been dictated, many find it extremely difficult to deal with free time. Even small amounts of leisure may bring on floating episodes, bouts of guilt, and other forms of anxiety. These reactions can be redirected through careful planning.

By making "To Do" lists, breaking activities into their smallest parts, and planning leisure activities, you can start developing a tolerance for "empty time." Each person will have different needs in this area. Some may need to fill time with activities that will help them socialize again, build interpersonal skills, and restore confidence. Others may need to reduce their compulsive behavior and learn to enjoy time alone and be at peace with themselves.

Find something that makes sense for you, fits with your personality, and creates good feelings. It might be spending Sunday afternoons with a beer and a bowl of popcorn watching sports on television or taking long walks with your dog. Think about the kinds of places you liked to visit before you joined the cult—museums, libraries, arts and crafts fairs, film festivals. Reconnect with activities you enjoyed such as riding a bike, hanging out at coffeehouses, participating in sports, playing music, taking evening classes. Be alert to what feels good to you now. Relaxation and doing enjoyable things is a vital part of postcult healing.

But don't push yourself. For example, you may have a feeling that you want to write, yet you may not want the discipline of a class, of knowing that you have to be somewhere at a certain time or be responsible for a product. Start casually and work toward goals. Most of all, remember: no pressure, no shoulds, no guilt. Learn to relax, take time off, and enjoy life again. It may not come easy, but it will come.

Become a good, sympathetic, and compassionate friend to yourself. Cult members are taught, directly or indirectly, to mistrust their own thoughts and feelings. This unhealthy habit must be reversed. Now you are free to perceive the universe through your own eyes, interpret it through your own mind. Being a good friend also means being a good listener. Part of the process of rebuilding trust is to learn to listen to your own heart and mind.

Some ex-members describe breaking into a cold sweat whenever someone asks their opinion about something—a meal, a movie, a current event. Because they believed for so long that they were *right* about everything, now they are either ashamed to admit they don't know what they think, or are afraid they may be coming across like a know-it-all, as they did in the past when they were in the cult. It may take time to find the right balance. In Part Three, *Nancy Miquelon* writes about the joy she felt at realizing she had her own opinion about a particular color—a telling example of the kind of mental tentativeness one feels upon leaving the controlled world of a cult.

Some of you may remain troubled by cult-related thoughts and reactions, sometimes becoming confused about which thoughts are yours and which were instilled by the cult. You may find that you have to work at discovering for yourself which beliefs are yours and which are alien.

If you have such problems, ask yourself where a specific thought or reaction came from. If after examination you determine that it was induced by your cult training, make a mental note of this. Dissecting your thoughts and opinions to find their origin can help distance you somewhat from each one, allowing you to gain control over it. Once you see that a troublesome thought is separate from you, is not part of you, you will feel free to reject it or to accept it. By repeating this exercise whenever you are uncertain about the origin of your thinking or behavior, you will free yourself from residual effects of the cult indoctrination.

Another tactic is to begin your sentences with "I think," "I believe," and "In my opinion"—phrases that are forbidden in most cults. By jealously guarding your independence of thought, you will notice yourself becoming more self-confident and able to express yourself. You will get to know yourself again, take pride in what is yours, and rediscover the courage of your convictions.

Another option is to take an assertiveness training class. These are sometimes offered at reasonable cost at adult education centers. After having been conditioned to unquestioningly follow the leader's teachings and rules, this may prove a helpful way to relearn your basic rights as an individual. The following is a list of rights each person is entitled to in relation to self-expression.

Assertive Bill of Rights

1. I have the right to evaluate my own behavior, thoughts, and emotions, and to take responsibility for their initiation and consequences upon myself.

2. I have the right to decide whether I am responsible for solving other people's problems.

3. I have the right to change my mind.

4. I have the right to make mistakes—and be responsible for them.

5. I have the right to be illogical in making decisions.

6. I have the right to say I don't know.

7. I have the right to say I don't understand.

8. I have the right to say I don't care.

9. I have the right to set my own priorities.

10. I have the right to say no without feeling guilty.(3)

The Fishbowl Effect

Because of a general ignorance in our society about cults, cult members are often stereotyped as having something wrong with them, either socially or psychologically. This sometimes causes former cult members to feel that people are watching them all the time. This may be particularly true for those who go back home to live with or spend time with their family.

Margaret Singer named this uncomfortable cult-related phenomenon the "fishbowl effect." She writes: "A special problem for cult veterans is the constant watchfulness of family and friends, who are on the alert for any signs that the difficulties of real life will send the person back. Mild dissociation, deep preoccupations, temporary altered states of consciousness, and any positive talk about cult days can cause alarm in a former member's family . . . . New acquaintances and old friends can also trigger an ex-cultist's feelings that people are staring, wondering why he joined such a group . . . . [Ex-members] have managed to deal with these situations [by] focusing on current conversation until the sense of living under scrutiny gradually fades."(4)

Families and friends may feel uneasy about broaching the subject of your cult involvement. Counselors have suggested that "initiating a discussion of the group involvement may be the best way to deal with the issue. Once the ice has been broken, others can discuss the matter and question freely without fear of hurting the ex-member. Through discussion, the ex-member can dispel their misconceptions."(5) In essence, it becomes your responsibility to educate those who love and care about you so that they will give you the necessary space for healing while also increasing their own understanding of cults and your postcult adjustment needs.

Family members describe the feeling of "walking on eggs," worrying that too many questions or a wrong comment will upset the ex-member, perhaps even cause him or her to want to return to the group.(6) Former cult members can help by reassuring their families that saying some good things happened in the group is not a danger signal that they are apout to go back. Families, for their part, must avoid playing a caretaker role, which is an extension of the unhelpful blame-the-victim mentality. When family members assume that they need to protect their relative from further victimization and social pressures, they are reinforcing the idea that the former cult member is weak.(7)

Talking about Your Cult Experience

Related to the fishbowl effect is the embarrassment you may feel about having been involved with a cult. This is particularly common right after departure or when a person has not sought out counseling or education.

Some former members may decide keep the entire experience private. Others may decide to be more open about it. Sorting through the cult experience, the good and the bad, will take some time.

First, remember that you only need to discuss what you feel ready and able to discuss. Don't let anyone force you into talking about your cult experience.

Second, you only need to share as much as you are willing to share. Some former cult members feel a compulsion to talk about their experience to everyone, which is generally a holdover from the cult-instilled confessing behavior and telling all. Remember, now that you are out, you are allowed to have boundaries and private areas again.

Third, if you do decide to share your experience, keep in mind the following helpful pointers from therapists Bill and Lorna Goldberg, who have led a support group for former cult members in the New York–New Jersey area for the past 15 years. The Goldbergs have a "Question and Answer" column in *FOCUS News,* a newsletter for ex-cult members. In a recent issue they addressed the question: "I feel embarrassed by my cult experience. How can I explain it to my friends and family?" The following are excerpts from their answer:

> Remember that when you joined the cult, you chose the best course of action available to you with the information you had at the time . . . . It may be helpful to review in your mind the reasons you joined and what you thought you were accomplishing by joining. Should you be embarrassed for wanting a better world or for searching for ways to serve God? Should you be embarrassed for wanting to better yourself or to get help with problems? For the most part, the qualities you had that made you vulnerable to the cult were positive qualities. Your good qualities [were] used against you.
>
> We all make mistakes in life or do things we wish we hadn't done. The degree to which we're embarrassed by these mistakes depends on how public the mistake is, the amount of support and understanding we have from those around us, and the difficulty we have in accepting our human limitations. It's important for you to examine the degree to which you are continuing the same harsh, judgmental attitude towards yourself that was expected in the cult . . . . Instead of focusing on your supposed failings, you may want to recognize that when you were able to see what was happening in the cult, you had the courage to leave . . . . Give yourself credit for that.(8)

The bottom line is: *you* decide what feels safe and what you feel prepared to discuss or explain. Most former cult members don't talk openly about their cult experience to new acquaintances, coworkers, or distant family immediately after leaving the cult. Often they don't disclose to anyone for months, sometimes a year or more, though they may speak sooner to close friends and immediate family members, therapists, counselors, and other former cult members. The delay, however, may have more to do with the stigma society places on a person who has been in a cult than with former members' acceptance of their own experience.

Restoring Former Relationships

Membership in a cult usually means estrangement from family and former friends—unless they are also involved with the group. Outside relationships become difficult to maintain either because of the internal contradictions that are raised by seeing noncult persons or simply because there is no time for the outside world. Some people may be neglected or dropped at the cult's direct demands.

Many members exiting a cult may not have seen or had meaningful contact with relatives and friends for many years. They may have been unable to attend important family events or spend private time with friends. Their relatives and friends probably went through a range of emotions—guilt, anger, anxiety, sadness—about their loved one's cult affiliation.(9) A great deal of pain is caused by these prolonged separations and an important stage in postcult healing is mending these relationships.

Reconnecting with those who were cut off

In most cults, pressure is put on members to cut all ties with the past. Messages from family and friends often are discouraged, not responded to, or answered with cult rhetoric.

Some families may have had a prior history of difficult relationships. Parents may have been too controlling or overly involved in their children's lives. Privacy may have been discouraged or nonexistent. Expressing feelings, especially negative ones, or differing points of view may have been impossible. Some family members may have been estranged from one another even before the cult involvement. Others may be angry about their loved one's behavior while in the cult or resentful about the expense and complications that were necessary to arrange an exit counseling and rehabilitation. These negative conditions need to be changed in order to construct new and improved ways of relating.

Reconciling with family is an important and often difficult task. Just as you have to educate yourself, it is important to encourage your family to get educated about thought reform to really understand what happened. Your family probably has no idea what you went through. They may be puzzled, angry, or anxious. Gaining their support and understanding can be extremely helpful, particularly if you had close family ties or will be living at home during the postcult adjustment period.

If there were communication difficulties before, the unresolved problems will still be there. Both sides should remember that cult involvement is not voluntary and the focus of blame needs to be placed where it belongs—on the cult. Many families choose to believe that everything will be okay once their loved one is out of the cult, then are surprised and dismayed to discover that there are still issues to address, some cult-related and some not.

This may be a time to consider family counseling or professional assistance, especially if there has been a prior history of family problems. Some mental health professionals consider family counseling invaluable. For example, Arnold Markowitz, director of the Cult Clinic and Hot Line of the Jewish Board of Family and Children's Services in New York City, believes that "family therapy is essential following a cult member's departure from the group to allow the entire family to be 'deprogrammed,' or defused, to address long-term patterns of dysfunction, and to help parents give up old expectations in exchange for more realistic expectations that accommodate the overall needs of their son or daughter."(10)

For the most part, families and friends are overjoyed to see their loved one leave the cult. In spite of the stresses and strains, it is often a homecoming unlike any other. Former friends are often as important as immediate family members, especially for those who were adults when they joined the cult. It may be vital for former cult members to look up old friends—to heal the pain on both sides, as illustrated in the following example.

> *Edith* joined a political cult when she was 30. She had many friends in the area, one in particular, Beth, whom she had known since college. Edith tried hard to recruit Beth, to no avail. Not only was Beth deemed a "hopeless" recruit but also, because she asked too many questions in the recruitment meetings, she was declared "an enemy" of the organization, a nonperson. Edith was ordered to cut Beth out of her life. While carrying out cult-related work, Edith occasionally ran into Beth; following orders, Edith would turn and walk away, unable to acknowledge her former friend. This went on for 10 years.
>
> When Edith finally left the group, and after some time in therapy, she decided to try to make contact with Beth. Nervous and afraid that Beth would hang up on her, Edith dialed Beth's number and tentatively opened the conversation. She explained that she was no longer in the cult and that she regretted many of her past actions, in particular the way she had treated Beth. She asked if Beth would like to get together for lunch; Beth, with some caution, said yes. They met and talked for hours, reestablishing their connection. Beth was able to satisfactorily vent her feelings about the experience. It was important, although painful at times, for Edith to hear how her cult membership had affected

Beth. The reconnection helped Edith's recovery process for she was able to learn how others saw her during her time in the cult. The two remain good friends.

Restructuring relationships with those who were also in the cult

Many people find that when they join a cult together with others they are close to, the quality of their relationships changes drastically. This is due to a combination of the suppression of all unapproved feelings and the lack of time for positive interactions. A cult's goal is to instill distrust and exert control. In some cults, couples are deliberately separated, children taken away, friendship networks broken up.

When people come out of such restricted environments, they often find that their relations with these others have been stilted and damaged, sometimes irreparably. The postcult divorce rate is high, which is not surprising since in many cults marriages are arranged by the leader. Others, who meet and marry while in the cult, may look at each other afterward and wonder who the other person is. Because of the emergence of the adaptive "cult personality," two people may enter a relationship, even marry and live together a long time, and realize only later that they have little in common.

Couples leaving cults face many challenges to make their relationship work. Those who manage do so with great effort, usually with the help of couples counseling and a lot of time focusing on communication and repair of the relationship. A number of the personal accounts in Part III speak to relationship issues concerning spouses, children, family members, or friends.

An important, related issue may be a need to reestablish relationships with one's children, who may have been in the cult with one or both parents, full- or part-time. *Ginger Zyskowski,* a mother of three and a former member of the Divine Light Mission, wrote the following about her experiences.

> When I finally got out of my group, I clung to my boys both physically and emotionally for fear of losing them again. They were all I had left of my original identity. The positive aspect of this was that we became a close-knit group, very concerned about one another. Being the best mom I could be was top priority. If there were dirty dishes or laundry waiting, they waited—sometimes until 2 or 3 in the morning—until I had spent time with the boys and their homework, music lessons,

sports, games, books, favorite TV programs, dinner, and so forth. As you might imagine, the negative side of this closeness was that I became too dependent on them for my emotional support. I felt pulled to extremes. Fortunately, I recognized this dependency and decided that I had to plan some sort of life or career for myself. At some point in the future the boys would be grown and leave home, and if I didn't have any identity for myself, I knew I would be devastated and lost again.

The cult experience caused me to view all of life from a different perspective. Priorities and values changed and magnified. My children learned that truth and honesty come first, that without these as a foundation everything else is an illusion. One of the truths I taught them was that I am not perfect, either as a person or a parent. They got to see me cry and hurt, fall in and out of love, be happy, angry, confused, abused, and simply trying to get us all through to the next day, week, year. We didn't have much money since my job was at minimum wage, and it seemed as though there were major expenses all the time. We agreed that one night a week the boys would fix dinner. We had a "No TV" night when we read books, played games, or did jigsaw puzzles together. I taught the boys to be open and ask questions. They have rights, and being able to question everything is one of them. I had and have respect for them as the persons they are and for their feelings.

Because they were initially so young, only four, five, and seven when I got out, I had to give them bits and pieces of information about the cult experience. Along with my own processing of the information and posttrauma issues, I was able to explain to them some of the effects of the cult experience on us all. This past spring, 15 years later, the four of us were able to attend the American Family Foundation conference for ex-members, where much of the boys' past was put into perspective for them. Their understanding of cults and mind control is greatly increased, plus they have a more accurate picture of how and why I made certain decisions.

One thing that worried me was that there might be consequences to them as students if their friends and/or teachers found out that I had been in a cult. Indeed there were—most of them positive. The negative reactions can be chalked up to people's lack of understanding of the whole cult phenomenon anyway, so we learned to "consider the source," as it were.

I suppose if a list of guidelines developed for us to live by, it can be condensed into the following:

- Remain flexible.

- This too shall pass.

- Expect much from yourself to avoid disappointments.

- Expect little from others to avoid disappointments.

- Treat yourself and others with love and respect.

- Always tell the truth.

- It's okay to fail—failing doesn't make you a failure.

- Don't be afraid to change.

- Trust your gut feelings.

- Learn who you really are and be the best you can be.

The entire cult experience, as devastating as it was, offered us a closer relationship, a more honest relationship, and a chance to evaluate our thoughts and feelings for ourselves and one another. We have more courage and strength, and I especially realize that there are extremes that I went to and would go to again in a given traumatic event. My fear has turned a warrior loose within me. It is comforting to know that my children are not ashamed of my cult involvement and are supportive of my recovery. I am not ashamed either. I can say that freely now. Although we may still have a long way to go, truth, love, and understanding bring solidity to each footstep we take along the way.(11)

Ginger's guidelines could be applied to all relationships. Honesty, flexibility, clarity in communication, and a sense of perspective are key. In some cases, distance or time apart may be necessary to regain a sense of self before a person feels both comfortable and safe in resuming a relationship with a significant other who was also in the cult. In other cases, a reconciliation may not be possible.

Dealing with those left behind in the cult

One of the most difficult tasks for ex-members is figuring out how to deal with certain people they left behind in the group. The pain of leaving behind a spouse, a lover, a child, or a parent can seem almost intolerable. Occasionally an intervention by a team of exit counselors may help reunite the whole family. All too often, though, healing must go on without them.

For those who still have loved ones in the cult, support from others who also deal with this loss is essential. By contacting resource networks, families can find and support each other. Often former members with relatives and friends in the same cult meet to work on mutual issues of support, public education, and action. Good advice for keeping in touch and maintaining relationships with those still in the group can be found in *Cults: What Parents Should Know* by Joan Ross and Michael Langone.

Where issues of guardianship, divorce, and custody are concerned, it is advisable that the former cult member seek legal counsel—if possible with a professional familiar with cult-related cases and precedents.

There is also the unpleasant possibility that people from the cult will call or seek out those who left in an effort to lure them back to the fold. Lorna and Bill Goldberg had this to say about cults' attempts to contact former members:

> The goal of the telephone call may not be to really see how you are or to find out why you left. The real goal may be for cult members to discover if they can talk you into rejoining. Since the cult member is using legitimate, friendly questions as a *ploy* and a *smoke screen* to manipulate you, you should respond to the real purpose of the call (i.e., the attempt to manipulate) rather than to the "friendly" words. Saying "I have no desire to speak to you about this. Please don't call me again," followed by hanging up is a legitimate response to someone who is trying to manipulate you. If you are concerned about sounding angry, you can say this in a neutral but firm tone. We are recommending that you respond in this manner rather than give the cult member an explanation because any explanation you give will engender a response and will imply that you're willing to enter into a dialogue on your decision to leave. Remember that the cult member's job is to have you return— he or she rarely cares about your true needs.
>
> On the other hand, it is also difficult to close the door on those you knew well and cared about in the cult. If the caller falls into this category and if you are feeling sufficiently strong to explain your position without undue stress, you can explain that you no longer wished to remain in the group, that your way of seeing things has changed, and if the caller wants to hear another point of view, you can suggest some people for him to call and some books to read. After the cult member has spoken with these other individuals or read the books, you can decide whether or not to continue a dialogue with him.(12)

It is really up to you.

Resolving Identity Issues

We define ourselves (and are defined by others) within such categories as gender, age, nationality, marital status, religion, and job or profession. We give ourselves and others labels: male or female; old, middle-aged, young; single, married, divorced; blue-collar or professional. Feelings, behaviors, and self-judgments are part of the inner dialogue that reinforces our ongoing sense of identity. Some parts of identity are either difficult or impossible to change—for example, skin color, nationality, and height. Other parts, such as job, religion, or marital status, we can more readily change.

For those who were born in a cult and then leave it as an adult, and for those who spent many years in a cult, especially a highly restrictive one, the sudden opportunity to expand upon or change one's identity may be overwhelming, frightening, exciting, or a mix of all three. Sudden freedoms, no matter how long they were dreamt of, can be terrifying. *"Frances Lief,"* describing the period after her escape from the Children of God as a teenager, writes:

> If young people manage to escape from the cult they grew up in, most likely they do not like the person they were obligated to be in the cult. By leaving the cult, they may remove themselves physically from that environment, but the task of creating a new identity is left and takes a lot of effort. This may seem like an unnecessary quest from the outside, but it is vital to us if we are to truly separate our inner selves from the cult.(13)

Changing one's identity is not the sole province of cult children; it is an important part of anyone's postcult healing process. And it does not mean adopting a totally new identity. It is a process of making some changes and adding new dimensions to the desirable traits you already have. The following questions and suggestions may give you some ideas for coming to terms with yourself and making changes in your identity:

1. What were you told about yourself in the cult that either is no longer true or never was true? Use the Disarming Triggers Worksheet (see Chapter 7) to help evaluate erroneous beliefs.

2. Give yourself permission to grow and change. People change all the time; it's okay.

3. Whom do you admire now? What do you find admirable about them? What is not admirable? Are there behaviors, skills, attitudes, or values they have that you would like to have?

4. What are the things about yourself that you do not particularly like but cannot change? This might be your age, height, nationality, certain physical disabilities or medical conditions. Make a list. How can you help yourself to accept these things?

5. What are things you would like to change that may be difficult but do-able? This may include going back to school to continue your education, learning skills so you can choose a career or make a change, eradicating certain unpleasant temperament traits that were enhanced in the cult, and healing the hurts and wounds of the cult experience.

6. What are the easiest to change? Even small changes go a long way in boosting self-confidence and self-esteem. They prove that you do have control over your life.

7. What parts of your personality do you like? What are aspects of yourself that you want to keep?

Your new freedoms and choices are all part of you. Each time you make a new choice or a new friend, each fresh accomplishment and victory—whether large or small—is a positive experience that will produce good memories. In this way you are reinventing yourself. Obviously, making changes in yourself is not going to be easy, but the hardest part has already been accomplished: you are out of the cult and moving toward a new life.

CHAPTER
TEN

FACING THE CHALLENGES
OF THE FUTURE

In rebuilding your life, besides dealing with the task of reestablishing former relationships, you will also need to figure out how to have new ones. This will again raise issues of intimacy, trust, and establishing boundaries. Other key challenges will be choosing or recreating a viable belief system—after many of your deepest beliefs may have been violated, or at least betrayed—and choosing a career or vocation that fulfills your true needs. These are discussed in more detail below.

Loneliness, Trust, Intimacy

Perhaps the single greatest difficulty ex-members face in postcult life is isolation and loneliness. This is especially true for those who walk away without any counseling or support, without a network of family, friends, or other former members. To fill the void created by the loss of the group or relationship, some people return to their cult or abusive partner, while others may inadvertently join another destructive group, a pattern known as "cult hopping."

A person leaving a cult leaves an intense experience. Strong and unique bonds are forged through sharing ideals, goals, and values as well as intense suffering and deprivation, group confession, and enforced intimacy. Emotional highs and mystical/spiritual experiences also serve to increase this sense of belonging. Immediately after leaving, the person may feel—and be—very isolated. Precult friends may be long gone, or may be unwilling to hear about what you went through.

This isolation may be intensified by the difficulty some ex-members have—especially soon after cult departure—clearly explaining the dynamics of their recruitment and the group's thought-reform and control program. But establishing social and emotional networks is vital to resisting the pull to return to the cult, and it is imperative that the former cult member reach out and try to restore former friendships and make new ones.

Learning to trust—again

Cults demand absolute trust. Members have no choice but to trust the leader or the group. Anything less is considered a gross imperfection, disobedience, the sign of Satan or the enemy or worse, and is often a punishable offense.

Many ex-members leave their groups with deep suspicion about people's motivations and attitudes. The recognition that their trust has been profoundly betrayed is often accompanied by feelings of hurt, rage, and fear. The experience leaves a scar. Knowing whom to trust and how much takes time. The cult experience teaches you—the hard way—that people who present themselves as friendly, interested, and helpful may have hidden agendas.

In a world based on reciprocity, trust cannot be demanded and should be based on mutual feelings and proof. Trust comes in stages and should never be absolute. The key is to proceed slowly. People who desire to get close to you must earn your trust. Trusting is a process, not an act.

Because perceived imperfections and mistakes are judged so harshly in cults, learning to trust again also involves learning to tolerate other people's ways, sensitivities, and eccentricities. This, in turn, increases your ability to tolerate and trust yourself, to accept your imperfections and idiosyncrasies.

Dating and sex

Many former cult members and abused partners have difficulty with intimate relationships. Getting involved in a normal relationship after leaving a destructive one can be a challenge, for a variety of reasons:

- You may have had little or no dating experience before joining the cult.

- You were born or raised in the cultic environment and therefore had no positive role models.

- You lived in a milieu where strict celibacy was enforced.

- You lived in a milieu where sexual promiscuity, enforced prostitution, or other forms of sexual abuse were practiced.

- You lived in a milieu where marriage and childbearing were directed by the leader.

- You had no time to develop mature adult relationships.

If you exit from a cult with little practical experience to serve as a basis for future relationships, or you have a limited capacity to judge other people's motives, dating and socializing may seem quite strange and even frightening. You may feel uncertain whether the behavior within the relationship, both your own and the other person's, is healthy. You probably fear making a commitment to another person. Popular television, movies, and books often present a distorted picture of life and relationships, compounding the confusion you might be experiencing.

Many former cult members may need sex education, especially those who were in very isolated situations or in an environment where the sexual practices and ideas were particularly perverse or corrupted. Learning about AIDS and safe-sex practices is crucial in such instances. For this, we recommend Magic Johnson's *What You Can Do to Avoid AIDS* (Times Books), a basic, nonthreatening book with an excellent state-by-state resources section. Magic Johnson and Arsenio Hall have also created a videotape on AIDS education, *Time Out: Truth about HIV, AIDS, and You,* which should be available for free rental at most libraries and video rental outlets. Additionally, every state has an AIDS hot line (a toll-free 800 number) which you can call with specific concerns or questions.

There are also a number of good basic books on human sexuality. Look in the health and sexuality sections of any good-sized bookstore. You should be able to find reliable texts for both heterosexual and homosexual men and women, as well as books for children and adolescents.

Most former cult members say that the most important advice anyone gave them regarding new relationships was to go slow—in both friendships and intimate encounters. Trust needs time to develop. It is okay to not rush into something. Remember, personal healing is primary; with that will come healthy relationships with others.

Setting boundaries in a relationship

Learning to recognize and set personal boundaries is an important postcult exercise. Because of the restrictions on privacy that exist in most cults, it is likely that your boundaries were violated time and again—until you lost a sense of which boundaries were appropriate.

Boundaries help define who we are, what separates us from the world. We all have a personal, private physical space that we are not comfortable sharing with just anyone. The same is true on a psychological level, and a significant part of maturing emotionally involves learning how to define and maintain these invisible boundaries.

For many, the cult replaced the family. If you came from a family with a history of alcohol or other substance abuse, severe medical or mental illness, divorce, domestic violence, or other trauma, then what you found in the cult may not have been very different from the environment in your family of origin. Arnold Markowitz and other professionals who work with families of cult members at the Cult Clinic in New York City have found that in many cases where there is a cult-affiliated family member, there is evidence of an "enmeshed" family. In enmeshed families, personal boundaries between members are ignored and overrun.(1)

Relearning respect for personal boundaries—your own and others'—is a crucial task. For some, this may mean learning to be emotionally independent for the first time. Failure to achieve this personal autonomy may result in a series of unhealthy and potentially destructive relationships, or in cult hopping.

The following list describes boundary invasions that are physical, emotional, and sexual. The distinction between the individual and the group is blurred. There is a loss of a sense of self. Becoming familiar with these signs of unhealthy boundaries may help you unravel the cult experience as well as steer you away from similar dangers in the new relationships you may be forming.

Signs of unhealthy boundaries

- Telling all
- Talking on an intimate level at the first meeting
- Being overwhelmed by and preoccupied with the group, leader, or other person
- Being sexual for others, not yourself
- Being asexual for others, not yourself
- Going against personal values or rights to please others
- Not noticing or disregarding when someone else displays inappropriate boundaries

- Not noticing or disregarding when someone invades your boundaries

- Accepting food, gifts, touch, or sex that you don't want

- Being touched by another person without having been asked

- Giving as much as you can for the sake of giving

- Taking as much as you can for the sake of getting

- Allowing someone to take as much as they can from you

- Letting others direct your life

- Letting others define you

- Letting others describe your reality

- Believing others can anticipate your needs

- Believing you must anticipate others' needs

- Practicing self-abuse, self-mortification

- Being subjected to sexual and physical abuse

- Living with food and sleep deprivation

- Being unable to separate your needs from others' needs(2)

The checklist below may also help you to evaluate your cult experience. How many items describe your cult experience? How many describe the new relationships you are forming now? The more items you check, the more you need to examine these relationships and their potential destructiveness. When using the checklist, also ask yourself the following:

1. Were there signs of unhealthy boundaries in my own family? What were they?

2. What signs of unhealthy boundaries existed in the cult?

3. Did these things make it more difficult for me to realize that my rights were being infringed upon?

4. What do I need to do to make my family or personal life more positive and rewarding now?

Checklist for evaluating relationships

☐ I assume responsibility for the feelings and behaviors of the leader, group, or other person.

☐ I have difficulty in identifying feelings: am I angry? lonely? sad? scared? joyful? ashamed?

☐ I have difficulty expressing feelings.

☐ I worry about how the group, leader, or other person might respond to my feelings or behaviors.

☐ I am afraid of being hurt and/or rejected by the group, leader, or other person.

☐ I am a perfectionist. I place too many expectations on myself. I have difficulty making decisions and I am glad that I don't have to make many decisions in my relationship with the group, leader, or other person.

☐ I tend to minimize, alter, or even deny the truth about how I feel.

☐ Other people's actions and attitudes tend to determine how I respond.

☐ I put the group's, leader's, or other person's wants and needs first, believing that their needs are more important than mine.

☐ I am afraid of the group's, leader's, or other person's feelings (e.g., anger) and that determines what I say and do.

☐ I question or ignore my own values in order to be part of the group or relationship.

☐ I value the group's, leader's, or other person's opinions more than my own.

☐ I judge everything I do, think, or say harshly, by the group's, leader's, or other person's standards; rarely is anything I have done, said, or thought good enough.

☐ I believe that it is not okay to talk about problems outside the group or relationship.

☐ I remain steadfastly loyal even when the loyalty is hard to justify and is personally harmful.

☐ I believe the group, leader, or other person knows what is best for me.

☐ I believe the group or relationship is more important than my family or friends.

☐ I believe the group, leader, or other person cares more about me than my family or friends do.

☐ I believe the group, leader, or other person has my interests at heart even when I don't understand how.

☐ Everything that is good and right is due to the other person, the leader, or the group's philosophy.

☐ Everything that is wrong or bad is my fault.(3)

Issues of Belief

The cult experience is often described as a spiritual rape. The wound is very deep and takes time to heal. Because of the cult's indoctrination techniques and use of deception, members become convinced that their "spiritual" experiences come from within and are a result of their allegiance to their particular leader and spiritual path. In secular cults, the goal is fulfillment of one's potential as a human being through unquestioning belief in a particular philosophy and participation in a group espousing that philosophy. Religious or secular, the realization afterward that an enormous betrayal has taken place may cause considerable pain. As a result, the former member tends to reject all forms of belief. It may take many years to overcome the disillusionment, and to learn not only to trust the inner self but also to believe in something again.

Although it is a widespread misconception that all cults are religious, it is true that all cults tend to disrupt a person's fundamental or core beliefs. This tends to have an effect in all areas of life, which is why it is sometimes said that a cult experience has an impact on the "spiritual being," or the inner person. Coming to terms with spirituality or personal beliefs may be the most upsetting part of some people's postcult experience. Father Kent Burtner, who has years of experience counseling former cult members, describes this aspect of cult recovery:

> The emotions of wonder and awe, transcendence and mystery, are a deep part of each person.... While in most of us those feelings are directed toward God, creation and the discovery of the "really real," like

any other emotion, they are subject to manipulation. Ex-cultists have experienced these manipulations profoundly and the memory of them remains vivid. If they have not rejected those feelings totally as a result of their "heavenly sting," they question whether they can find that sense of transcendence anywhere other than in the cult.

The cult has told them that no other path exists beyond that of the group. In essence cultists have never really made a choice for the group, but rather have experienced a program that causes them to progressively close the door on alternatives. The only "choice" that remains to them is the group itself. The lingering question of where to experience that sense of transcendence needs to be addressed.... In leaving such a group, the ex-member finds himself in an enormous vacuum.(4)

A related difficulty may be the persistent nagging thought that you may have made a mistake in leaving the group—perhaps the teachings were true and the leader right; perhaps it was *you* who failed. Because of the cult's "mystical manipulation" and the human desire to believe, a person may search for a way to go on believing even after leaving the group. This is one reason why many so-called "seekers" hop from one cult to another or in and out of the same group or relationship. Since every person needs something to believe in—a philosophy of life, a way of being, an organized religion, a political commitment, or a combination thereof—sorting out matters of belief is a major part of postcult adjustment.

The cult involvement is often an attempt to live out some form of personal belief, so the process of figuring out what to believe in may be facilitated by dissecting the cult's belief system. Father Burtner suggests doing an evaluation of the group's ideology, philosophy, and worldview, defining it in noncult language; then, going back and researching the spiritual or philosophical belief system that you were raised in or believed in prior to the cult involvement. Through this process you will be better able to assess what is "real" or "safe" and what is "off base." You will gain a basis for comparison that will enable you to question and explore areas of belief that were systematically closed to you in the cult.(5)

Most former members shy away from organized religion or any kind of organized group for quite a while after leaving their cult, and pastoral counselors are advised to do no proselytizing to former members at this time.(6) Those for whom a religious affiliation is important sometimes find comfort in their precult religion and return to the church, synagogue, mosque, or previous place of worship. That scenario, however, seems to be the exception rather than the rule. Most ex-members advisably take time before choosing another religious affiliation or group involvement.

When you do start to become involved in something new, if you have any concerns that it may be another cultlike group, contact one of the resource organizations listed in Appendix B to see if there have been any complaints against the group in question. Compare the new group against the checklist in Appendix A. Above all, if you have any doubt, trust your own instincts and check out your suspicions with others who are *not* in the new group.

Vocational and Career Issues

"So, what do you want to be when you grow up?"

If you have just left a cult, you may find yourself asking that question when you are 30 or 40 years old, or older. Whether you were born and raised in a group, joined before starting on a career, or interrupted education or career, you now have to face earning a living and deciding what to do with your life. You may have been provided for by the group, and now must provide for yourself for the first time—or for the first time in years. Or, the work you did in the cult may have been your first job. At some point after you leave the cult, you will begin the search for employment and will need to address vocational and career issues.

Once you get past your feelings of resentment about lost time, you need to take stock of your skills, talents, and interests. In their anger about the cult's betrayals and manipulations, many people resist looking at the positive side. It can help immensely, however, to remember that some good must have occurred—if only that you managed to survive a difficult situation which has made you stronger and wiser. A positive outlook will be an asset in facing the future. You may be surprised to find that you learned real skills in the cult which you can take advantage of now, such as in marketing, cooking, writing, selling, art, construction, computers or mechanical repairs.

Many people go to school after leaving the cult, sometimes to pursue a new career, sometimes to complete a program they had abandoned. In making a decision about school, talk to as many people as possible. Most campuses have offices with staff counselors who can help. Remember, no decision needs to be made immediately—and even if you make one, you are allowed to change your mind. To avoid putting too many demands on yourself at once, you might consider starting with an evening class or a junior college. Too much pressure too soon can be a hindrance to sorting out other things going on in your life that also need attention.

What you decide to do will depend in part on whatever your situation was while you were in the cult. Some people never work "outside" jobs during cult membership, and emerge from the group quite out of touch with the working world. Others might have had jobs in the main cult organization or in cult-related businesses, while still others held outside jobs unrelated to the cult. It is often a good idea to get a simple, undemanding job first to get some money coming in. Generally in such jobs you do not need to be too concerned about your dress or having to go through an extensive interview process.

To assess your prospects for a meaningful job or career path, you might consider going to a career counselor or placement service at a college campus, unemployment office, business college, or other career resource centers. They give aptitude tests coupled with lengthy interviews to help sort out personal interests and skills. Another good place to start is your local library or bookstore. Two useful books to consult are *What Color Is Your Parachute?—A Practical Manual for Job Hunters and Career Changers* by Richard Nelson Bolles (Ten Speed Press), a long-time bestseller, and *When You Lose Your Job* by Cliff Hakim (Berrett-Koehler), which deals with both practical and emotional issues in coping with the job market. Surrey Books publishes a handy series called "How to Get a Job," focusing on major metropolitan areas—Atlanta, Chicago, Boston, Seattle/Portland, New York, the San Francisco Bay Area, and so on. Each book provides listings of over one thousand major employers in a specific area, with job-hunting and résumé tips.

©Chronicle Features, 1986

Am I a team player? Are you kidding? I was in a cult.

To reorient yourself in the working world, it might be helpful to look over fashion magazines to see what dress styles are current or to skim magazines like *Working Woman* or *Inc.* which can provide you with a general sense of present-day issues in the workplace. If lack of clothes and lack of money are holding you back—that is, you have nothing appropriate to wear, especially for interviews—try to find a friend, relative, or former cult member who can help you shop or even loan you clothes and accessories. Most towns have thrift stores or consignment clothing shops where you may be able to find one or two suitable outfits.

Another strategy is using your cult experience to get a job. For example, if you cooked for your leader, think about restaurant or catering work. If you led seminars or training sessions and were good at it, think about becoming a teacher or working at a child-care or adult-education center where you would be qualified to teach. If you handled the cult's finances, look for jobs as a cashier or bookkeeper. The important thing is to not underestimate your skills and value as a worker. Having been in a cult, you are likely to be more hardworking, more dependable, and more honest than many other employees.

Some former cult members, however, feel absolutely repulsed by the kind of work they did in the cult. Because of triggers and other bad feelings, you may find that you simply cannot do work that has cult associations. In that case you will need to find new ways to earn a living, either through training in a new career or following an apprenticeship program in a new field.

At the same time, avoid throwing out the baby with the bathwater. Do not allow yourself to starve or become indigent by refusing self-sufficiency. Remember that a job, although it may bring up awful memories, is *not* the cult: You do get to go home at the end of the day. They don't own you. And when something better comes along, you can quit without reprisal. If you need to take an unpleasant job, perhaps temporarily, review the section on triggers in Chapter 7 to ease the impact of any cult-related associations and set clear goals for yourself so that you can move on to something else in time.

Résumés are an important concern if you were in a cult for a long time, and especially if you were not employed outside the cult context. There are a number of books that show effective formats for résumés, and many small typesetting shops (often located at copy centers) can help you put your résumé into an attractive format on good stationery.

In preparing your résumé, evaluate your strengths, weaknesses, and skills as objectively as possible. Make a list of everything you did before you joined the cult, as well as what you did while in the cult. Separate the list into activities and accomplishments that could translate to the working world. What were the good things that you learned from your cult experience? The following list grew out of discussions among former cult members on just this topic:

- self-discipline
- sales, fund-raising, and public speaking
- the value of honesty
- interpersonal skills and getting along with people
- time management
- patience
- survival techniques
- self-control
- teaching skills
- personnel administration
- administrative techniques and organizational methods
- publishing, marketing, and publicity
- economizing
- managing other people
- leadership skills
- meeting deadlines under stress
- juggling multiple tasks

Review the list to see what applies to you, or make your own list for your own situation. If you cannot think of anything right now, come back to it in a few months when you have been able to put more distance between you and your cult experience.

To cover a long span of time spent in a cult, you will need to be somewhat creative in writing your résumé. Consult with other former members who have faced this same problem. Some cults have "reputable" front organizations, such as printing or publishing operations, medical offices, yoga centers, restaurants, and charity groups. If your group had such businesses, evaluate the pros and cons of mentioning employment at one of them on your résumé. Maybe another former member of the group whom you are in touch with could be listed as a reference. Experience as a grass-roots organizer, a church recruiter, a missionary, or a homemaker is not necessarily a bad thing and may not look odd on a résumé. Ultimately, you will have to use your best judgment in how to fill in the gaps.

Generally, on your résumé and during interviews you are not going to want to refer directly to your cult involvement. This is something only you can assess with time and experience. In the beginning it is advisable to camouflage as honestly as possible so that you do not find yourself in an awkward situation with a prospective employer. You may be able to discuss your background with a career counselor, who might be helpful in resolving this issue. Chances are you will not be the first former cult member to have strolled into the counselor's office. Role-playing with friends and relatives can also be helpful here.

Other job-related matters that some former members have no experience with concern benefits. Since there are few, if any, in most cults (who ever heard of a cult pension plan?), when former members start new jobs they are sometimes overwhelmed by the array of questions and masses of forms to fill out. How many deductions to claim on tax forms? Who should be the beneficiary of your company-sponsored life insurance policy? Which HMO to choose? Do you want to participate in the company's 401K plan? Even before that, what benefits should you be sure to inquire about during a job interview? Most of these questions are addressed in reference books related to job hunting and job interviews, or they can be discussed with career counselors, friends, or family. Many companies have human resources or employee benefits personnel whose job it is to explain benefits and policies. Don't be afraid or too embarrassed to ask questions—even during an interview. A straightforward question will always get you further along the way, which is far better than getting stuck in a morass of confusion and ignorance.

One final note: you do not have to accept a job just because it is offered to you. If it does not feel right or meet your requirements, allow yourself to pass. There will be other opportunities. Remember, it's your life.

CHAPTER
ELEVEN

HEALING FROM SEXUAL
ABUSE AND VIOLENCE

"**Y**ou too!"

"Are you sure you're not talking about *my* leader?"

"I guess I'm not alone."

These are some of the typical statements heard when former cult members get together for support and to exchange information.

Off to the side, quiet and withdrawn, may be others who do not completely identify with the larger gathering. Their experiences set them apart: the violence and abuse they have witnessed or experienced carries a burden of terror, shame, and guilt that is often difficult to share. They may have already experienced rejection on other occasions when they tried to talk about the horrors of their cult experience. This is especially true of those who have come out of groups known for their violence and anti-social behavior, such as Posse Comitatus, Church of the First Born of the Lamb of God, and some satanic cults.

Yet others are silent for a different reason: they were born and raised in cults. For them, discussions of precult personalities and returning to the community or family of origin are depressing and isolating. Their only family may still be in the cult and their only identity may be the one they brought with them to the meeting. Although able to benefit from discussions on different aspects of mind control and common recovery issues, some of their basic issues remain unexplored.

In this chapter we address matters pertaining to cult-related violence and sexual abuse. A further discussion of children in cults can be found in Chapter 22.

Different levels of psychological, emotional, or spiritual abuse experienced in cults may cause differing degrees of difficulty in the postcult transition period. Children, for example, or those subjected to extreme forms of abuse, have an increased potential for damage. This is not to diminish the needs of those who were in less physically abusive groups. All women, men, and children in cults are at risk because of the irrational, erratic, and sometimes delusional nature of the leadership.

Physical cruelty and sexual abuse are common in many cults. Violence is present in many forms, from sporadic physical abuse to orchestrated punishments. Sexual abuse may masquerade as "marriage" to the leader or as spiritual practice, or may be the overt seduction of vulnerable females or males by those in power. In some cults, physical violence and sexual abuse are incorporated into elaborate rituals and endowed with mystical and magical meanings. Encouraging a devotee to have sex with the "guru" or "Prophet of God" is a slick combination of sexual coercion and mystification. A refusal to participate is seen as disobedience, and disobedience is sin. In occult groups and many one-on-one cultic relationships, terror and pain may be used to bring about altered states or to ensure control. Vows of silence and pledges of obedience help perpetuate the cruel and violent system.

Sexual Abuse in Cults

In many cults, members' sexuality is controlled and manipulated along with other aspects of their experience. Cult leaders soon learn that controlling a person's sexuality can be a source of power. People joining cults generally have certain values and beliefs about their sexuality. Through peer pressure and thought reform these beliefs are altered, often radically. When a group or leader demands sexual submission from a follower, it could be considered the final step in the objectification of the individual.

The incidence of sexual abuse in cults is a topic that cries out for solid research. At a recent postcult recovery conference, 40 percent of the female ex-members present attended an impromptu workshop for women sexually abused in their cult.(1) In addition, there were a number of workshop leaders and observers with histories of cultic sexual abuse who did not or could not take part, and there may have been other female attendees who had been sexually abused but who chose not to attend. There were also male attendees who had experienced sexual abuse in their cults but who, at the request of the women, were excluded from this particular workshop. So, we surmise that 40 percent is the low end of the scale of cult members victimized in this way.

When sexual abuse begins within a relationship of trust—for example, therapist-client, educator-student, clergyperson-parishioner, lawyer-client, doctor-patient, supervisor-employee, or between any two individuals where there is an unequal distribution of power—any other benefits of that relationship are contaminated if not destroyed. Because of the power imbalance and the potential for harm, sexual relations between an authority figure and those in his or her care are never justifiable. We believe that gaining more knowledge and increasing the general awareness about this issue can assist both the abused and those helping them make greater steps toward understanding and healing.

The incidence of sexual abuse within the mental health profession was explored in a landmark study of psychiatrists. The researchers noted that 6.4 percent of respondents acknowledged having sexual contact with their patients, some admitting multiple episodes. Three national studies of psychologists between 1977 and 1986 reported that 9.4 to 12.1 percent of male therapists and 2.5 to 3 percent of female therapists had had explicit sexual contact with their patients. A 1987 study showed a significant drop to 3.6 percent for male therapists, possibly due to increased public and professional awareness, increased litigation, and even criminal penalties for abuse.(2)

It is a violation of the Hippocratic oath for medical doctors to have sexual contact with their patients. This is the standard of ethical practice to which all professional mental health associations subscribe. Similar ethical restraints are found in pastoral and educational counseling. And it is by this standard that we should judge cult leaders and those in positions of power over others.

Varieties of cultic sexual abuse

We define sexual abuse as the misuse of power in a cult or cultic relationship whereby a member or partner is sexually exploited to meet the conscious or unconscious financial, emotional, sexual, or physical needs of the leader, other partner, or group. Sexual abuse can range from unwanted touching to rape. Safety and the redress of wrongs become impossible because of the power dynamics of the situation.

In a broad sense, reproductive and sexual control through enforced celibacy or mandated relationships are also forms of sexual abuse. In many groups, if not the leader, then the husbands are given absolute control over their wives (and sometimes their children), including a license for sexual conduct without mutual consent. Marital rape becomes an accepted standard.

In many cults, members are told that a sexual encounter with the leader is an *honor,* a special gift, a way of achieving further growth. A devotee may be asked, for example, to help the leader relax or feel better. In cults where the leader is regarded as God, sex with him or her may be interpreted and rationalized as spiritually beneficial. Often, members submit to a leader's advances out of pure *fear*. Given the imbalance of power, it is difficult to say no.

Testing is another practice used by leaders to manipulate followers, often to achieve sexual satisfaction. The more a leader demands, the more power he gets, until he intrudes and controls every aspect of life. The justification is that nothing is too sacred to withhold from the leader. Giving oneself, and sometimes even one's children, is viewed as a noble sacrifice. (Rosanne Henry's story in Chapter 20 is an example.) In some cults this testing is done in a sexually sadistic manner, further debilitating the follower and increasing dependence on the leader.

Some groups demand sexual abstinence or *celibacy,* or enforce certain *sexual prohibitions,* for example, against homosexual relations or unsanctioned relationships. At first glance such rules may provide a relief from the confusion of trying to master the intricacies of sexuality and intimate relationships. In reality, however, they merely serve as yet another cult manipulation. By controlling sex, marriage, and procreation, the cult is better able to control its membership. In some cults women are discouraged from bearing children, with sterilization and abortion used as means of birth control. In other cults childbearing is expected and sometimes ordered by the leadership.

In many cults there is a demand for *female subservience.* The women's behavior is strictly controlled and often placed under the command of her spouse who may not have been chosen or approved by her. Yet she is expected to be totally submissive to all demands placed on her by her husband—or by the cult leaders. Certain groups also condone punishment of women in the form of beatings or forced sexual intercourse. Women learn to take the blame, feel the guilt, and carry the shame of others' behavior.

There are many other possible scenarios for cultic sexual abuse, and some are illustrated here with case examples.

Sex therapy. A former member of a psychotherapy cult, *Noreen P.* made a complaint to the state licensing board and filed a civil suit against her psychotherapist for sexual abuse. With no special training in sexual disorders or gynecology, Dr. G. conducted "sexological" exams on Noreen to uncover the cause of what he identified as her "sexual inhibitions." He began his seduction on the therapy couch, each time sitting closer and closer to Noreen until she tolerated first an arm around her shoulder, then a hand under her skirt. Any protestations or squeamishness on her part were interpreted as frigidity and lack of trust. Genital exams occurred in the office unaccompanied by a nurse and were frequently a prelude to other molestations. Within a few months, intercourse and oral sex regularly occurred in the therapy hour for which Noreen was expected to pay her usual fee. Dr. G. lost his license to practice for five years and was fined several hundred thousand dollars in a well-publicized lawsuit that was brought against him by five of his patients.

Drugs. In a New Age healing cult, *Laurie W.* smoked marijuana and hashish as part of the group experience which combined drugs and mysticism. Occasionally heroin and cocaine were also used. Once the members were high, the leader chose his partner for the evening. With godlike authority—and the aid of the drugs—he coerced men and women to submit to him or to others in the group. The occasional child that was born in the cult was reared collectively. When Laurie left the group, blood tests were the only means to determine the identity of her son's birth father. A bitter custody battle ensued between Laurie and her group-assigned "husband."

Rape. *Lena C.* worked 16 hours a day in the offices of a large mass transformational group. In between her double shifts she spent all her time and money taking group-sponsored courses in an effort to improve her spiritual condition. Late one night her supervisor, Don, who had the power to demote her or assign her to unending menial labor, propositioned her. Lena refused and was given demerits for improper attitude and put on a punishment detail of 18-hour days doing heavy cleaning. On several occasions she was encouraged by other members to get out of the work detail; then Don would proposition her again. Exhausted from lack of sleep and poor nutrition, she could no longer adequately fend off Don's advances, and eventually he raped her. He continued to coerce her sexually until he tired of her and found a new victim.

"True love." *Murray D.* was well-known in dog-breeding circles when he first met Lida. At her invitation he attended one of her workshops and fell under the spell of Alesha, Lida's 100,000-year-old channeled goddess from the "sixth dimension," who told Murray that he and Lida were soul mates. Convinced by Alesha and Lida that his destiny was entwined with Lida's, he "fell in love" and married her at her request. With Murray's skill and knowledge, they raised and trained pedigree show dogs, which they marketed profitably to Lida's followers. Three years later Lida divorced Murray, leaving him virtually penniless and without health insurance. When he tested HIV positive, he contested the divorce settlement, which he claimed left him financially unable to procure proper medical care.

Ritual sex. Tapestries, icons, and works of art adorn the walls of the mansion's meditation room, known as the sanctuary. It is here that *Brenda J.'s* Master intones "Surrender to guru," as he gives private meditation instruction to selected pupils. Only after passing obscure tests is a disciple ready for initiation and a new name. Since the tests are never spelled out, Brenda never knows what life event has been planned by guru to help her advance to the next level. Only the subtle pressure of "surrender to guru" is continually maintained during the sessions, as guru and Brenda sit closer and closer until they are entwined. Brenda only knows that she must please guru and is left to guess just how that might happen. In this way she is led to increasing acts of sexual intimacy. Sex is justified as "tantric," part of the secret sexual practices of certain Buddhist and Hindu sects. Enlightenment, of course, is never attained. Shame and secrecy are the only outcomes of the sessions. Like the other disciples at the ashram, Brenda believes that she is the only one intimately involved with guru, though she occasionally observes others making their way to the sanctuary. Each disciple is told that the sexual contact is for her benefit, as guru is celibate, and that he is making the ultimate sacrifice for her. This manipulative logic produces an added load of guilt and confusion for Brenda and the other abused disciples.

Another extension of all this sexual abuse and manipulation within cults is *coerced prostitution* and *pornography*. Some cults force members to use sexual favors to attract new members, blackmail opponents, or gain political power.(3) Charles Manson's "Family" and the Children of God are best known for using sex as a tool for recruitment.

Seduction, rape, drug abuse, induced altered states, fear, manipulation of emotions, and misuse of power all surround the sexual abuse perpetrated in cults and cultic relationships.

Exploring the aftereffects

In their study of the dynamics of therapist-client abuse, Maurice and Jane Temerlin isolated three factors that can lead to abuse: idealization, dependency, and failure to maintain professional boundaries.(4) There are, in fact, many similarities between those who were abused in a cult and those abused in the course of psychotherapy (which can sometimes be defined as a one-on-one cultic relationship or even a cult if the therapist is involving his clients in group activities).

Because of *idealization,* which is encouraged by the leader or the therapist, the leader is viewed as enlightened, superhuman, blessed by God, or the prophet of a new "sacred science" or special belief. Members become *dependent* on the leader through viewing him as having all the answers and being capable of ensuring their psychological, spiritual, or economic security and growth. Dependence is increased by isolating members from family and friends, and by encouraging lifelong membership (or in the case of cultic therapists, endless treatment). *Personal boundaries are erased* through increased control. Members no longer have realistic responses to the leader. They become increasingly dependent, submissive, and depressed, and exercise less and less control over their own lives.

Current literature documents the potential for harm when there is sexual exploitation by professionals and others in positions of power.(5) One researcher describes the resultant effects as a distinct syndrome with at least 10 major damaging aspects that can have acute, delayed, or chronic effects.

1. **Ambivalence:** feelings of anger, fear; desire for, clinging to, and wishing to protect the abuser.

2. **Guilt:** feelings of having betrayed the abuser. These come from having exposed the abuse or discussed it with another. Victims become convinced that they were responsible for and take the blame for the abuse.

3. **Emptiness and isolation:** the abuser is given so much power that separation diminishes the abused person's sense of self. Without this magical person, life seems to lose meaning.

4. **Sexual confusion:** sexual thoughts, feelings, sensations, and impulses are contradictory and conflicted. The abuser usually exploits the victim's initial sexual confusion with overt molestation.

5. **Impaired ability to trust:** victims doubt their ability to trust another person or their own judgment.

6. **Identity and role reversal:** the abused is manipulated into taking care of the abuser. Sexualization of the relationship sometimes begins with the abuser talking about his problems to gain sympathy, which is then used to manipulate and exploit the victim.

7. **Emotional lability or dyscontrol:** intense, chaotic, and unpredictable emotions are experienced and expressed, from laughter to sobbing to raging. Sudden and profound depressions may appear just when emotional balance seems to be emerging.

8. **Suppressed rage:** like other survivors of incest, rape, or physical abuse, victims may have had to deny, suppress, or hide their an-

ger. This may result in a deep and powerful rage, which they were unable to act upon, talk about, or even acknowledge for long periods of time.

9. **Depression and increased suicidal risk:** rage toward the abuser may be turned against the self. Irrational guilt or shame may lead to feelings of hopelessness and helplessness, and suicidal thoughts.

10. **Cognitive dysfunction:** attention and concentration may be disturbed by flashbacks, intrusive thoughts, unbidden images, nightmares, and other symptoms of posttraumatic stress disorder.(6)

There may also be *intellectual impairment* caused by the cult's thought-reform program promoting fallacious beliefs and distorting the person's reality.

At some point, former cult members who were sexually abused need, to confront the issue of their sexuality. This can be difficult, so the feelings related to sexual abuse may be the deepest and last layer of cult-related trauma to be explored. Because acknowledging that one was sexually exploited can be so painful, a person may deny, rationalize, minimize, and distort the meaning of the experience. In the extreme, they may dissociate, separate from, split off, and even "forget" the experience in order to tolerate continued membership in the group.

Unearthing and confronting these experiences and feelings may be beneficial, if not necessary, for restoring the capacity for intimate and sexual relationships. Working through guilt and shame, and sorting through sexual values, beliefs, and preferences are major developmental tasks. Journal-keeping, creative self-expression, support groups, and counseling with a trusted therapist can be helpful in this process.

Violence in Cults

Sexual abuse is one form of violence found in cults. Beatings and physical punishments, assault against others, and occasionally even murder are other forms of cult violence. Violence may be used as a means of control, an expression of power, an outlet for rage or frustration, or for the sadistic enjoyment of the hierarchy. It may be part of the modus operandi of a profitable criminal enterprise engaged in thievery, drug or weapons dealing, kidnapping, prostitution, or pornography; or it may be part of the cult's rituals or initiation rites. The violence may be random or planned. Violence against others or their property is a criminal act.

Cult leaders coerce members into participation in violence or other criminal activities by leading them into increasingly difficult situations and limiting their options. Some regularly engage in violent acts, while others are forced to witness them. Involving members in criminal activities also gives the group the potential for blackmailing members, making it even more difficult for them to leave.

The following is a sampling of cult-related violence:

A 1990 police report in Melbourne, Australia, recommended an investigation of the activities of "The Family," a cultlike group led by fugitive Anne Hamilton-Byrne. Matters to be investigated included the deaths of three women followers soon after they sold their homes and gave their money to the sect, the disappearance of eight adopted children, two cases where mothers were coerced into giving up their babies for adoption to sect members, the forging of passports, and the transfer of large amounts of money from Australia to the United States.(7)

Bhagwan Shree Rajneesh, an Indian guru who preached free love and East-meets-West mysticism, died in 1990 after being deported from the United States in 1986 and charged with illegal immigration. Around that time a number of his followers at the group's ashram near Antelope, Oregon, were charged with various crimes, including intentionally poisoning food in several restaurants (which made hundreds of people ill), illegally tapping phones of opponents, allegedly plotting to murder U.S. Attorney Charles Turner, and conspiring to murder Rajneesh himself.(8)

Joe Hunt, founder of the Billionaire Boys Club, was accused (and acquitted) of the murder of a wealthy Iranian immigrant in 1984 to get money for the club. Hunt, 33 years old, is serving a life sentence for the 1986 killing of a fellow con man who got involved in Hunt's scams. Hunt espoused "paradox philosophy," which allowed members of his group to feel that they were above society's rules and laws. Members, some from among Southern California's wealthiest families, subordinated themselves to Hunt and his whims.(9)

One of the most bizarre and violent cults in the history of North America was described in 1993 in a Canadian weekly newsmagazine. Called the Ant Hill Kids and led by Roch Theriault, the group lived communally in remote Canadian locales. Theriault, who is serving a life sentence, "killed at least two of his followers, castrated two others, and severed the arm of another. He is known to have fathered at least 25 children with eight different women."(10)

Not all cults are as violent. Some use a more subtle, less visible brand of violence, which is harder to detect and prosecute. The following report concerning the Democratic Workers Party, a now-defunct left-wing political cult, illustrates more typical expressions of cult violence,

> After Helene's formal expulsion from the organization, as a finishing touch, a small squad was sent to physically intimidate her. One evening Helene was stalked at her job and chased home by women who had been her comrades just days before. They stormed her house, pushed her around, ransacked her belongings, and threatened her. They were well aware that Helene was recovering from major surgery; this did not prevent them from carrying out their orders which were to intimidate her into silence about the organization. This was the first use of goon squad tactics which the group became known for in ensuing years.
>
> Such tactics were used against other groups on the Left, against groups within the local labor, peace, and antinuclear movements, and against certain former members. Cars were spray-painted. Homes and offices were ransacked. Documents were stolen. Political meetings and conventions were disrupted. Certain persons were surveilled and threatened; others beaten up. In one case, two recently expelled members were assaulted in front of their child . . . .
>
> Similar methods were used inside the group as well. Militants being punished for something or awaiting "trial" could be suspended (removed from party life), put on punitive suspension (could not be spoken to by another member, that is, lived in total silence, sometimes for as long as six weeks), put under house arrest, or guarded around the clock. One militant sat for hours with [the leader], drunk, holding a gun at her head. Expelled militants were threatened and subject to extortion, told to repay the organization for the "training" they received. Sometimes this involved thousands of dollars.
>
> The leader set up an elite group within the organization called the Eagles, whose job it was to carry out many of these assignments. Eagles received special training in security and physical fitness from an ex-Marine member. Eagles served as the leader's personal bodyguards, as monitors during demonstrations, as disrupters, goons, and rabble-rousers whenever needed.(11)

This kind of abuse, intimidation tactics, and violence is perhaps more common than the extremes described in the earlier examples. The sad fact remains, however, that within the world of cults there are masses of evidence of abuse and violence of all kinds. The cultic organization thrives on the abuse of power, which often manifests itself in violent and brutal acts. As one cult researcher wrote, "Most cults undoubtedly are neither utopian nor infernal. At any given time, a number may be relatively harmless. But most—if not all—have the potentiality of becoming deadly . . . . Some cults that currently may appear harmless are in fact already doing serious damage about which the general public knows nothing, damage that cult leaders cover up and deny, damage that apologists for cults consistently refuse to admit or inspect."(12)

Satanism

Satanic cults and their victims are often regarded with skepticism or as unwanted stepchildren by professional and anticult groups. Organizations such as the American Family Foundation, the Cult Awareness Network, and the International Society for the Study of Multiple Personality and Dissociation are frequently divided over the reality and incidence of Satanism, particularly the phenomenon of multigenerational ritual-abuse cults. The controversy is hotly debated at meetings, in the media, and at professional conferences.

Carl Raschke, professor of religious studies at the University of Denver, has done extensive research on Satanism and occult groups. In *Painted Black: From Drug Killings to Heavy Metal,* Raschke relates the history of modern satanic practices and the phenomenon of "teen dabblers," and documents criminal activities of satanic groups, such as drug trafficking, murder, child prostitution, and pornography. The social problem of young teens dabbling with Satanism or becoming fascinated with satanic rituals and symbols has become commonplace. A survey conducted in Provo, Utah, found that 62 of 92 psychotherapists (or 67 percent) had treated adolescents involved in some form of Satanism.(13)

A well-researched and balanced view of the subject is presented in *Satanism and Occult-Related Violence: What You Should Know* by Michael D. Langone and Linda O. Blood. Besides a historical review, the book has sections on why people get involved in Satanism, effects and signs of satanic involvement, what families can do, suggestions for mental health professionals, legal issues, and resource organizations. David Sakheim and Susan Devine have edited another thoughtful volume, *Out of Darkness: Exploring Satanism and Ritual Abuse*. The contributors address many of the controversial aspects of ritual abuse.

We have chosen in this book not to separate satanic cults from other types of cultic groups. We believe that abuse in cults exists on a continuum. Satanic cults may be at one extreme, but they are not alone or unique in the horror or perversity of their actions.

Healing the Pain

Many cults perpetrate violence against the human body and the human spirit. Control is exerted in a variety of ways: through some form of threat, such as spiritual disfavor (i.e., being told that you are displeasing God or the leader); through the withdrawal of the leader's or other members' emotional support; through group pressure to conform; through withdrawal of privileges, food, or rest; and through overt physical abuse including confinement, paddling and birching, beatings, sexual mistreatment, and torture, sometimes resulting in death.

When physical or sexual violence is used in a group, it affects all the members. Witnessing or knowing of the abuse of others produces guilt and fear, and it is traumatizing. To be forced to abuse others further compounds the guilt and trauma.

Margaret Singer says that it is an "intellectual mistake" to equate the sexual abuse found in cults with the sexual abuse in outside society. Sexual abuse in society is more random, furtive, and associated with guilt; sexual abuse in cults may be an integral, open, and accepted part of the system.(14) This may have an impact on a person's recovery issues.

If you are just leaving a group or relationship where you were physically or sexually abused, consider the following suggestions:

1. Find a safe place to stay: your family, a trusted friend, a parish shelter.

2. If necessary, seek the safety of a battered women's shelter. In almost all cities there are nonprofit homes or residences where women and children in danger can find refuge. Sometimes they are able to network with social service agencies that provide counseling that will enable you to start planning for your life out of the cult.

3. Seek medical attention for any physical wounds or injuries, even old ones.

4. If necessary, go to or call a rape crisis center or the police. If you have been abused or threatened, you may be able to file criminal charges or obtain a restraining order to prohibit contact by the group, its members, or your former abusive partner.

5. Refer to the list of organizations in Appendix B. Some will be more helpful than others. Finding the appropriate help for your particular needs is key. Don't give up!

Besides getting immediate assistance, there are other things you should do. First of all, talk about the violence. This will help you process and work though the related emotions. Finding someone with a similar history or a therapist knowledgeable about cults will be the most helpful.

Expressing the emotions you have about the sexual abuse or other violence may also prove helpful for recovery. Art, music, writing, poetry, dance, drama—all forms of personal creativity can serve as a release and a means of healing.

Reading about violence and abuse can help increase your understanding of victims and perpetrators. Such books as *Trauma and Recovery* by Judith Lewis Herman, *Trauma and Its Wake,* edited by Charles Figley, and *The Nazi Doctors* by Robert Jay Lifton may provide you with insight and self-understanding. Another useful book is *Women, Sex, and Addiction* by Charlotte Davis Kasl.

There are many support groups around the country which may also be beneficial. Where alcohol or substance abuse has been a problem, attending meetings of Alcoholics Anonymous or Narcotics Anonymous can be very helpful. In general, however, we caution you to proceed into the 12-step world with your eyes open and your antennae up. It is an area rife with abuses and incompetencies. Hustlers use 12-step programs as a hunting ground for income and glory (see, for example, Holly Ardito's personal account in Part One). Some counselors and group leaders are not credentialed. Some programs are fronts for cults. Even a well-meaning program may inadvertently promote long-term victimization. Although the groups are set up to be against codependency, many participants become completely dependent on their 12-step meetings and friends. For a critical perspective on the widespread recovery movement, read *I'm Dysfunctional, You're Dysfunctional* by Wendy Kaminer.

If you were subjected to extreme forms of abuse, seek out a therapist or counselor experienced in working with survivors of trauma (see Chapter 12 on how to evaluate a therapist). Also review the sections in this book on anger, fear, dissociation and triggers, relationships, and self-expression. In all cases, denying the abuse will only prolong your misery. Our best advice is take the bull by the horns, so to speak, and work through the trauma so that you can move on.

CHAPTER TWELVE

MAKING PROGRESS BY TAKING ACTION

Healing takes place in many different ways. Each person is different and responds to different things. In this chapter we address some of the paths to recovery that have helped people after their cult experience. One general method is self-help, which includes attitude as well as effort, and is the key to regaining your wholeness. Many former members also find professional counseling useful. Finally, there is anticult activism, which usually begins at the middle or end stage of healing, when a person feels ready to take direct action against those who abuse and manipulate.

Self-Help

The primary sources of self-help are education, creative expression, and support networks. Each of these is described here.

Educating yourself

Education is one of the most important ways to cope with the aftereffects of a cult experience and integrating it into your life. Most ex-members go through a period where they read everything they can get their hands on. This is a crucial phase in the healing process since it helps to correct many misconceptions about cults and the people who get involved in them.

By reading about cultic influence processes and thought-reform techniques, ex-members can begin to comprehend and assimilate what happened to them and why. This can help them shed self-blaming stereotypes and attitudes and also provides ammunition for explaining the experience to others.

There is a growing body of literature on these subjects, including books and articles on specific groups, types of cults, and theoretical issues. Organizations such as the American Family Foundation (AFF) and the Cult Awareness Network (CAN) have compiled useful bibliographies; they also sell selected books, journals, pamphlets, and packets on cults and cult-related topics. Other educational and research organizations who also do work in this field are listed in Appendix B, and some of the most useful and informative materials are listed in Appendix C. Unfortunately, a number of good books are out of print, but can often be found at libraries and used bookstores.

Other means of education are associating with other former members who are likely to share their knowledge and information; and attending conferences, seminars, and workshops sponsored by the various cult information organizations.

Expressing yourself

Self-expression—whether through writing, art, dance, music, drama, or some other medium—is key to taking back your precult identity and shaping a postcult one. Expressing yourself about the cult experience can help purge, clarify, and educate your newly emerging self.

One of the most healing exercises is to write about the experience. Putting your thoughts and feelings on paper will allow you to look at them objectively, and sort out jumbled ideas and emotions. This journal does not have to be shared with anyone else—it can be a private, personal record. The decision whether or not to show it to others can be made later and depends on how you feel.

A chronological, autobiographical account is sometimes the easiest way to begin. What was happening before you were recruited? How were you vulnerable? What was the appeal? What were your first impressions of the group, the leader, the beliefs, the goals? What did you like? What, if anything, did you distrust or not like? Which types of persuasion were used? Which thought-reform techniques? When did you start to doubt? What led to your leaving? How did you leave? How are you feeling now? What are you doing to cope with and heal from the experience?

A broader autobiographical sketch can help make sense of the experience and put it into perspective. You will begin to regard your cult involvement as a chapter in your life, not as your whole life. Even for those who were born or raised in a cult, the experience is still only a part of your life, albeit a large one. Once you are out, a whole new chapter begins.

Writing an account of your experience also allows you to put into your own words the often intangible, subtle, and hard-to-explain dynamics of the group or relationship. Most former cult members need to explain to family and friends why they joined, how it was possible, how they got out, and so on. Being able to explain it to yourself will enable you to explain it to others.

Anna Bowen, who has done considerable work in developing guidelines for keeping a journal, believes that journal writing and art are two effective methods of expressing thoughts and feelings that may have no other safe outlets. She states, "The purpose of keeping a journal is to provide a safe avenue for self-awareness, self-expression, personal discovery, and a safe outlet for fantasizing, exploring new ways of communicating with dissociated aspects of the self, and working through trauma. Artwork allows for the expression of feelings there may be no words for; or it can elaborate, accentuate, and enhance the messages contained in writing. Talent is not a requirement." She recommends the following techniques for keeping a journal:

- See it as a personal commitment. Take it seriously. Accept it as an important part of your healing journey. It is important to remind yourself that the journal is your private property and no one else should access it without your permission.

- Use a large, blank book. These are often available in art supply shops, stationers, and bookstores. Write in pen, not in pencil, so that you cannot easily erase your work. Always date your entries (month, day, year) and include the time of day if it is relevant.

- If you don't like to use blank pages, write on whatever type of paper you are comfortable with, then tape or slot these entries into the blank journal page. Keep paper handy at all times so that even when your journal is not available you can write when needed.

- Write spontaneously, honestly, and deeply. Write about thoughts, feelings, images.

- Don't edit or censor your writing or artwork, especially when spilling out feelings. Record whatever and however it comes to you even though it may not make any sense at that time.

- Let go of traditional rules of grammar, spelling, punctuation, and neatness. *You don't have to be perfect!* Remember you are doing this for yourself. Nobody will judge how you choose to utilize your journal.

- Find a comfortable place to write, a place in which you will be free of interruptions and distractions. In nice weather, choose places outside where you can sit and write or draw.

- Make an effort to use your journal daily, even if all you write is "Today I don't have time to write." If you find yourself neglecting it, however, don't feel guilty. Don't use missing a few days as an excuse not to continue writing.

- Don't destroy what you have written. If it is too painful or disturbing, you can tape a piece of paper over it or find a safe place separate from your journal to keep it. One of the benefits of journalkeeping and artwork as a therapeutic tool is having a record of recovery and growth.

- Use your journal as a safe deposit box. It will hold important documents: your memories, pain, sorrow, feelings of hopelessness, fears, and so on. It will also hold your joys, accomplishments, dreams, hopes, and questions.

- Use your journal to fantasize. Make wishes, imagine safe places, describe what you would like the future to hold. Or use it to write letters (without the intent of sending them) to whomever you choose, saying whatever you choose. Also write letters to yourself. Your journal can also be a safe and private place for you to explore and become comfortable with sexual issues.

- When you are ready, go back and read your entries. Try reading out loud. When you feel comfortable doing this, share some of what you have written and drawn with a person you trust (therapist, friend, partner). Then write about how this felt.(1)

Movement therapy has also helped some people to work out the trauma of the cult experience. A former member writes:

When I reentered college, I turned to dance to reconnect myself to life again. I began with ballet but quickly rejected it because of its rigidity of form. I found modern and African dance, tai chi chuan, and choreography to be more liberating.... We helped one another find ways to bring out the best in each of our own works, free of jealousy and criticism. My senior honors thesis was based on the experience and what it did for me in my recovery. It earned Highest Honors, affirming the improvements I'd made in my critical thinking skills.... Utilizing my creativity has given me routes to explore my experience and discover my feelings and memories. It gives me a variety of voices to share them and I get to choose with whom I will share them.(2)

Another former cult member describes her healing through self-expression: "I am personally experiencing each step in this growth process. My painting and especially my poetry help me to know myself and my environment better, to feel more alive and connected to life and to transform my wounds into wholeness.... Therapy helped guide me down the path, but poetry allowed me to express my rage, grief, and forgiveness."(3)

Creative acts such as these will allow you to transform the hurt and the feelings of humiliation. It gets the feelings out of you, and the results may be something powerful and beautiful to behold.

Finding a support network

Without a support network, it can be extremely difficult to heal. Talking to trusted friends, family, former members, or clergy about your cult experience is a necessary part of the postcult process. Sharing thoughts and feelings with those who care begins the process of understanding and working through the experience.

Talking about it rather than silently rehashing it within will help put it in perspective. Without that outlet some ex-members feel compelled to return to their cult or choose other cultic situations. Talking to other former members is an effective way of getting support, sharing information, and solving problems. For many, such a support group—formal or informal—may be the only "exit counseling" they receive. Through a support group you will find others who have gone through similar experiences, usually in quite different ideological frameworks.

One avenue for support is FOCUS, a network of people who have been in cults or other thought-reform situations. There are a number of FOCUS groups nationwide meeting on a regular basis, usually monthly. Meetings are free and voluntary, and there is never any pressure to attend. Some former members of specific cults have their own support group or newsletter, such as *TM-Ex* for former devotees of Transcendental Meditation.

Through contact with others who have been through similar experiences you will begin to better understand yourself and what you are going through. As you hear others' stories and share their pain, you will identify with them and feel compassion. In this way you will start to have compassion for and forgive yourself. You may also benefit from hearing how others have dealt with various postcult problems, such as learning to recognize and identify specific postcult symptoms (for example, floating). You will also gain insight on dealing with and eliminating side effects as well as facing general life issues. You will be able to measure your own growth and healing as new people come into the group and you find that you are offering them help and support.

You can also *leave* FOCUS groups. It is nice to know that this postcult phase will pass. Many people attend for some time, then drop out, returning occasionally because of a specific need or interest.

Conferences offer another avenue for combining practical learning and personal healing. At most of the conferences sponsored by cult information or research organizations there are sessions and workshops specifically for former cult members. At a recent workshop dealing with women's issues, for example, 27 women participated and represented experiences in 32 different groups!

Professional Help

By evaluating your psychological health—that is, your capacity to work, love, relax, enjoy life, and, for those who have religious faith, pray—you will best be able to determine if you need professional help. There are many aspects of life—physical, psychological, and emotional—that require personal attention during the postcult period. Some of these are best addressed by using professional services. Consider theological or philosophical beliefs when choosing a counselor or support organization. For example, the religious affiliation or lack thereof of some counseling professionals may or may not be helpful to your needs.

Public assistance

Some people come out of their groups seriously ill or disabled. Temporary reliance on state or federal public-assistance programs may be an excellent way for them to get back on their feet. State agencies can help in finding housing, health care, and employment.

If you were employed before joining the group, you probably paid state and federal taxes. If you dislike the idea of using public assistance, consider those taxes as money deposited for the future. If you had earnings withheld for social security and disability insurance, you are entitled to use that money now if you are disabled. This is not charity—this is survival.

As soon as you are well and working, you will be paying taxes again, and contributing to the same programs that assisted you. In that way you will help others as you were helped.

Individual counseling

Former cult members seek professional counseling for a variety of reasons. These include the following conditions:

- You find that emotional difficulties that you had prior to your cult involvement are resurfacing.

- You have difficulty functioning fully or enjoying life. You have difficulty working, relaxing, or loving.

- You feel overwhelmed by emotions such as depression, anxiety, guilt, shame, fear, and rage.

- You continue to lapse into disturbing altered states, or have nightmares, insomnia, intrusive thoughts about the trauma experienced in the group, panic attacks, numbing of emotions, a feeling of deadness inside, or detachment from others.

Many of these symptoms are related to post-traumatic stress disorder (PTSD), which is commonly found in survivors of rape, incest, and war, and victims of natural disasters, such as floods, tornadoes, and earthquakes. These symptoms often require professional care.

When choosing a counselor, particularly if you have not been through a formal exit counseling, try to find someone with experience in counseling former cult members or someone who is at least willing to learn about typical cult-related problems.

Without study, few professionals truly understand thought reform and its consequences. In addition, many psychiatrists, psychologists, and social workers believe that cults were a passing fad, now gone. There is also a tendency for some professionals to say that a cultic involvement is the result of some pathology—that is, some kind of abnormal condition—in the person who joins such a group or gets into such a relationship. Other professionals believe the problem lies with the parents, and that if the parents had not been peculiar in some way the children would never have joined a cult. This is an example of the unfortunate and damaging practice of blaming the victim (or the victim's parents), similar to the type of blaming found in rape cases.

There are specific cult-related issues that professional counselors need to be aware of if they wish to help clients who were in a cultic situation. If mental health professionals do not have an understanding of mind control or are quick to use hypnotic techniques (which may exacerbate problems in ex-members already suffering from dissociation), they may do more harm than good (the story of Jessie in Chapter 23 is a good example).(4) Perhaps most important, therapy should start with the client talking about the cult experience, not her or his childhood.(5)

In your search for a counselor, consult resource organizations, close friends, family, clergy, and medical professionals. Basically, there are several types of counseling professionals who can be of assistance: exit counselors, pastoral counselors, and psychological counselors. Remember that selecting a counselor is a very personal choice. You may feel comfortable with one type of counselor, while a friend or partner may prefer a different approach. You might take advantage of different types at different times during the healing process. In all cases, shop around and feel assured that you have found someone you can talk to and confide in.

Exit counseling

If you left the cult voluntarily or were kicked out, you may benefit from meeting with a professional exit counselor. It is important to remember that exit counseling is *not* psychotherapy. Exit counselors offer short-term counseling and can be helpful on a temporary basis to gain an understanding of cults and thought-reform techniques. In a postcult situation exit counselors are often used in conjunction with another type of counselor.

The advantage of an exit counseling is that it can provide you with a basis for understanding your experience in a way that will promote further healing. Often, former members are not aware of the specific manipulative techniques used in the group, or their potential aftereffects. They may find it difficult to distinguish and separate the cult beliefs and values from their own. Illogical, magical, and black-and-white thinking, difficulties in concentrating and making decisions, and erratic behaviors and feelings are all problems that are more easily eradicated when their source is known. A day or two—or even just several hours—of exit counseling may be all you need to sort through the various cult mind-control issues.

To choose an exit counselor, start by interviewing those who have expertise in your particular group or type of cult. Ask other former members about their exit counseling experiences. Read as much as you can about cults and mind control beforehand, and read *Exit Counseling: A Family Intervention* by Carol Giambalvo. Although the book is written primarily for people planning interventions with loved ones still in a cult, it will give you a sense of the support, sensitivity, and mutual respect that you should expect from an exit counselor.

Be sure to interview several counselors before choosing one. In making your final selection, consider the following:

1. Is the exit counselor a former cult member?

2. What is the exit counselor's level of experience?

3. What is the exit counselor's philosophy of exit counseling? What approach will be taken?

4. What is the fee structure? Will you be able to contract for one or two days? Can you travel to the exit counselor's location? Where would you stay? Can you afford to pay for the exit counselor to come to your location?

Select someone you feel comfortable with and can afford, who has a clear grasp of how mind control works. Familiarity with your particular group may be an asset. More important, though, is the exit counselor's ability to help you sort through your experience even if little is known about your specific cult.

Pastoral counseling

Pastoral counseling is particularly helpful for those who previously had a strong religious affiliation and for those coming out of religious cults, to help clarify distortions in the Scriptures. As with other professional help, it is helpful to locate a clergyperson who has familiarity with cults and mind control. Churches and religious organizations are hard hit by the loss of their members to cults and increasingly are confronting the cult issue.

The following suggestions from Father Kent Burtner may help former members evaluate a pastoral counselor:

The pastoral worker's job will range from "first aid" for intense crisis moments to long-term therapy, sharing reflections and helping clients in the task of rediscovering their ability to choose everything from vocation to spirituality .... The counselor will also have to learn from the client and collaborative sources something of the group's ideological structure and how it worked, together with the guilt-specific practices of the group. . . . All the theological language that is used by the counselor should be carefully defined as the counseling proceeds . . . so that words do not bring along by association concepts [other than those intended].

The theological task is not usually the one taken up immediately after departure from a cult. Counselees often will need to learn to handle more mundane, less abstract emotions first, before learning to cope with larger abstractions. The counselees themselves will generally tell the pastoral counselor when the theological issues can be dealt with.(6)

Psychological counseling

A variety of mental health professionals with different titles and degrees offer psychological services. Counselors and psychotherapists may have masters or doctoral degrees (M.A. or Ph.D.) in social work, marriage and family counseling, nursing, clinical psychology, and psychiatry. Clinical psychologists (Ph.D., Psy.D.) are trained to evaluate and treat emotional and mental problems. Psychiatrists (M.D.) first train as medical doctors and later specialize in the treatment of mental and nervous disorders. Clinical social workers (M.S.W.) and nurse clinicians (R.N., C.S.) receive advanced clinical training in their fields.

To qualify as a counselor, there are professional standards that must be met: a certain number of hours of internship, supervised clinical experience, and/or licensing exams. Most professionals belong to a recognized professional organization that subscribes to a code of ethics. Depending on the type of training, each professional is limited in what he or she can do. Because psychiatrists have medical degrees, they can prescribe medication, whereas most others cannot. Psychologists receive formal training in assessment and therefore can administer personality and intelligence tests, whereas others cannot. Clinical specialists in adult and/or child psychiatric or mental health nursing are nurses with advanced degrees and training in psychotherapy. Some nurses in advanced practice are licensed to prescribe medication as well.

Fees vary, with some clinicians offering a sliding scale for low-income clients. Lower fees and sliding scales are also found at some mental health clinics. Many health insurance policies cover a limited number of visits for psychological counseling, within certain restrictions set by the insurance company. Check your policy or ask the human-resources administrator at your workplace. Your discussions will be kept confidential.

Other considerations in choosing a therapist or counselor

A therapist or counselor should view cult experience as a major contributing factor to your current problems and believe that it should be addressed early in the therapy sessions. This person can then assist you as a coach, an ally, in a psychoeducational process.

A therapist should be willing to learn from you and offer explanations to you. If your therapist belittles or disregards your cult experience or insists that your current issues are exclusively related to childhood and family dynamics, or to an underlying need to be controlled, it is time to change therapists.(7)

If you cannot find a therapist familiar with cults and mind control, consider seeing an exit counselor first. That way you will be less likely to confuse cult-related issues with other difficulties, and you will have a better chance of educating your therapist about cults and mind control. This is also good time and money management. It will shorten therapy, save you money, and tap the talents and knowledge of both the exit counselor and the therapist to your best advantage.

An excellent resource that addresses many topics related to how psychotherapy works and what to expect is the book *When Someone You Love Is in Therapy* by Dr. Michael Gold (Hunter House).

The following questions and guidelines may be useful in your selection of a therapist.

Questions to ask in the first session

Consider asking the following questions during the first session with a therapist or counselor. Remember, you do not have to select the first person you talk to. Don't be afraid to "interview" the therapist to make sure he or she will be able to meet your needs.

1. What is your educational background? Are you licensed or accredited?

2. What is your counseling experience? How long and with what types of clients?

3. Do you have an area of expertise?

4. Do you have training in cults and mind control?

5. Are you a former member of a cultic group or relationship? What kind of postcult counseling did you have?

6. What type of therapy do you practice (for example, Freudian, cognitive-behavioral, humanistic, transpersonal, bodywork) and what will it involve? Do you utilize hypnosis or other trance-induction techniques? (Some types of therapy utilize New Age concepts, guided-visualization techniques, and hypnosis, which may trigger you and compound your difficulties.)

7. Do you believe in "therapeutic" touching of clients? What, in your opinion, is permissible touching?

8. Do you believe that it is ever appropriate to have sex with clients or former clients? (Run—don't walk—out of the office if the answer is anything other than "Never.")

9. Are you reachable in a crisis or an emergency? How are such consultations billed?

10. What is your fee? Do you have a sliding scale for those who can't afford your full fee? What is your cancellation policy?

11. What is the length of a regular therapy session?

12. How do you feel about the New Age? Do you incorporate any New Age techniques in your therapy (for example, using crystals, past life regressions)?

13. Would you tell me a little about your philosophy of life?

14. Do you believe in setting treatment goals? How are these established?

Questions to ask yourself after the first session

1. Did you feel accepted, respected, and comfortable with the therapist?

2. Did anything in the environment make you feel uneasy? Don't feel strange if you react to the furniture, paintings, books, or other objects in the office.

3. Was the therapist direct and open in answering all your questions, or did he or she dodge some?

4. Did the therapist give you the impression that she or he has all the answers (if so, consider going to another therapist), or did she or he seem interested in exploring issues with no preconceived expectations?

5. Did you get the feeling that the therapist is sensitive, intelligent, and mature, someone with whom you could feel safe?

6. Did the therapist overreassure you that you now had the right counselor to take care of you? In other words, were you being set up to idealize him or her as the perfect therapist, the only one who could heal you?

General matters to keep in mind

1. Trust your own judgment. You have the right not to trust immediately. Trust needs to be earned—there are no shortcuts.

2. Interview several therapists—after all, you wouldn't buy the first car or stereo you looked at.

3. Get information from friends, other former members, AFF and CAN, and agencies such as rape crisis centers (the latter generally know therapists skilled in dealing with trauma issues).

4. You can stop therapy any time you want. Therapy is for you, not the therapist.

5. Touching is a highly personal issue. Some therapists will hug a client. This should be initiated by the client, not the therapist. Touching should be discussed openly, early in therapy. If touching makes you feel uncomfortable, say something right away.

6. It is *never* okay to be touched on the chest, genitals, or anyplace else that makes you uncomfortable.

7. It is important that the therapist interact with you during the session. People coming out of cultic experiences need a therapist who is interactive without telling you what to do.(8)

Taking Action

An important stage in the healing process arrives when you begin to think of yourself as a victor over mind control rather than a victim of it. At this stage you are beginning to meet the great challenge of turning a negative and destructive experience into a positive and strengthening one. Some people use this as an opportunity to take an active stance against cults.

Anticult activism

When you are ready for it, and only if you so choose, you can utilize your newfound freedom and understanding to educate and help others. Telling others about the cult issue in general or your personal experience in particular can be an excellent and healthy way of channeling your anger. High schools, hospitals and clinics, churches, synagogues, parent and educational associations, and youth groups often look for speakers about cults.

Writing about your experience and having it published can also be very rewarding. Writing letters to the editors of local papers or to your government representatives helps to solidify your understanding of cults and mind control and at the same time educate and warn others of the menace to society that cults pose. Letters or phone calls to persons in charge may also be useful to heighten the awareness of organizations whose facilities are being used by a cultic group for their meetings. A number of groups, for example, meet at local libraries, school buildings, churches, and other places with meeting halls.

The following letter to a public official is a good example of how one former cult member took action against a cult she was in. To protect the individual's privacy, names and locations have been deleted or changed.

> The Honorable _____
> Mayor of _____
> City Hall
>
> Dear Mayor _____:
>   I am writing to alert you of a potentially dangerous situation in our city. A nonprofit organization named _____ will be seeking a zoning permit so that they may hold their public "recovery" meetings in their building at 123 Main Street.
>   I caution you, this is a very destructive group. I speak from first-hand knowledge, as a victim of their mind control. I was first approached by this group in 1986, at a vulnerable time in my life, and was offered a new way of living. The group claims to utilize a 12-step approach to treatment of various addictions. Little did I know I would be subjected to years of emotional exploitation, sexual abuse, and personal humiliation. Today, after three years of therapy, I have come to accept the fact that I, an intelligent, well-educated woman, was cleverly deceived. I fear for our town and its surrounding communities if this group is allowed to establish itself. Residents will be drawn into the psychological abuse that I and others have suffered.

Enclosed please find some articles which I think you will find interesting. Feel free to call me as well. I would be happy to talk with you in greater detail and provide additional references. My daytime number is _____. In the evening I can be reached at _____.

I am sending copies of this letter to the offices of the Chief of Police and the planning and zoning commissioners, in hopes that your joint cooperation can help prevent _____ from causing further injury in our community.

Sincerely,

_____

After receiving this letter the mayor called and spoke with the sender for over an hour. Later two detectives called and interviewed her for several hours. They were planning to do a full-scale investigation of the group.

If you consider writing a letter of this sort, be sure to have solid, verifiable information. You do not want to put yourself in a situation of making false or libelous claims. To be certain, consult a lawyer.

Another way of becoming active is to join FOCUS, where your support for others who have left cults is welcome and meaningful. You could also serve as a local contact person—either for ex-members in general or for ex-members or families of current members of the particular group or type of group you were in. Many ex-members are especially in need of a good listener, a calm friend who can ease them through those first months out of the cult. Many families with relatives still in a cult also need sympathetic listeners.

Legal remedies

According to Herbert Rosedale, a New York City attorney with more than 15 years of experience with cult-related cases, custody or damage awards are "not going to solve the cult problem." But, he states, "there are numerous ways lawyers who have an understanding of cult-related litigation can be of great help to clients." Lawyers can make a difference by educating social workers and judges in family court about cultism; by assisting the elderly and disabled who are often coerced via undue influence to give large gifts to cults; by advising families on guardianship, custody, and conservatorship; and by helping rebuild ex-members' lives in practical ways through providing sound legal advice. "We may not eliminate cults," states

Rosedale, "but by helping people one at a time we can make the law responsive to new needs, and thus help formulate public policy toward cultism."(9)

Unfortunately, it may be some years before the legal profession embraces Mr. Rosedale's advanced thinking. Today the legal system most commonly deals with cult-related issues in cases concerning child custody, civil, or criminal issues.

Child custody

When one parent is in a cult and the other is not, the noncult parent frequently attempts to gain custody of the child or children. In such cases the legal issue is to decide which environment will be "in the best interests of the child." According to an attorney experienced in matrimonial law, successful litigation of cult-related child-custody cases is helped when the client and lawyer pay attention to the following:

1. Emphasize the destructive and dangerous influence of the cult on the child.

2. Focus on the cult leader as the surrogate parent and stress the amount of control the leader has within the cult environment.

3. Keep multiple cases before the same judge, and as much as possible consolidate actions for hearings and trials.

4. Make special use of expert witnesses.

5. Enlist the help and support of other ex-members.(10)

Precision is key. Particularly when religious cults are involved, it is important to demonstrate how the group's practices are physically or psychologically detrimental to the child without questioning the truth or falsehood of the religious doctrines. Another attorney emphasizes the importance of carefully collecting relevant facts and using appropriate language: "Remember, accurate characterization of the facts and proper framing of the legal issues can go a long way toward determining how the litigation will proceed. In this regard, judicious use of language is imperative."(11)

Criminal cases

If a crime has been committed against you by the group, you have the right to press charges. Crimes may include sexual abuse, extortion, or unlawful restraint. You do not need your own lawyer for this; you can file a complaint at the police station nearest to where the crime or crimes were committed. If the police do not seem interested, don't give up. Proceed to the sheriff's or district attorney's office. If you get no response there, go to the state attorney general's office.

Most groups fear negative publicity. If you think the group may try to sue you, get legal advice before you go public. Be certain of your facts, and present all your information accurately. Anything that happened to you personally or that you witnessed can be made public. If going public frightens you, review the steps in Chapter 8 concerning safety issues.

If you committed criminal acts during your involvement, consult a lawyer. Criminal acts include assault, theft, drug dealing, or any scam where money was taken from others by deceptive means. While your criminal acts may never be uncovered or reported, the fear of possible legal charges could prolong or block your recovery. You may also be vulnerable to blackmail attempts by the cult.

Do not go to any lawyer employed by or in the service of the cult. Your own lawyer can advise you how to protect yourself legally. As a witness against the group, you may be able to avoid prosecution for any illegal activities you may have committed while in the cult.

Civil cases

If you were injured by the group or relationship, you can pursue compensation by means of a civil suit. Fraud, deceit, sexual abuse, and undue influence are some of the charges brought in civil suits. Even if the group has not broken any laws per se, you may be able to initiate a suit against them.

You will be required to demonstrate that the group or abusive individual harmed you in some way—emotionally, physically, sexually, or financially—and that you are entitled to a monetary settlement for damages. There are lawyers with expertise in these matters, and in recent years, there have been several successful suits against well-known cultic groups, with juries sympathetic to the plaintiffs.(12)

If you plan on undertaking a civil suit, make sure that you have a good support network. While lawsuits may be an effective weapon against the spread of cult mind control and victimization, as well as a powerful aid to your own recovery, they can also be expensive, time-consuming, and personally draining, and they may become an impediment to healing. You need to weigh the physical, psychological, emotional, and financial risks against the possibility of a positive outcome. Suits may take years from start to finish. You may fight and not win. You may win but never collect. If you decide to not fight at the legal level and go on to other things in your life, that does not have to mean that the cult won. You have your mind and body back—that's the victory!

Getting On with Your Life

"When will I be done working on this stuff?" "When will my past cult involvement stop being such a big thing in my life?" These are questions you may ask yourself from time to time as your recovery proceeds. The answers are not simple. Gradually, preoccupation with feelings, thoughts, and behaviors associated with the cult will lessen. As you resume responsibility for your life, your sense of personal empowerment will increase. You will start to look forward to your personal relationships, career, and even simple pleasures, and memories of life in the cult will recede into the past and cease to be the overbearing shadow it once was.

For some, the cult experience becomes transformed into something useful, in some way influencing their life work. Many ex-members, for example, become therapists, exit counselors, and lawyers working on cult-related matters. Others continue friendships and relationships with other ex-members. For most, recovery means coming to terms with the past through self-acceptance and self-forgiveness and healing through finding a new view of the world and life. The world may never again seem quite as safe, fair, or rosy. Human nature is no longer viewed with the same naïveté. But even though they may now be less gullible and less vulnerable, in many ways former cult members have an increased understanding of and a new compassion for themselves and all humanity.

If they avoid the challenge of recovery, former cult members run the risk of allowing cynicism, pessimism, and bitterness to become defenses against further vulnerability, and of using isolation and denial as weapons against future pain. Recovery means full acceptance of one's humanity— the good as well as the bad. It means accepting the struggle to grow while recognizing one's own and others' imperfections.

SUCCESS IS THE
BEST REVENGE: STORIES
FROM EX-CULT MEMBERS

You gain strength, courage, and confidence by every experience in which you really stop to look fear in the face. You are able to say to yourself, "I lived through this horror. I can take the next thing that comes along."
—Eleanor Roosevelt

CHAPTER
THIRTEEN

REFLECTIONS OVER TIME
GINGER ZYSKOWSKI

Ginger Zyskowski was a member of three different cults, one of which was the Divine Light Mission, an Eastern-style group. Ginger has been free of cults for 13 years and provides here a heartening perspective on the postcult recovery process. She owns and operates a drum school and teaches percussion.

It is 4:30 in the morning. I sit at the kitchen table with an old edition of the "new" Webster, an even older and yellowed edition of Roget, and the DSM-III-R. I am hoping to find just the right stuff to condense into a 10-minute oration. I am going to be on a panel at the annual Cult Awareness Network conference. What emerges is the following. (I do take a small liberty by choosing to drop the Υ and use simply "recover." I do this because—even after 13 years of postcult life—recover is what I do a little every day.)

So picture with me, if you will, the word *RECOVER*—broken up letter by letter, each hung separately on an imaginary wire creating the beginning of a giant mobile. Under the first *R* in recover I've decided to hang the word *RECONSTRUCTION*. What an overwhelming process! The cult experience is like starting out as a beautiful piece of glass—like a big picture window overlooking a wonderfully scenic view—and then a pebble flies into this glass causing a slight fracture. The crack spreads, soon the entire surface is cracked. The view is totally distorted. This is how a person coming out of a destructive group often sees his or her life. Then the reconstruction process begins. This process is filled with anger, fear, pain, resentment, and anxiety, and can only be approached with tentative and small steps exploring different directions with extreme care.

Second, the letter *E*. After perusing both Roget and Webster, I have singled out my E-word—*ENDURANCE*! I was sure I heard a slight chuckle from old Webster when I checked the definition: "the ability to withstand hardship, adversity, and stress." I think that endurance can hang on its own with no further explanation necessary.

The next letter—*C*—is a little difficult to work with because there are so many choices, but I decide to use the phrase *"CUT TO THE CHASE."* If you are unfamiliar with this phrase, it comes from the film industry and describes when, in a movie, instead of staying with the slow paced activity or "fluff," they cut to the fast action chase scenes. So, out of the fluff and into the action.

I'd like to take a moment here to divert and speak of patience. Patience takes on a different perspective after a person has been in and out of a destructive, highly controlled group. In some cases I have more patience now than ever before, especially with regard to those who have been victimized or traumatized. On the other hand, I have no patience for manipulation, closed-mindedness, ineptness, laziness, lies, or procrastination. What does this have to do with "cut to the chase"? It means that I have patience to a point, then it's "get off your hoo-ha and cut to the chase!"

The fourth letter—*O*—presents a bit of a dilemma, but I have come up with what I think is an interesting concept: *ORCHESTRATE.* After another consultation with Webster, I found that orchestrate means "to arrange or combine so as to achieve maximum effect." Makes it sound easy, doesn't he? But, in reality, orchestrating my life is what I am trying to do. And it is within this concept that I would like to add two other O-words: *OPERATE* and *OPPOSE.* To operate with some degree of success in the orchestration definitely requires a positive attitude, along with a heavy sense of humor. I've picked out some of the positive aspects of my group involvement and kept them. Not everything that happened within the group needs to be negated, and I've learned that it's okay to take all the time I need to sort all this out. Remember, we started with that crackled glass, and until at least a part of it is repaired, those positives are not clearly visible. By oppose, I mean—to question! I question authority, I question everything! And I have had to learn to keep in mind that what other people think of me is not as important as what I think of myself.

The *V* was easy at first—*VALUES.* This word flashed at me as I imagined my mobile growing little by little. Values and priorities have taken on a new look, a reevaluation, if you will. The ultimate value—truth—makes old priorities dissolve. For example, it's not how much gold is in the ring, but how the golden ring of truth and free minds sounds out, is heard, and is amplified. I thought for a moment that I should use *victimized* here, for which Roget listed "cheated, swindled, deceived, duped," and, my personal favorite, "bamboozled"! Suffice it to say that as an ex-cult member, I am already familiar with this bamboozlement thing and I really didn't want it hanging around on my RECOVER mobile!

The sixth letter, another *E,* has brought two important concepts to add. The first is *EDUCATE.* We must educate ourselves if we are to begin to educate others about this phenomenon. In order to keep moving forward, I continue to learn and gain more understanding about the issues of mind control and post-traumatic stress disorder (PTSD). You may think that PTSD applies only to the Vietnam veteran—it doesn't. It is, however, through Vietnam vets' severe difficulty with this disorder that PTSD is recognized as the long-term shadow it can be in a person's life. The symptoms of PTSD, such as nightmares, flashbacks, anxiety, sleeplessness, fear, are identical to those symptoms occurring in postcult survival. And it is with this education that I must *EDIT*, continually edit my life, my choices, my decisions. I must continue to update and improve within my day-to-day living, my career, and my relationships. No person can act beyond his or her knowledge, and there is no excuse for ignorance!

Under the last letter—*R*—I choose to hang *RESPECT.* No matter what situation I've been in, knowing that I have survived this experience and continue to regain my independent thought and reconstruct my life—this deserves respect. With respect comes compassion for those who are still victims, mesmerized by false truths and power-hungry, rich, manipulating, self-ordained gods. Respect and compassion for other now-free minds struggling to reconstruct and discover their real potential, strengths, and talents. Respect and compassion for myself. The human element of fallibility will raise its head occasionally. There is no "perfect"; there is no "normal"; there is only "cut to the chase and give it my best shot!"

My father quoted an old Native American adage to me when I was very little: "Do not judge a person until you have walked a mile in his (or her) moccasins." I've learned to apply this not only to others but to myself as well. Think back, and imagine walking a mile in the moccasins you wore then; give yourself respect and gentle judgments for the distances covered.

To summarize:

R—RECONSTRUCTION
E—ENDURANCE
C—CUT TO THE CHASE
O—ORCHESTRATE—Operate—Oppose
V—VALUES
E—EDUCATE—Edit
R—RESPECT

My imaginary mobile has expanded sufficiently for the moment. The irony, it seems, is that the mobile will never be finished, never be complete. It is only a foundation for more and more parts to interact. As it hangs out there, in its precarious, delicate balance, I realize that there is no way to box up my cult experience and store it away somewhere. It will not disappear; it will always be a part of my life. And it is through this experience that I have gained expanded knowledge, a deeper trust in myself, the courage to question, and compassion and self-respect.

In closing, I must say that it is through the eyes in front of free minds—eyes that feel pain, joy, love, anger; eyes that show compassion, consideration, and honesty; eyes that look at me with understanding, gentleness, and truth—it is in these eyes that this mobile of my life is reflected, and it is these reflections that give me the courage to continue and recover.

CHAPTER FOURTEEN

SOMETIMES YOU JUST HAVE TO GO FOR IT
JANET JOYCE

Janet Joyce was a member of the Sullivanians, a psychotherapy/political cult, for 17 years. She writes about regaining self-confidence and self-esteem. Since leaving the group she has reconnected with her family, is pursuing artistic and musical interests, and is working with teen mothers.

When I was recently asked to write about recovery from my cult experience, I was excited. I had already written a short piece on how I got involved in the group and found it extremely helpful (see Chapter 2). It was especially helpful to read that piece in a service about cults at the Unitarian Church I had become involved with in the past year. Becoming a resource on cult issues has been important to me and, I think, useful to others in that community. It's been an eye-opener to many people that I, an idealistic, socially conscious young woman, had slowly but surely become enmeshed in a destructive cult. I was not some weak or weird person who willingly gave up control of my life to follow the teachings of a paranoid fanatic; rather, I was an intelligent, caring person who was slowly and methodically manipulated by my therapist (who was ultimately directed by the cult leader) to turn my life over to the group.

I've have had a lot to deal with in the 6 years since I left the Sullivanians, which I was a member of for 17 years. Although I had been thinking seriously about leaving for about a year before I did, and toying with the idea for several years before that, it took a major life event to push me to leave. In December 1987 I was diagnosed with breast cancer. I had surgery and was physically fine by February, but something crucial had changed in my view of the world and my life. Having faced my own mortality I realized more than ever that there were many things I wanted to do that I would not do if I stayed in the group.

For one, I wanted to have children, something that I had been told I was not ready to do. I had always loved babies and animals, but in the group I was told that I was too angry to be around children and that I would be a terrible parent—even to a pet! I knew that even if I convinced my "therapist" that I was ready to have a child I would run the risk of having the child taken away from me. I had seen many children taken from their parents and given to others in the group to raise.

When I left and got my own apartment in another part of the city, one of the first things I did was adopt two kittens. It quickly became clear to me that I was able to love and take care of them. They are now five years old: friendly, playful, and loving. They have been an important part of my recovery, as they are a constant reminder of a part of myself and my self-esteem that had been taken from me while in the group. Three years ago I adopted a dog who had been mistreated as a puppy. Charlie was about six months old, an Akita-Chow mix, very cute but very wild. He has also become very friendly, not always so well-behaved perhaps but a wonderful pet. Having pets again has been very important to me since in the cult I had been forced to give them up.

When I first left, I contacted other former Sullivanians. I started with people I had been friends with who had left long before. In the five years before my departure there had been a lot of publicity about the Sullivanians, generated by child-custody cases brought by ex-member parents who were seeking to get or keep their children out. The leadership fostered a hatred of anyone who left the group, especially those who were seen as troublemakers getting the media interested in the group. I was very nervous about being identified with such clearly defined "enemies," so I contacted people I thought were safe; however, I also ran into people who were not so safe. These ex-members were friendly, glad to see me, and glad I was no longer in the group.

When I was invited to a party at the house of two of the most hated ex-members I said I didn't want to go—I still believed that they were truly horrible people. After talking with several other ex-members I decided to go anyway. I had a wonderful time. I talked to people I hadn't seen for years and heard many stories of what their lives had been like since leaving the group. Lo and behold, they were not all dying of depression (a common prediction on the part of therapists in the group). Nor were they all ecstatically happy. They were getting used to living in normal society again, with varying degrees of success.

In the beginning I had a hard time with the word *cult*. Cults were things that religious fanatics got involved in, I thought. I was not religious. You had to be crazy to be involved in a cult. I was not crazy. I rationalized by telling myself that the group was a progressive political and psychological community that just was no longer what I needed in my life. Then an ex-member who had been a therapist in the group gave me an article on psychotherapy cults by Margaret Singer and Maurice Temerlin. I read it with astonishment. They were describing the group precisely. The experience of reading that article and discussing it with other former Sullivanians started me on a quest to learn as much as I could about cults. I went to the library and took out all the books I could find about cults. I spent that first summer reading—really devouring—anything I could get my hands on about cults.

I hadn't seen my family for almost 17 years and was very confused about what I thought about them and what part I wanted them to play in my life. I was also terrified of calling them up after such a long time. I didn't know what to say. After I had been out of the group for about six months, I asked a friend if he would call my parents and prepare them for my call. He was delighted to do so, but my parents were out of town at that time. I finally reached them at home before my friend did, but the support of knowing that he would talk to them was enough to get me through that first call.

A few weeks later I was able to meet with my parents and my oldest sister. I brought along two ex-member friends and several videotapes of news programs about the Sullivanians to help explain what I had been doing all those years. I was glad to see my family again, but I still didn't know how much I wanted to be involved in their lives or have them involved in mine. Since I was just starting life on my own when I got involved in the group, I felt I now needed to pick up where I had left off.

One of the few things I had when I left the group was a career in which I could easily support myself, so I decided to stay in the New York area and make a life for myself there. I then started thinking about what I wanted to do with my life in general. When I entered the group I had been working with people as an activity and recreation therapist. I wanted to go back to that kind of work—I even considered pursuing my lifelong dream of going to medical school. The group had steered me in the direction of a technical career. In fact almost everyone who had entered the group as a teacher, social worker, psychologist, or other helping professional was told to change jobs and get training in something more lucrative, such as computer programming or technical writing. I now had the freedom to go back to what I had originally wanted to do. Since I also very much wanted to have or adopt a child I decided to stay in the computer field while I figured things out.

A recurrence of my illness pushed me to think about what I wanted my life to be like, and I began working to create that life for myself. I rented a cottage to live in, fixed and decorated it, and planted a garden. I made many new friends through various community activities, volunteer jobs, and support groups. Unable to have a child, I began volunteering at a teenage parent program, where I spend several days a week with babies and their young mothers. When I first volunteered there I still believed what I had been told in the group—that I was dangerous and could not be trusted with children—but since I had shown myself clearly that I had not been a danger to my pets, I decided to give it a try with infants.

Once again I realized that what the group had told me had little or nothing to do with me and everything to do with the leaders' agenda. Having and spending time with children was used by the Sullivanians as a tool to manipulate members and destroy their self-esteem. The "privilege" of spending time with the children was routinely taken away if a member was perceived to have broken the rules in any way. It could also be taken away at the whim of the leaders. If Saul, the leader, wanted to keep people in line, he would simply accuse them of being psychopaths and take away their access to the children. When a trusted group member was suddenly "taken off" baby-sitting, everyone in the group became more conscious of following the rules, knowing that they might be next. The little time I did spend with children in the group was filled with anxiety that I might do something wrong. What a relief it is to find that in the real world I am good with babies. They like me, and their mothers trust me!

Although it has been five years since I left the group and I have many new friends, I still find it useful to talk about my cult experiences. I am still in the process of figuring out who I am and how the "real me" was manipulated and destroyed by the group leaders. My experience was not all bad though, and I am now starting to bring some of the good stuff back into my life. While in the group I went to art school to develop my skills as a painter and sculptor. I enjoyed it, but had little time for art other than the work I had to do on group-related graphic design. I now realize that I can create whatever art I want, show it to whomever I want, and spend as much time on it as I want. It's my life!

I also made a lot of music while in the group. I sang, learned how to play the bass guitar, even wrote songs. Now I have gotten back into choral singing, something I had enjoyed for many years before the cult involvement. I'm thinking about writing songs again. Writing songs in the group was always a bittersweet experience. Writing the music and lyrics was fun, but having them changed according to the dictates of the director of our political theater company was painful. I eventually stopped writing, and am pleased that I'm getting ready to start again.

When I left the Sullivanians I became an "enemy" of the group; none of my friends who stayed would speak to me. When I ran into members on the street they would quickly turn away and walk in the other direction. Even though Saul, the original leader, died a year and a half ago and the group seemed to be splitting into several factions following various of the more powerful members, it was unclear who of my former friends might speak to me. I knew that many members had become disillusioned. Some moved away to start a new life, many stayed in the city to try to salvage whatever they could of their friendships and lifestyle.

On a recent trip back to New York I decided to just call people who had been my closest friends, the ones I had thought about often. Although I had written to some of them and even left messages on their answering machines, I had never received any response. This time, deciding to just go for it, I made a number of calls. Although some people still did not call back, I did get together with one of my closest friends and spoke to several others. It was exciting to see people I had known in the group and to help them begin the process of their recovery. And, as I said before, the more I talk about my experience in the group and my recovery, the clearer it becomes to me.

CHAPTER FIFTEEN

HUMANS ARE FREE BEINGS
"FRANCES LIEF"

Frances Lief (a pseudonym) grew up in the Children of God, a neo-Christian cult. She escaped several years ago as a teenager and speaks strongly about the adjustment and identity issues for children leaving cults. She is now in college.

Somebody told me the other day, "Nobody owes it to you to understand you." In that light, having been born and raised in a cult, I am hesitant to write about what it feels like to live in the outside world. Yet, I would not be writing this if I did not expect somebody to understand. I will qualify what I am about to say: if people outside cults expect a young person who grew up in a cult to adjust, then it would be helpful if those people would try to understand the difficulties and dilemmas.

When I ran away from the cult, it was not like one fine day I was sitting there and it dawned on me that because I'd decided the cult was wrong I could get up and walk out. Leaving the cult was the biggest, most fearsome thing I could ever dream of doing. The process took me more than five years. At age 13 I had a gut feeling I didn't like it all that much, but it was a long road I traveled until the day when, at age 18, I got up early and like a zombie followed the plan I had laid out.

I didn't believe I would ever dare leave the Children of God (COG/aka The Family) until the moment I actually slipped through that opening in the gate and began to run. Even then I felt like I was watching somebody else doing it. In leaving I was abandoning everything I knew. Granted I had ceased to believe certain things—for example that evil spirits actually existed. But for a long time after I left I still thought (much more than I realized consciously at the time) that in "turning my back on the truth" I had exposed myself to hell on earth and judgment hereafter. I had such a terrible year after running away (and before I was able to come to the United States) that the COG's prophecies about "backsliders" loomed large in my mind, threatening. Yes, I had consciously decided to reject the cult, but few people around me seemed able to grasp how difficult it is to erase such an experience. (When people are able to do it completely, it's called amnesia.)

I was afraid of many things after I left the cult. When I expressed a fear, people would say, with the best of intentions, "No, that's not a problem, you're safe here." I remained uneasy, however, which becomes tiring as a permanent state. The cult's belief that almost all outsiders are enemies had me expecting that people would be eager to support me when I brought up my grievances against the cult, many of which I was expressing for the first time. I needed assurance. I was newly emerging from a terrible storm and wanted badly to set things straight in my mind. It was disappointing to find most people quite eager to pass over the matter quickly. Some seemed to be waiting the whole time I was speaking to give their answer, and when they did it was: "Case (nicely and neatly) closed." Sometimes people would answer a different question from the one I had asked. I still needed people to tell me I had done the right thing in leaving. I did not know when I escaped that Children of God is a cult.

I am learning to live with a totally new value system, way of life, and culture. If people understood that, they might understand some of the emotional turmoil I go through. In the COG, for example, higher education was of the Devil. When I was admitted to a university and began to study I explained this to some people, who responded, "Oh, really?" Ironically, in the COG I was reinforced for things I did that were in accordance with the cult much more than I am now reinforced for doing things society values but the cult condemns.

I am realizing that I disagree with some of the values in this culture. I have been given light reprimands for saying I don't feel some kind of emotional "allegiance" or gratefulness toward the college I go to. Nor do I experience pride through the school. The pride I feel (and pride was the worst sin in the COG) is for my achievements, in college or elsewhere. I don't feel the need to seek endorsement by attaching myself to something external to me. If others could put themselves in my place, they would see that I operated on that same value when I ran away from the cult. If approval from an authority is what I'm looking for, it was stupid for me to escape and live as a runaway for one year and suffer what I did; the COG had a ready-made system you could appeal to for approval. And in the cult at least I knew how I could receive endorsement if I wanted it. Not so in the outside world. I soon discovered that I had no clue what the rules are.

Reading good, nonsuperstitious books by ex-members of cults or experts, attending a CAN conference I received a John G. Clark scholarship for, and speaking with other former members have helped me the most. Spending money on airfare to the conference, buying books, calling long distance to a childhood friend who also left the COG—these may seem like a waste to some, considering I work for minimum wage, but it is also considered "sensible" not to run away from home.

Sometimes people say, "But, you know, they were false prophets. The Bible says many false prophets will arise and that the Devil mixes the truth with lies, and that's what so-and-so does," and on and on. We were taught all that in the cult, too, only the false prophets were just somebody else. Many people are very concerned about "my relationship with the Lord," or they want me to know that "He was taking care of me the whole time." And when I question that, they respond, "God has a plan." I will leave this subject here: I'd say, questionable ethics on His part.

One of the hardest things for people to understand, I think, is that when a person escapes from a cult alone, he or she still has the cult mindset in many ways that can make life difficult. I didn't know any other way to think than "magical" thinking and the black-versus-white kind of reasoning I'd been taught. What probably helped me most to learn to think are the math and philosophy courses I've taken. At first it was very distressing to try to do an algebra assignment; I would look at the problems and go blank. It was difficult to sit still long enough to get anywhere. Eventually, however, I found it oddly reassuring that I could follow the given steps and arrive at the exact same number that was printed on the answer sheet. I learned that by following steps I could arrive at an answer; not everything follows whims, as the COG leaders did. The quadratic formula is not a revelation from God—therefore it is not likely to be suddenly changed before an exam.

I have learned there are rewards in reasoning in ways that do not end with absolute answers. For example, I was dumbfounded at a professor's comment on my literature essay that I needed to present reasons for the other side when I had presented my argument as an open-and-shut case. Also, I had to chuckle when I read a sentence in a book on critical thinking that said, "Of course, we all know when we read something that we don't have to believe every bit of it." I felt like stomping my feet in anger—I'd always had to.

In the COG those of us who were born in the group were treated especially harshly. A lot was expected of us. It didn't matter that we had been selling literature on the street since we could toddle about, nor did it matter how hard we worked as we got older. We were relentlessly told how ungrateful we were for the sacrifice our parents' generation had made to give us this way of life; we were exhorted to become more thankful, willing, humble, spiritual, sacrificial, and so on. We, of course, were in this for life. We were treated like public property, with no room for individuality. The climate of the large "teen homes" was armylike. They even said it was an army, a boot camp. I would think to myself, "Not even soldiers stay in boot camp for years on end!" Even when we were living in a community with our parents, emphasis was placed on "firm discipline," and "delinquent" parents were punished. Since parents were judged by their children's behavior, parents could sometimes be harsher to us than our "teen shepherds." In connection with this I now feel it is so important to always treat people, including oneself, as Kant said, as an end in themselves and never simply as a means.

When young people leave a cult they need autonomy, including the right to make their own mistakes. Personal dignity and autonomy are the basic rights each person has by virtue of being a human. These rights are overridden when others decide they will use influence, pressure, or whatever to get you to do what they "know" is best for you.

The experiences I had in the cult make it difficult to trust people, especially if they have a paternalistic outlook. They may mean well, may think they know what is best, and may work to try to avoid what they feel would be pitfalls on my part, but they should realize that if I am to recover from the cult I cannot be expected to continue in the cult modes. For example, it is very difficult for me to sit still, look attentive and receptive, and listen to drawn-out dissertations. When I feel caged in or feel that people are being "hands on" or intrusive about what is really my business, I feel my lungs will explode—I clench my teeth, my ears ring.

I'd never been allowed to show anger and I still generally keep it in, which leads me to behave toward myself in ways I don't want to. But when I do express anger I feel so guilty I usually end up running to apologize and doing whatever is wanted. I can understand that this may be a sticky subject for people who believe anger is wrong. However, one of the basic needs of a young person leaving a cult is permission to be angry. I should clarify that: first, we should be given permission to disagree and choose for ourselves. We were never allowed to do that, so that now when we feel backed into a corner that old feeling of never having any choice emerges, followed by anger. If some disagreement and choice of options are allowed, anger about something can probably be greatly curbed. A sense of control over my life (not over others or outside things) and feeling that I have a say and can actually do what I choose are vital.

As far as anger goes—toward the cult or other things—I think if people were able to truly grasp what it means to be in and then leave a cult, they would be willing to put up with a bit of anger and/or attitude. They would see it is as an encouraging sign. For us not to have anger should bother people; it indicates that we still identify with the cult or think the cult was right in how it treated us.

If young people manage to escape from a cult, most likely they do not like the person they were obligated to be in the cult. By leaving they may remove themselves physically from that environment, but the task of creating a new identity is left and takes a lot of effort. This may seem like an unnecessary quest from the outside, but it is vital to us if we are to truly separate our inner selves from the cult. On the surface everything may look fine, but it can be extremely depressing to go through the ordeal of escape and then not feel any progress. If you have never had to step back, reconsider, and discard most of your past life, creating an identity may seem like an abstract notion. For a young person leaving a cult, it's concrete. Change—or remain who you were in the cult.

Two aspects to keep in mind are, first, that life in the cult was very rigorous, gray, and not the way most people spent their youth. Once out a young person will want to live. Life was structured and very restricted; now a young person will want to have options, live more flexibly. Second, appearance is one of the cult's strongest methods of erasing individuality and controlling a person's self-image. I would ask people to take it seriously when a young former cult member tries to change her or his appearance. I know it may look like vanity to some, but especially if we explain our reasons, people should try to respect our needs.

I believe humans are free beings and that we are ultimately responsible for shaping our lives. For a young person who's been in a cult, however, the emotional price of going forward, no matter how others may or may not respond, can be steep, especially if previously that person's life happiness and relative peace had been contingent on others' approval. If a young person has to figure it out alone, it may take a while for her or him to see that one can be independent and still be accepted, and then decide to take the risk.

If we admit mind control exists and that it can exert tremendous pressure and leave aftereffects on adults who have had prior experience living in the outside world, consider how much of an impact being born and raised in a cult might have on a young person. It may be necessary to relieve that young person of the feeling that he must go along with whatever he's told. It may even be necessary to show a young person that she truly has a choice. When a young person raised in a cult sees that autonomous action brings no dire consequences, the fear will diminish and obedience will take on its appropriate character.

CHAPTER SIXTEEN

RETURNING TO HUMANITY
"MEREDITH O. MAGUIRE"

Meredith Maguire (a pseudonym) spent eight years in a left-wing political cult. She discusses struggling to find herself and her values after leaving the group, and the importance of establishing a real relationship with her young son, who was born in the cult. Meredith is now self-employed.

I began my experience in a radical political group by consciously choosing to dedicate my life to making the world a better place to live for all people. I had gotten married in 1977 at age 27; two months later my husband and I moved 1,800 miles from home in order to join the group. As it turned out, my acceptance of a rigid political belief system set me up to be manipulated and abused. My beliefs blinded me to the destructive techniques used in the name of bringing about political change.

In our group, criticism/self-criticism, used daily, was the primary method of control. I remember so clearly one of the first sessions that targeted me. Sitting in the circle being berated and accused of misdeeds by the group, I felt like my head was literally being yanked from my shoulders, turned around 180 degrees, and set down backwards. I stopped seeing, stopped thinking, stopped speaking my mind. In that experience, I began to surrender my vision, my mind, my personal experience, and my soul, and to internalize the idea that due to my middle-class background, my own thoughts, ideas, and gut reactions were at best, suspect, and at worst, downright evil.

Over a period of eight years of criticism sessions, cadre training, and sleep deprivation, I began to view myself as a depraved individual incapable of functioning in the world without the leadership feeding "correct ideas" into my brain and without my comrades' constant criticism to keep me on track. The social pressure was great, with encouragement from the trusted friends who had recruited me. I became bound and determined to be a worthy member of this elite community, to meet the challenge of changing the world. Having been raised Catholic and having attended Catholic schools for 16 years gave me a strong and early experience with submission to authority and to a belief system. Before joining the group I had spent eight years freeing myself from the Catholic worldview. I thought I had learned to think independently and make my own decisions. What I recognize now, however, is that I had not even begun to chip away at my most deeply ingrained fear—fear of authority. That fear hooked me into the group and would not let me go.

Consciously trying to serve, I opened myself to the required self-sacrifice. I experienced high levels of anxiety as an imperfect person attempting to live up to the task at hand. On another level, I was being manipulated by deliberate practices designed to frighten me into submission. With hindsight I can see that in order to avoid the wrath of the leadership and the ultimate consequence of being expelled, I lived for eight years in terror of not being able to adequately control my thoughts and actions, my feelings and words. I had fully internalized the belief that there was no life outside this group and that I might as well be dead as expelled.

Maintaining such a level of self-control on a daily basis was difficult, and fairly often my "self" would slip out to be smashed up against the wall. I especially remember the time the membership was being interviewed to see how we were doing. "How is your life? What are you feeling?" they asked in a very friendly manner. I spontaneously responded that I felt like a caged animal pacing back and forth with no outlet and ready to blow at any moment. The leadership's response was swift and terrifying: I was suspended from participating in the life of the group and not allowed to leave my house for a period of time; no one was allowed to speak with me, including my husband and my other housemate. I was expected to spend all of my time writing self-criticisms and purging myself of these feelings until I could parrot back the party line. I was eventually let back in but from that time on I had an awareness that I was a "thorn in the side," incorrigible, unreformable.

My son was born in 1983 despite expressed wishes from the leadership that we remain childless. Daily life was structured according to the needs of the group; within that structure I carried the primary responsibility for my son since my husband was given little time or encouragement to take on his role as father. When my son was about six months old he entered day care from 9 A.M. to 5 P.M. In the evenings he was in our group-arranged child care, where parents took turns caring for the children. If I was lucky I was able to spend one evening a week with my son, along with several other children, as well as a little time on the weekends.

We believed that we were raising our children in the most healthy manner—a collective childhood. We believed that to children all adults were interchangeable, that it didn't matter if and when children saw their actual parents. We believed that we were raising children who would not be spoiled by the individualism and selfishness of our culture, that they would grow up with a strong sense of their responsibility to society. We had high ideals but little actual knowledge of child development and child needs. Our theory and words honored children but our practices always put their needs as the lowest priority. The political work always came first. This is an example of how my belief system blinded me to the realities around me. The only way to live within this system as a parent was to refuse to think about your child or children. From the time I would drop my son off in the morning until I picked him up anywhere from 11 P.M. to 2 A.M., I had very little awareness of being a parent.

My son was two and a half years old when our world appeared to fall apart. In 1985 the inner circle surrounding the leader broke the bond of silence and began exposing to the membership the true nature of the group. The explosion from within left many shattered lives in its wake. I was 36 years old at the time. It had never been easy to be committed to the organization 24 hours a day and be a parent of a young child. But it was even harder to emerge from that insulated, cocoonlike world, feeling dead inside, into a world where I had to figure out what I thought and what I felt, into a world where I needed to make decisions not only for myself but also for my child.

There I was: a parent of a toddler I had hardly seen for two years and in a marriage that lacked any positive feeling. Even though we had joined the group together, over the years my husband and I had gone in very different directions. The group frowned on couples having any life separate from the organization or even talking with each other about their work. Because of his professional training he had been promoted into a leadership position, while I functioned as a workhorse in the lower echelons. Emerging from the group we were at opposite poles on every issue; we had very little shared experience, no ability to communicate with each other, and a huge pool of unspoken pain between us. Several years later, we got divorced.

Reentering the world brought feelings of confusion and anxiety about my identity, self-worth, and ability to function as an individual, but I knew I didn't want to fall into a pattern of daily life by default. I wanted to be able to think through what had happened to me, understand it, and not repeat it. There were a number of things I did to regain my self-respect, to practice thinking, and to find a place for myself in the world as a parent and as an individual.

The first and most crucial was to allow myself time: time for myself and time with my family, particularly my son and my parents, brothers, and sisters. I would have chosen to spend time with my husband also but his needs were different from mine and he didn't make that choice. My first goal was to reestablish my relationship with my son and make a conscious decision to be a mother. Even though my child already existed and I was his mother, sometimes my eyes would peer at him while my brain tried to figure out where he came from. I felt entirely disconnected from any thoughts or actions that may have brought him into existence.

The more time I spent with him, day in and day out, the more we reconnected. The feelings of alienation and anger over having to shoulder the responsibility for him began to subside. After one year, having spent about six months caring for my son and six more caring for myself, I wrote in my journal: "I do want to be his mother. I feel this is a choice I make now because I don't know really who decided or how it was decided to have him in the first place. At the time, I was not in control of my life as myself to decide." This is a decision I have not regretted.

One of the things that enabled me to give myself the time I needed was the necessity to give my son what *he* needed: time to play. When I talked to my therapist of my fears about being a mother, knowing I was incapable of thinking or feeling for myself, she suggested I take the view that my son and I could grow up together. That was one of the most helpful things that anyone said to me.

By taking advantage of a combination of resources available to me (such as living with my family and being eligible for unemployment compensation) and by keeping my material needs to a minimum, I was able to survive working part-time. My son was with his father on the days I worked, so that when he was with me I didn't go to work. On those days we went to the park or to the beach. We played together in the sand, swung on the swings, slid on the slides, sat in the sunshine. Sometimes I would just sit and watch him play. That was such a relief—to have nothing to do but watch him play! The world began to be reborn in my soul in those moments. I was able to glimpse life after the walking death I had known.

Making decisions about my son's life, however, was the most difficult task I faced. Everything revolved around the decision I was making about my marriage. I began to read about child development, parenting, divorce, and effective child-custody arrangements. In our group, divorce was a regular occurrence and was always handled with a 50/50 joint custody split. I assumed that was the only choice. The more I learned through reading and talking with different people, the more I realized that there was no simple solution. It took me several years to sort out what I thought was best for my son and myself. Once it was clear that I needed to get a divorce, I pursued a custody plan that would give my son a primary home base with me and the most stability that I could provide, as well as an ongoing relationship with his dad.

The combination of both my group involvement and my marriage ending left me without any structures to fall back on. I often felt I was completely alone, fighting my way backward to remember who I was while simultaneously fighting my way forward to go beyond who I had been. An activity that served me over and over in coming to terms with the past and trying to map out the future was writing. I wrote down everything I could imagine. I wrote lists of ideas, lists of friends, lists of goals. I made timelines of possible life plans, being as specific as I could about what I wanted in each time period. I wrote out my values and beliefs, particularly in regard to parenting and family issues, reading them over to myself often, and allowing them to change and develop as I did. I often wrote down phone conversations, even as I was having them, so that I would be able to go back and think about the ideas that had been expressed. I had a hard time remembering anything. I wrote about my feelings, about the anger and the pain of separation and divorce, of being 36 and not having a clue as to who I was in the world. I worked on a chronology of my life's events. I wrote about the patterns I observed in my family that enlightened my understanding of myself.

I opened up as a person in a way I never would have thought possible. I made new friends, usually through work, sharing the realities of my life insofar as I felt safe to do so. I didn't want everything to be private and unspeakable. In the group we were never allowed to talk with each other about anything real; now I pursued that with a vengeance. I wanted people to know *me*. I visited a former group member a year later. After we talked for a bit, she said, "Your voice isn't quivering." She had never heard me speak without a tremor in my voice.

For me being in a cult meant giving up power over my own life. I believed that by giving up my own self-interests I could serve a greater purpose and accomplish something in the world. I think that desire to contribute to the world and live a meaningful life is a natural human desire, easily manipulated. The manipulation in our group was designed to instill a strong fear of authority and a fear of our own ideas. Once I had chosen to give myself up to those beliefs, with the group's manipulation process in full swing, it became too overwhelming to confront the fear and anxiety that surrounded a decision to take myself back.

Now, as a parent, I feel very aware of authority issues: How do you socialize and educate a child without instilling fear of authority? What is the best way to teach children to trust their instincts and trust their feelings, and to act upon them? At what point does individual self-expression produce more harm than good, and where does social responsibility begin? Since I am still trying to take the view that my son and I are growing up together, we work on these issues and answers together. He is now 10 years old: a daily inspiration and a constant challenge to me.

CHAPTER SEVENTEEN

AN INTERRUPTED LIFE
LANDY ONG TANG

Landy Ong Tang was a member of the Unification Church for more than seven years. He writes primarily about the issues of shame, evaluating his cult experience, and finding direction. Landy is now writing plays and comic books, and works as waiter and a massage therapist.

It's hard for me to imagine that it has been 10 years since I walked away from the Moonies. And it is equally difficult to speak of recovery because even 10 years removed I don't know how "recovered" I am, how healthy and adjusted I am.

Perhaps it would have been easier if my leave-taking had been as dramatic and definitive as my introduction. A sidewalk kidnapping, perhaps a visit home gone awry, days spent in a safe house away from the church, being supported and asked to examine the evidence—and then a burst of enlightenment followed by heartfelt denunciations and renunciation of Reverend Moon and the church. But that didn't happen for me.

Instead, I was one of the walkaways. A slow and gradual feeling of dissatisfaction crept into my bones and mind, a lingering malaise that began to fill my days and color all the "normal" activities I was expected to do, such as witnessing and fund-raising. It was a paralysis, along with more questions than I knew what to do with, that finally did me in.

I had joined the church when I was 19, and by my seventh year I was in New York working with the church choir, The New Hope Singers International. I was becoming more and more dissatisfied with being treated like a child. I longed to make my own decisions and start being an adult, responsible for my own life. At that point I got the chance to volunteer to go to Washington, D.C., to help start the *Washington Times*. It was the first conscious decision I had made about my future since I had joined the church—everything previously had been decided by the church bosses. It was also the seminal decision that led to my leaving the church.

Once I arrived in Washington I started making more and more personal decisions, from when I got up in the morning to how I spent my paycheck. In fact, this was the first time since I had joined that I had my own money. I rebelled and made several decisions without asking my church superiors—for example, finding my own apartment, moving out on my own, and deciding to go back to school. At the time I justified these rebellious acts by saying to myself that Reverend Moon wanted each of us to become little Sun Myung Moons and that meant that if I were the only church member left on the face of the earth, then I had to make my own decisions, and this was good practice. Mainly, though, I was reveling in my newfound independence and inner strength. Once I was back at college I turned all my attention to school; over time the church became a non-existent part of my life. And I simply pretended that it hadn't happened.

Perhaps the greatest difficulty I experienced and still experience is a sense of shame, a sense of being a pariah, or even worse, a fool. I had spent eight years in the Moonies telling my family and friends that I was doing the "right thing" and that time would prove me right. I had said that I knew what I was doing and they didn't. So, after leaving, how could I say to them that maybe they were right? And were they? Leaving didn't solve anything for me—it only opened up further questions. That is part of what I struggle with even at this moment and maybe I will for the rest of my life.

I know that the human mind and spirit are malleable. I know the subtleties of the techniques of persuasion. Yet there is a little voice inside me that simply says, "How could any sane person fall for that?" I know that is the voice of accusation, but I listen to it because there is a part of me that truly does believe it. I find myself simultaneously believing that I was manipulated by one of the most sophisticated mind-control organizations ever created and also that I was a weak-willed fool and an idiot. A dichotomy? Yes. A contradiction? Yes. Reality? Yes.

The recovery process has been a slow one for me. I started it at the same time I began leaving the church, for the act of leaving was the first step in separating from it. I look back now and see how the most powerful tool the church or perhaps any coercive group possesses is the ability to take what I call the best parts of ourselves—our goals, our ideals, our dreams, which lie hidden at the very core of our being, hidden because the world so loves disabusing us of those notions—and entwine them with the group. The group then comes to represent our noblest selves; to leave the group is to leave the best parts of ourselves behind. "If I left that," I would think to myself while in the church, "then what would I be but a hollow shell, eating, sleeping, and going through all the motions, but having no interior life."

Leaving the church, even through the "back door," was the first step toward reclaiming my life. It was the first step toward saying that my ideals were exactly that—*my* ideals. And that the best parts of me weren't lost simply because I left the church. These are my assertions and it's a constant struggle to remember them and find balance in my life.

Going back to the same college I had attended before I joined the church allowed me to pick up the pieces of an interrupted life. It provided me with the opportunity to examine all these issues without directly confronting them but as they were presented in the books we read. I became obsessed with the question of how one knows the right course of action. How does one *be* in the world? I used to think that period in school was a time when I shut off the questions by diving into schoolwork, but now I see that even then I was attempting to find some answers, or at least define the parameters of the questions more sharply.

When I finished school three years later I was still directionless, so I did what was most comfortable. Perhaps it was also a reflection of my self-image and self-esteem at the time. I believed I didn't deserve any better than to be a waiter, so that's the kind of work I got. Maybe I was still punishing myself for leaving the church. But underneath it all there was also a restlessness within me. I moved first from Annapolis, Maryland, where I had gone to school, to Washington, D.C., where I lived with another ex-member, and then to Tucson.

It was in Tucson that another turning point happened. One day I was in a used bookstore and found a copy of *Hostage to Heaven,* written by the woman who had brought me into the church and had since left. The last time I had seen it I had taken an unauthorized break while selling candy for the church and was wandering around a college bookstore. The prohibitions in me were so strong that I was unable to even pick it up. This time I did. I bought the book, took it home, and began reading it. It literally blew the emotional cap off for me, and for the first time I began dealing with the latent emotions I had about being a Moonie.

I remember driving to work and screaming at the top of my lungs, pounding the roof of my car with my fist, feeling so violated and abused. For a couple of weeks I felt very, very precarious, riding a fine balance between feeling my pain and being overwhelmed by it. On the other hand, it was the first *feeling* that I'd had since I left the church. I felt very, very fragile. This is not something I wanted to admit at the time, nor do I like admitting it now. I guess being so vulnerable and exposed in the church has made me uncomfortable with being really exposed now.

One of the tactics I adopted early on was to ask myself what I had gained from the experience. I would make lists of items, all of which seemed somewhat inconsequential to me. Then I would list what I lost. This, however, was very real for it more closely touched on the seething emotional turmoil boiling just below the surface of my conscious mind. As time has gone by, I have confronted more and more of those feelings within me.

Speaking with other ex-members has been of immense help since often I feel they are the only ones who can truly understand the experience without judgment. Although speaking with friends who were not in any group has also helped, since it makes me see that I am not a pariah. The anger and pain have receded into the background now, integrated on some levels and unintegrated on others. But, like a nest of hornets, they can be raised by a word or situation.

Life seems to be a process of confronting your demons and embracing them so that they become part of yourself. Throwing light on my fears, I move steadily forward, trying to find balance, love, and humor in all situations. I also recognize how wary I am now of any situation that calls for me to give of myself unrestrainedly. I cannot. I know this and accept it as part of the emotional scar that I bear. It is my red badge of honor—for I have gone through hell and come out with my life.

As I think about what all this means on a practical level, it means that I am still a waiter but have made an attitude shift about it. I am not here to save the world. I am here to be the best stonecutter, or waiter, that I can be right now. The church installed the thinking of looking only to the future. I am trying to live in the now and the future. Further, I am beginning to explore and embrace my past on many levels. Toward that end, I have made overtures to reintegrate my family into my life, I am studying Chinese martial arts and language, and I have begun writing again, have joined a writer's group and am moving forward.

It has been a long hard road, but I have come to believe that that is what life is for everyone. My detour and difficulty just had a different flavor. This is as near to defining recovery as I can come. It is a process— one that never really stops. But it can be rewarding and fulfilling—and that is all I hope for.

CHAPTER EIGHTEEN

REINVENTING MYSELF
NANCY I. MIQUELON

Nancy Miquelon, who spent 13 years in a New Age vegetarian cult, writes about finding her voice again, learning to make decisions and have opinions, and dealing with relationships and belief issues. She is the former national coordinator of FOCUS, a former members' support network, and is a psychotherapist.

I walked out of the Emissaries of Divine Light almost nine years ago. I had been involved for 13 years, from age 19 to 32. I was fortunate to have available to me immediately a lot of able support, in friends as well as in a therapist who had a little knowledge in this area. The biggest single thing was that they were willing to be educated. They believed me and they listened endlessly.

Information was extremely important. I couldn't get my hands on enough of it, both to educate myself and to start my mind working again. It felt so good to be thinking! Talking to other former cult members was and still is particularly valuable and helpful to me—to understand what happened, grieve, laugh, and find the value in it all. With these people it has felt the safest to share my pain.

I can remember intense moments of despair over having been had, as well as over having lost my elaborate and all-consuming belief system. I had been so dedicated, with a such a sense of purpose. When leaving I didn't know what I thought or felt, what I could trust in myself or others. I was desperate for direction, yet didn't trust any from outside myself and could find none within myself. One day I reacted to a man's shirt. It was a chartreuse color, and I remember saying to myself what an ugly color it was. Almost immediately I realized I had just expressed an opinion. I knew something about myself! I didn't like that color! It was little thing, but it felt so important to get a handle on a real feeling that was my own.

It was extremely important for me to redefine the language I'd come to use. I strongly recommend making lists of words, looking the words up in the dictionary, and reestablishing their use and meaning for yourself. I found it important to do this with feelings, too. It was very hard to identify emotions beyond good and bad. It was important to feel pain, to feel anxious, to feel confused, to feel melancholy, and to very specifically name each feeling. I've seen charts with lists of hundreds of adjectives of this sort. This process helped to reclaim *all* of myself.

Learning how to relate in healthy ways was a big deal. Relearning trust, both in myself and others, is only now becoming less of an issue for me. Being comfortable with ambiguity instead of demanding or at least longing for solid, black-and-white answers is something for which I now have a higher tolerance. About two years after I'd exited the Emissaries I went to an Al-Anon meeting (a 12-step program for loved ones, friends, and families of alcoholics). It was very helpful to see that others could understand my experience even if they had not been there themselves. This was healthy, I think, in that I could not become elitist or isolated in self-pity! Interestingly enough, the person who understood my experience the easiest was a Vietnam vet.

I know a lot of people have used 12-step meetings of various sorts for their recoveries. Although the fit isn't perfect it did help me in my healing process. Therapy helped me unravel the experience, the mental controls, and the thought patterns, but Al-Anon helped my heart. It gave me a means to have a higher power again, with nobody else telling me what that meant, which was so important to me. I had such a desire for a spiritual life before getting involved with the Emissaries.

I still have a very simple spiritual life. I have not been successful in reestablishing any affiliation (I grew up Protestant). This is sometimes frustrating to me because I really liked that in the cult. But I find that I have a deeper, more personal spiritual experience than I ever did before because I have had to struggle with my own answers and my own understanding of a higher power. I now know that no one else can give me answers, no one else knows for me what needs to happen in my life. I may gather information from many places, but *I* make the final choice.

A very empowering event happened in 1987, three years after I'd left the group. I was going to my first Cult Awareness Network conference, which in some measure terrified me. Who are these people anyway? I thought. A week before I left for Pittsburgh a long article came out in the Sunday *Denver Post* about Colorado's "Oldest Commune." It was a glowing report all about Sunrise Ranch, the international headquarters for the Emissaries of Divine Light. The writer had swallowed their propaganda—hook, line, and sinker. In response I wrote a letter to the editor stating that the surface was nice and glossy, but what went on in the name of spirit was deception and manipulation. Upon returning from the conference, which had been exciting, informative, validating, and supportive, I saw my letter in the Sunday paper. It was like standing in front of Martin, the leader, and saying "Fuck You!" I had my power back—it was a great feeling.

Keeping a journal was also very helpful. It gave me time to myself; it gave my thoughts importance. To write my ideas down and look at them helped to sort out "me" from the cult identity. I still use my journal for personal reflection. Private time has become very precious. In fact, I am fiercely protective of it and much more of an introvert than before. I've been out of the group nine years now and still feel this way. I find it healthy to have time alone, to be comfortable with myself alone.

One of the words I had the hardest time with after leaving the group was *want*. It was a word I had completely eliminated. In the cult, it was not okay to want anything. It took a long time to change that. Getting my very first apartment alone at age 34 helped. It was all mine—to keep to myself or to share, to decorate, to reflect me. I had deprived myself for so long that I was really into having "things" for a while and making up for lost time. This overcompensation meant my budget was not in great shape for some time, but I now give myself permission for having done that—it was such an important part of my healing.

I had been married while in the Emissaries, and my husband actually initiated our exiting. I am grateful that he had a good sense of timing and managed to say he wanted to leave when he did, because at a different time I might not have left. Once we left, however, our marriage quickly fell apart. It had already been in trouble, and because the whole relationship was based in the Emissaries it deteriorated rapidly after exiting. As glad as I was to be out of the Emissaries, to lose that experience and my marriage at the same time was devastating. My ex-husband and I are now friends. We share this history and went through some very trying times together. He will always be a part of my life.

Shame and guilt have been big hurdles. Shame at having been had; guilt for hurting my family; shame and guilt for having believed it all and having tried so hard to make it real. What I've said to myself often that has helped is that I did feel like a fool, and figured some people probably thought I was. So, since I had already made an amazing ass of myself, anything else I might screw up could hardly be as bad. That put everything in a positive light. I could take risks and not worry about looking foolish. This viewpoint has allowed me to speak publicly on many occasions, and I find that for the most part people are willing to learn and understand rather than judge or "blame the victim." In other areas of my life I have felt free to ask questions and not care if they were stupid questions. I have felt free to challenge authority and risk being shot down. Through trial and error I have developed a very strong sense of myself and a better grasp on honesty, manipulation, and deception than most people. I have the courage to risk being wrong.

I found a private place out in the mountains near where I live. There is a big gnarly old aspen tree there, and I have gone to that tree for quiet, solitude, comfort, and reflection. It is now my tree, I'm quite certain. I found this place soon after leaving the cult. It was comforting to think that this tree had seen seasons, a world war or two, many changing events. All that had come and gone, yet the tree was still there. This gave me a changed perspective. I realized after a year or two that this tree had been a higher power for me when I could not accept the idea of a god. It remains a powerful symbol for me, but I now have God in my life as well.

I have used a number of thoughts and quotations over the years to keep me going. A poem someone once gave me has become a favorite.

> To laugh often and much
> To win the respect of intelligent people
> And the affection of children,
> To earn the appreciation of honest critics
> And endure the betrayal of false friends,
> To appreciate beauty,
> To find the best in others,
> To leave the world a bit better,
> Whether by a healthy child, a garden patch,
> Or a redeemed social condition,
> To know that even one life has breathed
> Better because you have lived—
> This is to have succeeded.

A friend arrived in my town in 1987, just after she had left the Emissaries. We spent many long hours together as she began her exit and regained herself. We remain best of friends. I know she has breathed better as a result, and so by the poet's definition, I have succeeded. Anything else I do is gravy.

I can sum up the positives of this horrible cult experience by saying I've had the chance to reinvent myself. Few people ever have quite the same thorough opportunity as those of us who have been through a cult experience.

CHAPTER NINETEEN

RECOVERING FROM A CULT
HANA ELTRINGHAM WHITFIELD

Hana Whitfield was a member of a large pseudopsychotherapy/religious group. She discusses the difficulties of adjusting to mainstream society after 20 years in the group, finding herself fearful, alone, and without resources. She shares here the practical methods she discovered that have helped her in her recovery. Hana now works a cult educator and a consultant to families who have relatives in the cult she was in.

When, in 1984, I left the high-demand group I was involved with for 20 years, I was in bad shape physically and psychologically. Severe, constant headaches, which had started eight years earlier, prevented me from working several days a week. Never overweight, I had lost 20 pounds and was thin and weak. I experienced bone-deep exhaustion all the time. I longed to be able to go somewhere no one could find me and never wake up again. During my last five years in the group, suicide was constantly on my mind. I fought it, forcing my mind away from it all the time because on some level it seemed so much the right thing to do.

Before I left the group I was extensively threatened that I would be sued, followed, not given a moment's peace for the rest of my life, that I would die of some terrible illness or in an accident, or that even worse things would happen to me because I was betraying the group by leaving. I was terrified they were right, that my decision was wrong, and that I'd spend eternity regretting it.

I was obsessed with fear and guilt about myself, about what I was doing and not doing, about what I was feeling and not feeling, and about what I was thinking and not thinking. These emotions and thoughts never stopped. While in the group I'd come to believe that I caused everything that happened to me, including the constant pain, guilt, and fears. I had spent years dissecting the most inner parts of myself according to the group's teachings, trying to find the terrible misdeeds I must have committed sometime in the past to be in so much pain in the present . . . all to no avail.

Now I couldn't sleep at night because my mind wouldn't shut off. I heard multiple voices chattering, arguing, whispering, sometimes for days and nights. I felt I had fragmented into hundreds of "me's," each having its own perspective and arguing with one or more other "me's." At times I thought I was going mad with everything going on inside my head and with my vain efforts to stop the confusion and appear normal in front of other people.

While in the group I'd been largely out of touch with normal society. I didn't know how it worked, how to find a job, how to present myself to the world, how to avoid mentioning the group's name in a résumé. I could no longer speak proper English. My vocabulary was loaded with the group's clichés and terms, and I would stutter and stumble when I talked to outsiders. I had been manipulated so extensively for so many years that after I left the group I didn't realize I could have walked into any newspaper office or city council building and I would have received more help than I dreamed possible. I didn't think of doing it at the time because I believed that they were the group's enemies and would instantly reject me as a "cult nut."

I had no family in America—my relatives lived overseas. All my group friends disconnected from me after I left and was declared "persona non grata." I had no one to turn to for help or support. I couldn't move around independently as I didn't own a car and didn't know how to drive. I had no money or assets of any kind since I'd spent 20 years working for nothing. I had no means to go anywhere, particularly not overseas to my family who didn't have the finances to help me. I had a Green Card but no passport. My Rhodesian passport had been cancelled in January 1980 when that country elected its first black government and became Zimbabwe.

I was torn between wanting to believe in God and not being able to. If God existed and I didn't have faith in Him, I knew I'd suffer forever. But I needed tangible proof to believe, and there wasn't any. What faith I'd had, had been used up by the group. There was none left. It was a terrible conflict, one I could not resolve. And there was no priest, padre, father, or minister I knew and trusted enough to talk to about the conflict.

Without understanding what was occurring, I was "floating" all the time, in and out of guilts, fears, and altered states. I couldn't decide anything—what to buy, what to eat, where to bank, where to go, what to do or not do. A numb, dead, depressed, unthinking feeling stayed with me all the time, though I didn't realize it until years later in therapy.

I was constantly afraid that the group was after me, watching me and plotting against me. I was terrified, always watching my back. I was scared and distrustful of people, particularly men. I felt they were after me for sex only. The first year I mostly kept to myself and rarely dated or socialized.

I hoarded my money like a miser. I had frequent panic attacks at the thought of ending up homeless and in need. Sometimes after I bought food, or clothes at thrift stores, I got physically ill and threw up. If I put the stuff back and left empty-handed the nausea went away. I devised various coping strategies to help me through.

For example, I deliberately tried to live one moment at a time. At the end of each day I wrote out a "To Do" list for the next. I put everything down including things like getting up at 6:00 A.M., eating breakfast by 7:00 A.M., getting to work by 8:30 A.M., eating lunch in the park at 1:00 P.M., and so on. My "To Do" list kept my day predictable and lessened the depression, the guilt, and floating.

When the inner voices got too confusing or the depression got too bad I worked extra hours at my job or cleaned whatever I could get my hands on. Whenever I could I worked a full-time day job and a part-time evening job. This helped a lot. I slept better, thought more clearly, felt more centered and in control.

I started a journal because I got relief by writing down my thoughts, no matter how scarce or jumbled they were. Often all I could start with were disjointed words. For the first few months I took time each day to relearn English to replace the group's language. I read the paper daily. I joined a library and reread favorite authors like Charles Dickens and Emily Brontë, and, interestingly, I discovered Harlequin novels, too. But I was still too embarrassed to let anyone know I was reading them.

I worked at making friends with myself. Every day I'd congratulate myself for something I did or said that was positive. At the end of the day I'd review my "To Do" list and give myself a pat on the back for what I'd achieved, which gradually improved my self-confidence and trust.

I saved fanatically to afford driving lessons and bare necessities. It brought me a measure of independence to know I could rent a car if I needed one. Saving money was an obsession. I knew it and allowed it because it gave me so much satisfaction to see my little store of money grow.

To help the continual exhaustion I'd sleep as much as I could on weekends to relax and rest. I had dark rings under my eyes and people often asked if I was tired. It embarrassed me and I'd shrug off the question. I sometimes used makeup to hide the rings.

To learn about businesses and the job market I joined an executive search firm—one of my early bright ideas. I pored over résumés late into the night and on weekends. Three months later I got a better job, and later on, still a better one.

I've been in therapy now for almost two years and it has greatly helped me to turn my life around. There are problem areas I still have and need help on. For example, the suicide thoughts still come up occasionally. Sometimes they scare me, because suicide is still an option. It has been very hard to come to grips with. I get terrible mood swings. When the lows hit, they sometimes stay with me for weeks. The headaches still occur, sometimes enough to incapacitate me weekly. I am now under medical care for them. Loss of memory is exasperating. I forget things I've said or seen even on the same day. There are also guilt feelings. A major one is that I've abandoned the God of my parents' faith and *that* God may be the real One.

I experience awful fears, fears of so many things. I have purposely not written them down here because, reportedly, the group I belonged to would use the information against me. I still have nightmares about the group. They are always the same: cult members chase me with guns or machetes or lasers, either in trains or cars or aeroplanes or on foot and I run for my life across mountains, through tunnels, across water, in the dark.

It's been an awesome release to see how cleverly the cult turned off my feelings. Now I'm beginning to see that it's *normal* to have feelings—including negative feelings—and that I am *entitled* to my feelings. And there are ways to express them without tearing my environment apart in the process.

The loss of the best years of my life, the loss of the opportunity to have children of my own, and the loss of building a career are bitter pills to swallow. I can see now that in giving myself completely and unconditionally to the cult leader and his beliefs and practices, I gave myself up. I gave up my cognizance of myself in its entirety. I have started to reclaim this most prized possession in therapy. I've been on Prozac for over one and a half years and it has made a major improvement in my life physically and psychologically.

I am fortunate to have married an extremely loving, tolerant, and supportive husband with whom I share everything. We have started to work with families who have loved ones in the same cult we were in and we help educate these members so they can make a more informed choice about the cult—a choice my husband and I did not have.

Addendum: The above was written in 1991. My recovery is ongoing in the present, and I've been told it may continue for quite a while. My gratitude goes to the many kind, caring, and wonderful people who helped me so much along the way.

CHAPTER TWENTY

BLINDED BY THE LIGHT
ROSANNE HENRY

Rosanne Henry and her husband joined a New Age/Eastern-style cult, known as "Kashi Ranch." Rosanne was convinced by the group to give her newborn child to the leader, and then later Rosanne left the group. She writes about the pain of losing her daughter—and the joy of going back to reclaim custody of her. Rosanne is now completing her masters degree in counseling.

Harry and I had been married three years. Because of various confusions and tensions in our lives we decided to try therapy. To save money we went to the Free University and signed up with "Art Therapists" (who turned out to have journalism degrees). After six months of therapy they referred us to "Joya," their new spiritual teacher.

Within two weeks of the referral, Harry took emergency leave from his medical residency and flew two thousand miles to Colorado to meet Joya. She was perceptive, shrewd, and charismatic. She immediately began breaking Harry down and indoctrinating him. Concerned about Harry's welfare and our marriage, I followed him to Kashi Ranch, the ashram where Joya and her followers lived. Because of the vulnerable state we were in it took only a few months of concentrated efforts to push us into our contrived cult personalities.

The ashram moved from Colorado to Florida. Harry found a job with a health maintenance organization while I began developing a business that would serve as the economic base for the Ranch. Within a year Macho Products was in operation, manufacturing and distributing protective equipment for the martial arts.

Joya, whose name was now Joyce Cho, was trying to have a child. She had recently married a Tae-Kwon-Do master, and had two grown children and a teenager from her first marriage, but at age 40 wanted more. For months we heard about her miscarriages and her relentless desire to get pregnant. Then she devised a plan and whoever was pregnant on the Ranch became a target. We were all approached to give our babies to "Ma" (Joyce's spiritual name). Eventually, we were told, these children would be Ma's successors. All this was handled discreetly through "the girls," a group of women who took personal care of Joyce and handled her dirty work.

When I was six months pregnant with our first child, I was targeted. They worked on Harry first and had him work on me. After two months of hell I finally agreed to the plan. I remember the very moment when I flipped the switch: "There is nothing greater that I could do for my child than give her to the divine mother," I thought. Four of us gave our first child to this woman. She raised them as twins—like two matched sets of dolls.

Joyce had assured me that I would be very involved in my daughter's care. As it turned out, I got to watch all the children sleep a few hours a night, four nights a week. Near the end of the first year I was thrown out of the nursery after an argument with Joyce's tyrant teenage daughter. Shortly after that I left Kashi Ranch and joined Harry who had left five months earlier. I did not take my daughter with me though I desperately wanted to. I had just begun to see another very dark side of Joyce but I couldn't give her up—she was still my guru, my god. I had to truly believe this to leave my daughter with her.

Harry and I moved back to Colorado and started a new life. Six months later I got pregnant. When I gave birth to our first son, I learned how it felt to actually keep the child that I brought into the world. It was such a healing experience to love and nurture him, yet so disturbing to think about my daughter. How could I have done this? Two years passed; trying desperately to replace my daughter I became pregnant with our second son. For years I endured the deepest grief known to a woman: a longing for her child. Finally, I got up the courage to visit the Ranch and see my daughter.

My little girl, "Ganga," was six years old on my first trip back. She was so beautiful and full of life, and we connected right away, but I had to be careful because she thought Ma was her mother. Seeing her was both relief and torture. I wanted her back in my life but I didn't want to move back to the Ranch and surrender to Ma again. For four months Joyce and her cohorts worked on us to move back. Finally, I hit my limit—something snapped. I was breaking through the cult mind-set: I didn't have to accept Joyce's reality anymore. But what in hell was I going to do about Ganga?

I knew that I desperately needed good professional help. With a referral from a trusted friend, I started therapy with a Jungian psychotherapist. After four months of intense work my therapist suggested that I might want to go and get Ganga someday. My reply was total surprise, "You mean I can?"

From that moment on Harry and I worked to get our daughter back. We assembled a team of lawyers, cult specialists, therapists, and private investigators. Four months later I went to Kashi Ranch with my father, a private investigator, and the local SWAT team, and demanded my daughter back! With the cooperation of the local criminal justice system I had secured the necessary court order. Our daughter was reluctantly released to the police and had to wait in a foster home until the judge awarded us custody. Two weeks later Ganga was on the airplane with her "real" family, flying to her new home in Colorado.

This is what she wrote at the age of nine:

> A cult is a person that uses mind control
> and can make you gullible and you don't even know it.
> But you start to love her because she makes you feel special.
> A cult can hurt you very bad.
> She can even make you think she's god!
> A cult is bad.

Even though it is easier to express what is evil and wrong with Kashi Ranch, we try to keep it in perspective and let her express what was good about her cult experience. There were some positive things and these helped mold her to become the wonderful person she is today.

I feel very lucky. I got a second chance—a chance to be whole and live a full life with all of my children. Having my daughter back is a dream come true. Yet I struggle not only with the loss of those precious six years but also with the pain of the wound I inflicted on my daughter. Every day I search for forgiveness; the healthier Ganga gets, the easier it becomes.

In Chapter 22, Rosanne describes the challenges faced by Ganga and her family as she learns to adjust to life away from the cult.

CHAPTER
TWENTY-ONE

LEARNING TO LOVE
DAVID G. ROCHE

David Roche was in the Democratic Workers Party, a political cult, for more than 10 years. He writes about belief issues, self-esteem, and learning to recognize and express feelings and to love again. David is now a professional comedian, a massage therapist, and a nationally recognized spokesperson for facially disfigured people.

I was born with a birth defect called an extensive cavernous hemangioma —basically a tumor consisting of enlarged blood vessels—on the left side of my face, throat, and neck. When I was about a year old the hemangioma began to grow at an alarming rate, distorting my features, causing my lower lip, for example, to resemble a bunch of ripe Concord grapes. My parents took me to the Mayo Clinic where I had a variety of treatments. My lower lip was removed. Gold pellets of radon gas were imbedded in my lower jaw so that the radiation they gave off would kill tissue. My left eye is growing a cataract because of this; the radiation also caused my teeth to dry up and rot and the lower part of my face to stop growing.

Today, I feel that my face is a gift from God. Not the kind of gift that you rip open exclaiming, "It's exquisite! How did you know what I wanted?!" It was more like, "Oh God . . . you shouldn't have!" For much of my life my face was a continuous source of shame to me. It is only in recent years that I have come to see it as the elaborately disguised gift it is. Because of my face, my dark side—my shadow side—is on the outside. Although I have often tried to hide, to deny my reality, ultimately I have not been able to. What I have to deal with is out there for everyone to see, including myself. We all have wounds, and when they are on the inside it is more tempting to hide them, to pretend they don't exist. I lived that way for many years.

I was in my mid-thirties in the mid-1970s when I joined a communist political group, the Democratic Workers Party (DWP, sometimes referred to here as "the party"). Just as I had tried to be a "good boy" when growing up Catholic, I wanted to be an excellent communist—as a way of dealing with my lack of self-worth. We were totally dedicated to the cause of the oppressed. We strove to live up to an impossible ideal, using the most extreme criticism of the smallest errors or "incorrect" attitudes to change ourselves.

After working a typical 13-hour day at my political assignment, I would buy a pint of vodka on the way home, slug half of it down, and be asleep in about 15 minutes. This was one of the ways I repressed my own individuality and dealt with my doubts and fears about what I was doing. Selflessness was a natural choice when my self was not acceptable, or even known.

When the organization collapsed from within in 1985 the rug was pulled out from under me. I had to learn to rebuild myself. Emotionally I felt like a zombie and was heavily armored against love. My self-image had been savaged by the years of relentless criticism sessions. I lived on cigarettes, alcohol, coffee, sugar, and doughnuts. My resting pulse was 100. I had no vision of the future and could barely imagine myself being alive in five years. This was the legacy of being in a cult for 10 years.

Yet now, even though facially disfigured people are essentially children of the dark, craving anonymity, I am standing in the spotlight and performing as a successful humorist and public speaker (one of my topics is "How I Learned to Love Myself"). I have found that when I stand on stage I am not only comfortable but even feel beautiful. It has been a transforming experience to stand in front of hundreds of people looking at me, or to be on national television with millions watching. I am claiming who I am: in my humor and in my speaking I bring up issues about facial disfigurement.

Not only am I doing something that I thoroughly enjoy but also I have opened myself up to love as a result of beginning to love myself, and am now in a committed long-term relationship. In many other ways I have been through a profound transformation process of recovery from cult life.

In my first efforts at rebuilding myself I joined the YMCA and began battering away at the Nautilus machines, whanging the metal, my mind flooding with bloody fantasies of putting an ax in the head of one of our abusive leaders. This was my initial practice at getting in touch with intense feelings of anger, guilt, and fear.

Often I would awaken screaming from bloody inchoate nightmares as my long suppressed anger and other feelings struggled out of my sub-conscious. I still have dreams about the party. It is only in the last six months or so that they have changed and only in that period of time have I ceased looking at these dreams as literal and understood they have meta-phorical content.

In 1986 I went to a therapist who very quickly said that she would not see me unless I stopped drinking. I walked out, and it took me half a year of resentment before I listened to what she said. With the help of 12-step programs I stopped drinking, smoking, and using marijuana. With my background the notion of embracing powerlessness repelled me, as did any use of jargon. The idea of a "higher power" evoked a mental picture of an angry alcoholic god-with-a-stick. But it was powerfully liberating to be in meetings where individuals spoke from the heart and were listened to with respect.

It took me a long time to find the good in my party years. I did receive benefits from being challenged then, and particularly remember one transformative experience. I had decided that I wanted to speak on buses as an organizing tactic. My plan was to get on last, put in my fare, and start speaking. For two weeks, twice a day, I waited at the end of the line, pushing myself forward on resistant, numb legs. Each time my cour-age failed me. Then one day I actually started speaking, and my worst nightmare fantasy came true. Another passenger began heckling me furi-ously, screaming, "Get off the bus, you damned communist." I remember thinking, "How did he know?" and that it was not fair for him to call me a communist in public even if I was one. I babbled on while he raged, then stumbled to a seat. As I slumped, humiliated with failure, an elderly Irish woman in the seat in front of me turned and squeezed my hand and told me I had "done just grand." She turned and told the heckler that *he* should get off the bus. I was just barely assimilating this when another hand clasped my shoulder from behind. Two Latino guys congratulated me and said, "Look, some more people got on. You better get up and do it again." That was my debut as a performer.

Many feelings—especially positive ones—were new to me. I remem-ber weeding in the garden, feeling the warm sun on my back and experi-encing a brief moment of calm and contentment. I wondered and thought, "This must be what people call peace of mind."

After my cult experience I was intensely cynical about words. Fortu-nately, I found that I was able to believe and accept the healing touch of Karen, my mentor in massage therapy. This was especially important to me as a facially disfigured person and as a former cult member who had suppressed my feelings for 10 years. Massage was my primary recovery therapy and opened the door to learning to love myself. It helped to end years of dissociation and integrate the physical and spiritual. Now giving and receiving massage is a basic part of my spiritual practice. I have spent several years volunteering as a massage therapist at California Pacific Medical Center in San Francisco. In my private practice I always accept clients who are ill on a low-fee basis.

My recovery from the DWP also involved caring for two long-time friends as they died of AIDS in the late 1980s. When it was time to gather friends for the final weeks of Jon's life, I took responsibility to coordinate his care. In the years since the party I have consistently realized what I miss most is the sense of being of service and the sense of community. In the three months or so before Jon died I was able to immerse myself in a loving community where superficial concerns tended to give way in the face of impending death. I was not fully able to appreciate what was happening. I still judged myself as inadequate, failing to meet the needs of people around me and not equal to the "assignment." But in truth I was in an atmosphere of loving support, and incredibly fortunate.

In 1988 and 1989 I regularly flew to Los Angeles to help care for my friend David, also in the last stages of AIDS. This time I was more open to the experience, more relaxed. But still, time after time, I would plead with David to tell me what I could do for him. He would answer, "Just *be* here." I thought he was either not in touch with what he needed or was shy or embarrassed. Finally, after weeks, it got through to me that he meant *exactly* what he said. He wanted my full presence. So I have the memory of sitting on the couch for hours with David's head on my lap as we listened silently to the Mass in B Minor (and dozed a bit). What a wonderful gift, the realization that my presence had value!

In the early stages of my recovery I tried to pray, without success. The praying I had learned as a child and youth seemed rote, mechanical, and essentially meaningless. I had been in the seminary as an adolescent; when I would masturbate and then go to confession the priest would give me a number of prayers to recite as penance. So praying was presented to me as punishment for sin. At least it kept me praying!

It took me a long time to realize that prayer is simply the expression of truth, nothing more. It has many forms (including some useful rote forms). Gardening is prayer. So is the care of children. The moan of orgasm is prayer. Telling the truth when it is difficult. Standing in the sun. Massage is prayer.

One aftereffect of my cult experience is that I am very alert to any hint of guruism. The idea that anyone's relationship with what is sacred must be defined by and/or mediated through a "holy person" frightens and angers me—especially if that person receives riches, sex, or power for doling out holiness.

As a comedian I often perform as Reverend Dave, "the beloved founder of the Church of 80% Sincerity." The 80% Church is a postmodern church with absolutely no ideals. We are reality-based, adjusting our spiritual beliefs and practices to conform to reality rather than ideals. For example, I tried to look at myself in the mirror and say 30 times a day, "David, I love you. David, I love you." I soon realized that I did not love myself. No problem. In the Church of 80% Sincerity we simply change the words and you don't even need to make eye contact with yourself. "David, you are a nice person and you try hard. You do dishes very well. Sorry, I just don't love you. Maybe we could just be friends?"

A sense of humor is the opposable thumb of the soul. Freely expressed, I find it to be the antidote to dogmatism and rigidity and sure death to cultism. It involves a constant repositioning, a looking at beliefs and experiences from a fresh vantage point.

Humor and laughter were highly valued in my family. I always wanted to be comedian but never had the self-esteem until my mid-forties. As I started to express myself in my comedy classes and get approval, I found I began to come out, to tell my story and claim my own truth. This form of creative self-expression has become one of the key aspects of my recovery. I have come to understand from my experience that the primary manifestation of God is as creator. The more creative we are, the more we are in touch with the divine in ourselves.

I do not believe in being born again. My experience is that personal transformation, maturity, and peace of mind come over time, through effort and continuing choices. There *are* moments of inspiration and intense growth. My judgment is that these are hard-won moments, wrung from the past. Yet, as I look back over the past few years I am sometimes flooded with a sense of having been gifted. At these times my grim linear straining can seem suddenly ludicrous, and I open to grace.

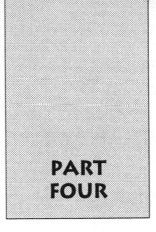

**PART
FOUR**

SPECIAL CONCERNS

Postcult recovery is a psychoeducational process.
—Margaret Thaler Singer

CHAPTER TWENTY-TWO

CHILDREN IN CULTS

Children are the least powerful and most helpless members of the cult. At best they become loyal members, dependent on the group's interpretation of their needs for parenting, education, medical care, and discipline. At worst they become the weakest pawns and victims of the cult, used as tools of recruitment, indoctrination, and control, often suffering neglect and physical and sexual abuse.

Children usually do not have to be converted because their induction into the cultic society begins so early. The cult world may be all they have ever known. Even if they attend mainstream educational programs, the outside world is carefully explained and kept separate (as exemplified in "Shippen's" story, told later in this chapter).

Cults recruit couples and whole families as well as individuals with children. As the family becomes invested in the cult, individual family members become increasingly subservient, childlike, and dependent on the group or leader. By giving up their autonomy the parents can no longer maintain the family as an independent unit, and their model for the family becomes confused. By default or intention, children often become the property of the group or the leader.

As discussed in earlier chapters, the cult leader or the dominant partner in a cultic relationship often dictates even the smallest details of everyday life of those under his sway. We also discussed the similarity in personality traits between many cult leaders and the classic psychopath. Since the psychopath has an emotional maturity equal to or less than that of a 10-year-old, his capacity for mature parenting is nonexistent.(1) Childlike in his own emotional development, the cult leader has neither empathy for nor an understanding of the needs of his followers. Adults and children alike are viewed by the cult leader as threatening objects to be controlled and as objects to be used to fulfill his needs and desires.

Sometimes there are serious or even fatal consequences of the leader's idiosyncratic beliefs about medical and dental care, education, upbringing and socialization, or sexual roles. If the group isn't already living communally, the cult leader creates an environment that extends into the members' homes and families. Nearly everyone becomes infected with the leader's obsessions, bizarre beliefs, and need for secrecy. And children especially become part of this cult-created family disorder.

For example, in the Sullivanians, the Manhattan-based psychotherapy cult described by Janet Joyce in Chapters 2 and 14, members had to receive permission from their therapists in order to have children. Children were separated at birth from their parents to prevent "contamination" from their biological parents' "neurotic" tendencies. Newborns and children were given to other group members to raise, and the parents had limited visitation rights. At an early age, children were sent to boarding schools to further separate them from their parents.(2)

Four areas of concern that are addressed in this chapter are the difficulties experienced by children who live in a cult environment and have to interact with the world outside; special health and medical problems caused by neglect and abuse; the psychological effects of physical, emotional, and sexual trauma; and the adjustment difficulties encountered after leaving the cult.

Difficulties of Living in Two Worlds

Many children who are brought up in cults may need to interact, chiefly in public schools, with the larger society. These children have to learn to balance a double standard of values, mores, and beliefs in order to function in both groups. What separates cults from other groups with varied religious and cultural beliefs is the imposition of an us-versus-them mentality, characterized by secrecy, isolationism, elitism, and a fear of outsiders that can border on paranoia. If the group participates in activities that are illegal or socially taboo, an added burden of shame and fear must be borne by the child.

For example, in the Children of God (COG), incest and child and adult prostitution are common practices—behaviors that are illegal and highly stigmatized in society. Forbidden to talk with outsiders about these behaviors, children within COG and similar groups are at a severe disadvantage when interacting with outsiders. This situation reinforces the isolation, distrust, and fear already experienced by the child. (For an example and further discussion of this situation see the account in Part Three by

"Frances Lief" who describes running away from COG as a teenager after growing up in the group.)

"Shippen's" story

Shippen's childhood presents us with an example of a child who was brought up in a cult (Ordo Templi Orientis) while also living in a noncult community. She describes growing up in her family, practitioners of "Ceremonial Magick" based on the writings of Aleister Crowley. Shippen took vows and had a role in her cult; at the same time she was a "normal" teenager who was involved in an honors youth symphony, wrote plays, and danced in school programs. At some point in her teen years she began to rebel against her parents and the group. She describes the difficulties of "having a foot in both worlds."

> I was taught that magick is about control of oneself, one's circumstances, and of others. It is also about becoming more than human, which in my family meant an ability to strip oneself of the trappings of personality in order to come to terms with some kind of essence. Ceremonial Magick, as I experienced it, used sex rites and sacrifice, but in very limited, controlled ways. Self-actualization was the focus of most of the disciplines and studies. My parents worked to train me in the meditative arts necessary for a magician and psychic. I remember vividly much of the training and many of the experiences. The most striking part was the sense of being specially endowed with gifts others didn't have, gifts that couldn't be talked about or shared with anyone but my parents.
>
> The uniqueness was a tremendous burden because it had to be developed by special exercises: I learned to chant almost as soon as I could talk. I was taught breath control and breathing exercises instead of learning to catch a ball. Instead of coloring in coloring books, I painted tarot cards and read the meditations that went with them. There was very little my parents studied that I wasn't fully involved with.
>
> The kids down the block did not know this. Nor did the school authorities. I was not unique outside of my own home, but neither had I been taught any skills that were even remotely useful in the schoolyard. I was a confused, lost, and alienated child who tended to talk with trees or, later, read during school recesses. Not only did I lack common experiences and skills to share with other children but also I had been warned about talking to others. I knew of two other children from my parents' community who had been removed from their homes by the authorities. I was afraid if I ever revealed my parents' practices,

there would be dire consequences to them, and to me. The outside world was terrifying. My lips were sealed, effectively, for 30 years by that terror.

As I grew older, I got snotty about the training, then I refused to go to the rituals. Once I dared to break the silence imposed on me to ask for help from my best friend's mother, then later the school authorities, and, later still, religious representatives in the community. My best friend's mother, who knew about my vows and the ceremonies, told me to put up with it till I got into college. The religious representatives discounted everything I said and lectured me about lying. The school authorities told me my mother was very ill and I shouldn't be bothering her. This was true, though I didn't realize it for many years.

Medical care was nonexistent in my family. They believed that all physical illness comes from incorrect thinking, so if your body is bothering you, you'd better straighten out your thoughts. I knew my mother's body was bothering her—in fact, she was dying. But my father told me that her thinking was bad, that she was getting what she deserved until she corrected it, and that there was nothing he or I could or should do. The school authorities probably saw me as a callous, self-centered, spoiled teen, when in fact I was merely behaving in the way I had been taught and had been treated myself when ill.

I graduated from high school, got into a good but free college, and ran away to it since my parents did not approve.(3)

Health Problems and Medical Neglect

In some cults, religious beliefs are used to justify lack of medical care or keeping children away from public school and the community. Lack of timely treatment for minor illnesses may lead to severe and often fatal complications, especially in the very young. Generally this type of abuse only comes to the attention of authorities when medical professionals, educators, or concerned witnesses call state protective services. Even then, First Amendment protections often shield or delay discovery of the nature of groups that use religion as a cover to avoid close examination.

One published study reflects the patterns of abuse and neglect in cults. A survey of 70 former cult members responding to questions about health issues provided the following results:

- 27 percent said children in their groups were not immunized against common childhood diseases.

- 23 percent said children did not get at least eight hours of sleep a night.

- 60 percent said their groups permitted physical punishment of children.

- 13 percent said that children were sometimes physically disabled or hurt to teach them a lesson.

- 13 percent said that the punishment of children was sometimes life threatening or required a physician's care.

- *[only]* 37 percent said that children were seen by a doctor when ill.(4)

There are plenty of examples of medical neglect, among them, two members of End Time Ministries were convicted of felony child abuse in a Florida court after their four-year-old daughter died of pneumonia. This was the second time End Time Ministries members were convicted for failing to get medical treatment for their children. (5) Also, six children of members of the Faith Tabernacle died from complications of measles, which health officials felt could have been prevented by timely medical treatment and avoided entirely by vaccination. The group does not believe in immunizations and medical care.(6)

In one Eastern meditation cult, a woman gave birth without the aid of medical personnel and her child failed to begin breathing for several minutes. The guru of the group, who was in attendance during the labor and delivery, was part of the effort to get the child to breathe. Members of the group are now convinced the guru has miraculous healing capacity, and the child—who is retarded—is seen as proof of the guru's love rather than the result of his disdain for proper medical care.

More common perhaps than the obvious medical neglect of these examples is an insidious form of neglect which is indirect and unspoken. In most cults, members simply are not given the time to attend to their own or their children's personal needs. And many members simply have no financial resources to pay for medical care. Thus their basic medical needs and sometimes more serious matters are shunted aside, put off month after month, year after year. This can have an even greater impact on children's developing minds and bodies.

Physical, Emotional, and Sexual Abuse

When the secrecy that surrounds a cult is broken by the harsh glare of publicity, only the most horrifying cases get media attention, and there is little awareness of the more pervasive but significantly damaging practices that are not as publicized. Despite the lack of large-scale scientific studies of the effects of cultic systems on childhood growth and development, there is a growing body of literature on the deleterious effects of cults on children when there is direct evidence of child abuse.(7)

Children are urged to follow the cult leader's example, and children of the cult leader are especially vulnerable. For example, Brother Julius, the messianic leader of The Work, a declining cult in Connecticut, has settled out of court various suits alleging that he sexually abused children in the cult, including those in his own family. Julius's son, Daniel Sweetman, was also indicted and held for the sexual abuse of children in the cult.(8)

Numerous other instances of severe physical and sexual abuse of children in cults have been reported in the past several decades. Paddling and birching, whipping, isolation, food and sleep deprivation are rampant among certain kinds of cults. Child prostitution, pornography, rape, and incest are also not uncommon.

Two followers of the Ecclesia Athletic Association were found guilty of beating to death an eight-year-old girl, and seven other members were indicted on charges of enslaving over 50 children.(9) The leader of the Christian Fellowship Church was sentenced to 31 years' imprisonment in Illinois for sexual assault, abuse, and child pornography. Charges against him and two others for similar abuses were also brought in California.(10) Although the suffering of children in cults may not yet be fully documented, anecdotal examples such as these fill the public records and the files of those of us who study cults.

Anna Bowen, a registered nurse and counselor who works with survivors of severe childhood trauma, writes: "Systematic, organized, malevolent abuse, such as that which may occur in cults, has devastating effects on a person's sense of self. The focus of an authoritarian group is to indoctrinate the child into the group's philosophy and demands by denying the child any opportunity to develop a sense of self through experiencing normal growth and development. The intent is to eradicate naturally deserved self-worth except as related to cult beliefs and structures . . . . Children may become convinced that they are a creation of the cult, their only purpose being to serve the system and their only usefulness defined by the system's needs and functions. The child, his or her needs ignored or minimized, has no purpose other than to be used by others. Every stage of growth and development that the child enters is interrupted or damaged."

The following personal account relates one scenario of abuse in a cultic environment, perhaps most typical of the one-on-one cult. "Jessica Kay" was five years old when her mother, "Rachel," became involved in a cultic relationship with "Fred" (see Chapter 1 for Rachel's story). Now 14, Jessica Kay shares her perspective on those years.

The truth is, I do remember
by Jessica Kay

For a long time now whenever someone asked me about him I said I didn't remember. Otherwise they would keep asking me questions I did not want to answer. The truth is, I do remember. I first met him when I was five years old. Right from the start I didn't trust him. Maybe I didn't like the look in his eyes when he first looked at me. I don't know how to explain it, but I just didn't like him.

I knew I was right about him was a short time later. I had just gotten home from school and my mother was still at work. I sat down to watch TV. It was the first time I was alone with him. All of a sudden he turned off the television and gave that look I saw when I first met him. He demanded that I stand up straight like a soldier. I was stunned but promptly obeyed. He told me to pull my pants down. I did so without hesitating because I was so frightened. Then he stuck his finger in my anus. He commanded that I turn around and he made me touch his penis. At the same time, he was touching my private part. I was very uncomfortable and extremely scared—too scared to say anything. There was really no ending, it just ended.

About five minutes later he told me that if I ever told anyone about what had just happened he'd kill my whole family, including me. [In this household, weapons, including dynamite, knives, and guns, were frequently in sight of the children—Authors' note.] I promised him I wouldn't say anything. I didn't . . . until he moved out three years later.

During the three years he was in my life there were numerous occasions when he abused me emotionally and sexually. He pulled my hair, hit me, was always saying negative things to me. He also made me stay in my room, sometimes for hours and hours alone. Sometimes he wouldn't let me eat. I constantly lived in a state of fear and anger. I was afraid, never knowing when he would do something to me again. And I was angry because I couldn't tell anybody. I didn't have any way of getting help or being able to feel safe.

When I was in third grade, I came home from school to find all his personal belongings gone. I was so relieved that he was gone—for good, I hoped. It took a while to feel safe and sure that he wouldn't come back. I had a lot of trouble sleeping at night. I was still afraid that he'd come back and hurt me and my family. After a while I got the courage to tell my mother.

I first told it to my therapist. I felt very guilty, like I had done something wrong for letting him do this to me. I went to therapy and tried to make that guilty feeling go away. My mother explained to me that what he had done was wrong. She told me that we could go to the police and report it. She explained that they may or may not believe me and that he may or may not be punished. If we brought charges against him, it would mean I would have to talk about what had happened to me over and over again to strangers. I was nervous about telling so many people for fear of breaking that promise with him and that he'd come back to kill my family and me.

After thinking it over for a very long time, I decided to go ahead and press charges. I was sick of living in fear of him and feeling so angry all the time. I am 14 years old now. My case finally got settled in court. I received a settlement for my pain and suffering, which made me happy that he had to suffer the consequences of his actions. I would have always felt that something had been robbed of me if he had gotten away with it for nothing. I don't care how he got punished as long as he did.(11)

I still have much healing to do and I'm working on it. I'm now living with my father. I have been since shortly after *he* left. I no longer felt safe living with my mother. I also felt much hate for her because I felt she didn't protect me. I've worked very hard on my relationship with her and I can spend time with her now without feeling angry all the time.(12)

It is unrealistic, in such a case, to expect that all the effects of the cultic involvement with its attendant emotional, physical, and sexual abuse can be easily undone. It is heartening to note, however, that many children can and do recover. Margaret Singer states, for example, that she has interviewed scores of abused former cult members who grew up to be well-adjusted, fully functioning adults.(13)

Psychological impact

Mental health professionals who work with traumatized children have noted several common aftereffects in children who have endured abusive, violent, and frightening experiences. Similar to the aftereffects experienced by adults who have exited cults, these emotional responses are experienced by children with an intensity unmodulated by growth and maturity.

"Repeated trauma in adult life erodes the structure of the personality already formed, but repeated trauma in childhood forms and deforms the personality," writes psychiatrist Judith Herman. "The child trapped in an abusive environment is faced with formidable tasks of adaptation. She must find a way to preserve a sense of trust in people who are untrustworthy, safety in a situation that is unsafe, control in a situation that is terrifyingly unpredictable, power in a situation of helplessness. Unable to care for or protect herself, she must compensate for the failures of adult care and protection with the only means at her disposal, an immature system of psychological defenses."(14)

Professor of psychiatry Lenore Terr studied 25 children who were kidnapped aboard their school bus in Chowchilla, California, in 1976, and were held in an underground vault for 16 hours, until they escaped by digging themselves out.(15) Their posttraumatic symptoms were intense, despite the relative brevity of the captivity and the lack of physical or sexual abuse. The symptoms identified by Terr, which parallel the emotional trauma suffered by children in cultic situations, are:

Terror. This may include the fear of helplessness, the fear of another, more fearful event (fear of fear), the fear of separation from loved ones, and the fear of death. Ordinary childhood fears such as fear of the dark, of strangers, and of being alone are often magnified and retained throughout childhood, and sometimes are never outgrown. Children in cults may fear the devil, outsiders, their parents leaving the group, and displeasing the leader.

Rage. Children who are frequently abused or terrorized may have difficulty controlling their anger, which may be expressed as rage when they are frustrated, bored, or annoyed. Children may identify with their aggressors and bully other children or act out in abusive or even criminal acts. Or children may turn the anger inward with such self-destructive behaviors as cutting or burning themselves, or taking a passive stance toward repeated episodes of victimization. In cults, the victim stance is more likely, while the few who are more aggressive and fanatical may grow to inherit leadership of the group.

Denial and numbing. With repeated trauma, children develop a mechanism of numbing, sometimes accompanied by a physical inability to feel pain. Children may develop either a withdrawn or fearful personality or its opposite—a hearty, charismatic style that camouflages a numbed and diminished sense of self. Dissociative disorders have been observed in adults abused as children in cults.

Unresolved grief. A child growing up in a cult, even without physical trauma, suffers many losses. Leaving the cult, sometimes without family, friends, and relatives, can produce feelings of isolation and desolation. As an adult looking back over the cult years, a person may feel a tremendous sadness for the childhood that might have been. This is experienced as a loss of self. The gaps in experience, in developmental stages, and in the development of normal trust and self-esteem, as well as a lack of common history with mainstream society, may severely affect a person's basic sense of identity.

Adjustment Difficulties of Children Leaving Cults

Children usually exit cults when their parents decide to leave. In some instances, the children are taken from the cult as a result of a custody suit between divorcing parents, one in the cult and the other out. In others, they are removed from the group by a government agency, due to complaints of child abuse or neglect. As discussed previously, how a person leaves a cult may influence recovery: Was there an exit counseling? Did the group disperse upon the death or abandonment of the leader? Did the young adult walk away on his or her own? Was the whole family excommunicated from the group?

Major adjustment problems encountered by children leaving cults center on issues related to their need for acculturation, lack of self-control, little experience with independent decision making, boredom living in a "normal" family, distrust of others, conflicting loyalties, developmental arrest, lagging social development, and lack of self-esteem.

Rosanne Henry's story in Part Three, "Blinded by the Light," is a poignant example of two parents who reclaimed their daughter after leaving her in the care of their cult leader. "Ganga" was six when she was rescued by her parents. In the section below Rosanne describes the challenges faced by Ganga and the family.

Adjusting to a new family and to life outside the cult environment has not been easy for Ganga. Here are some of the issues we have struggled with over the last four years.

1. Ganga grew up in such a controlled environment that she was out of touch with our culture in many ways. Her primary activity had been traveling around Florida in a Winnebago with teenagers as her nannies. She had never been to Disney World, though she lived only 60 miles away. We took her to amusement parks and zoos, on train rides

and picnics in the mountains. It was as though she had lived in a foreign country all of her life. She had a hatred for dolls that soon melted away, and we kept her supplied with Barbies, water babies, and even Madame Alexandres. She welcomed most of this because it allowed her to see much more of the world and to be a seven-year-old little girl. We let her explore many things and choose her own activities. Art, gymnastics, and swimming quickly moved to the top of her list.

2. Cults typically exert strong control and legislate members' morality; thus, Ganga was not encouraged to develop her own values. Fortunately, we got her back young enough to begin this process. Her development was delayed but did occur a year or two behind other "normal" children.

3. In the beginning our nuclear family of just five members was boring and tedious for her. She had lived in a home with close to thirty people and an ashram of almost one hundred. With fewer caretakers and only one set of rules, it was more difficult for her to manipulate and get what she wanted. I think she was relieved, however, to have the structure and support provided by the family. And for the first time in her life, she got her own room.

4. Ganga was lied to about who her parents and siblings were and even when her birthday was. From the beginning she was cast as a character in the leader's fantasy. How could she learn to trust after being lied to and deceived so completely? This is an issue we will struggle with for a long time. We had to start from the beginning and are building trust step by step. It has taken a lot of teamwork to be consistent, dependable, and especially honest with her at all times.

One of the first things we did was to find our daughter a safe place to talk about her cult experience. We searched for therapists who worked with children and had some knowledge of cults. After interviewing a few we selected one and started Ganga in therapy as soon as we got custody. She saw this therapist for two years and a school counselor for a year and a half concurrently. Her damaged sense of trust is slowly healing.

5. When we got custody, Ganga's emotional functioning was that of a younger child. She had not been allowed to develop a full range of emotions. She was especially not allowed to express negative emotions. We allowed her to express her feelings and tried to honor her pain. It took months before she let herself cry and feel her intense grief at losing her first family. The emotion she had the least experience with, however, was anger. We encouraged and allowed her to express anger in appropriate ways. Her younger brothers' fights showed her one way; we suggested others. She experimented and came up with journalkeeping as an effective outlet for years of repressed anger.

6. Ganga continues to struggle with loyalty issues—loyalty to her cult family and loyalty to her biological family. Four years after she joined us, she confided that her nightmare is to have to choose between the two. The best way we could find to help her bridge the two worlds was to occasionally let her see a few "safe" ex-members of the group. I vividly remember the day she was able to tell her best friend about her past. Fortunately her young friend was very healthy, and was curious and compassionate, not judgmental. Sharing the cult secret helped Ganga to unload a heavy burden and begin to integrate her two worlds.

7. There were gaps in her cognitive development. At first we thought she had a reading disability, but just spending time reading with her brought her up to her grade level within two years. She has probably stayed in the concrete operations level of cognitive development a year or two longer than "normal" children, but now seems to be moving ahead conceptually with her peers.

8. Ganga's social development was also a year or two behind her peers when we brought her home. In the beginning she looked like a teenager and acted like a toddler. Eventually she learned appropriate behavior from experience, gentle coaching, and most especially natural consequences. When other children threatened to beat her up because she loud-mouthed them on the bus, we stayed out of it; and when she forgot to hand in a critical paper at school, she suffered the consequences of a lower grade. It has been important, because she was so protected, to let her learn how the real world works. How else will she learn to deal with it?

9. Her self-esteem was very low. This is typical of most cult members, and growing up in such an environment is devastating for children. One psychologist who evaluated Ganga said, "She seems to have been persuaded that she must try harder to be good in a way that ignores her own basic needs of nurturance." We have helped her rebuild her self-esteem by creating an atmosphere of safety and trust. It is also nonjudgmental, cherishing, empathetic, and supportive of her feelings. We have belief in her, respect for her, and the expectation of success. My daughter's disconnection from and dislike for herself will take years to change, but we are on the way to wholeness. Today she is more self-reliant than most of her peers; she has lots of friends and is doing well in school.

10. In a gradual, informal way we have educated her about mind control and the dynamics of influence. We have shown her articles about other cults, discussing how this related to the Ranch (the cult's ashram). Sometimes we were too direct, and she would get defensive. Because she was the guru's "daughter," however, she saw a lot of what

went on behind the scenes in these groups and, in some ways, understood more clearly than many adults.

Two areas that we haven't explored but which might be effective are dreamwork and support groups. Our daughter seems to process her cult experience in cycles or waves. The peak of the wave is the anxious and pensive time when she tends to have vivid dreams about the Ranch. Working with a reputable therapist in interpreting these dreams might be very helpful. Ganga has also requested a support group of other children who have been in cults, but we have been unable to locate other children in our area.(16)

Margaret Singer and others, in addressing the needs of those born and raised in cults, stress the need for the following:

1. Immediate medical and dental examinations with appropriate vaccinations against childhood diseases.

2. Instant instruction to show that some of the attitudes and behaviors learned in the cult do not go over well in the outside world.

3. Exposure to educational and social experiences that will help the youngsters relate and adapt to the larger society, including its value systems.

4. Training in conflict-resolution techniques to learn how to mediate differences and to learn the art of compromise.

In addition, there are some specific concerns:

5. Children who identified with the cult leader may need therapy with behavioral management.

6. Children may need help with trust and safety issues.

7. Teenagers especially tend to rebel once out of the cult and are at high risk for acting-out behaviors and substance abuse.

8. Parents may need help in reestablishing their own leadership roles within the family structure.

9. Parents are advised to take an active role in working within the school system and in discussing the role of the cult in their child's life with teachers and administrators.(17)

Identity issues for cult children reentering society

Identity is a mental construct that provides a framework for relating to the world. In a cult, identity is rigidly molded, with little room for originality, spontaneity, or differences. The boundaries between self and others are poorly delineated, and one's primary identity is that of group member. This may provide a sense of inner stability and security, but at the cost of individuality and freedom. (Identity issues are covered more fully in Chapter 9.)

A person born and raised in a cult who leaves it as an adult may have different problems from the person who left the cult in early childhood or who was recruited later in life. The former's whole identity is attached to membership in the group. They have no precult identity to counterpoint the cult experience, no multifaceted personality as is taken for granted in the general population.

For good or ill, children growing up in a noncult society have a number of influences on which they can draw to incorporate desired traits into their own sense of identity. Cultural heroes and villains play a role in the child's inner world. Beliefs and values come from the family, the educational system, and the larger society. A variety of individuals model different behaviors and beliefs throughout a child's formative years.

In a cult, on the other hand, indoctrination into the group's worldview, beliefs, and values gives no options about who you are or what you believe. The outside world is monitored, interpreted, or denied, according to the cult's ideology. Major and minor life decisions about roles, relationships, worship, and the future are made by others, generally on the basis of what benefits the group or leader. Even so, children leaving a cult *can* develop a healthy identity, as Frances Lief's story in Part Three, "Human Are Free Beings," shows.

•

As new generations grow up and leave the cults in which they were raised, they will continue to impress us with the flexibility, strength, and regenerative capacity of the human spirit. We have a lot to learn from Ganga, Shippen, Jessica Kay, and Frances.

CHAPTER
TWENTY-THREE

THERAPEUTIC ISSUES

With cults moving into the mainstream and many cult members living and working in the larger society, psychological or emotional troubles resulting from a cult involvement may be more difficult to spot, even for professionals in the therapeutic community. Certain cult groups have even become fashionable. In television interviews and in the tabloids, movie stars and other celebrities offer testimonials to the benefits of membership.

At the same time, society in general has been influenced by certain trends. For example, meditation techniques are now taught in hospitals and clinics and featured in the media, and alternative medicine and health foods are capturing the attention and loyalties of a jaded population disenchanted with the conventions of modern medicine.

Not all meditation techniques, alternative medicines, and health food regimens are dangerous or cultic. However, many of today's cults utilize these socially acceptable routes as avenues to draw people into a cultic system. It is not surprising that many clinicians, who may have participated in New Age, transpersonal, or mass transformational therapies, fail to recognize in their clients the impact and aftereffects of a cultic involvement.

People rarely seek treatment because of current or past involvement with a cult. The most frequent presenting problems among former cult members are depression and relational difficulties. Often the person is unaware that there is any connection between previous cultic involvement and current life problems. This lack of awareness can easily be compounded if the person's therapist is unfamiliar with the role a cult experience can play in the production of psychological difficulties.

The mental health professional may discount the client's cult involvement by considering it to have been a voluntary choice. Like some parents of cult members, these may be apt to regard the cult involvement as a passing phase. The fact that so many people start and stop meditation or join and quit various church groups perhaps helps perpetuate this misconception. Rachel, the woman whose cultic relationship was described in Chapter 1, was fortunate that her therapist immediately recognized the nature of her involvement with Fred. Because of this, the therapist could evaluate the relationship appropriately and help Rachel withstand Fred's pleas for her to return to him.

In his work with former cult members, Moishe Spero has observed that "intensive psychotherapy is suitable if not mandatory for successful deregression from cultic commitment, for the return of adaptive cognitive and emotional functioning, and to dispose the ex-devotee to more healthy reintegration into normal living . . . . Diagnostic psychological testing objectively reveals significant forms of regression in numerous ego functions and cognitive processes as a consequence of cultic commitment and also reveals the dramatic reversal during and following psychotherapy of many of the indices of this regression."(1)

In this chapter we hope to clarify treatment issues, assessment, and the potential for therapeutic errors when working with clients with a cult experience, as well as to identify common postcult psychiatric disorders. The concluding section lists resources available to mental health professionals and others with an interest in postcult therapy. (See also Appendix B.)

The following case report exemplifies typical difficulties encountered in the treatment of a cult member who seeks therapy for "non-cult" problems. We will follow "Jessie" through her course of treatment after she leaves the cult in order to explore some of the therapeutic dilemmas that arise.

Jessie: A Case Study

Jessie had no history of emotional problems prior to her involvement with a charismatic entrepreneur and his cultic enterprises. Yet by the time she entered therapy, Jessie had become angry, remote, and distrustful. An attractive, intelligent woman in her forties, she briefly related the following account of her previous therapies, asking, with a considerable degree of skepticism, if her new therapist could possibly help her.

When Jessie was in her late twenties, already married 10 years, she had a good job in sales and management and put her considerable talents and energy into her marriage, home, and career. Then she met "Jerry," a marketing representative from a competing agency. Over lunch during a business convention they discovered common interests in psychology and the New Age. The lunch led to a friendship, a business partnership, and eventually a love affair.

Because of Jessie's business reputation and talents, Jessie and Jerry were able to open a marketing and advertising firm. They combined financial resources—mostly Jessie's and her husband's—and Jerry's flair for bringing together other people's assets and hopes. Jerry conducted marketing seminars, mixing the latest pop psychology with a smattering of Eastern mysticism and the enthusiasm of a preacher at a church revival meeting. He developed a growing organization of true believers in his methods and business schemes. In the beginning everyone appeared set to prosper.

But the promised fruits failed to appear. "Tom," Jessie's husband, became disenchanted with Jerry, which led to frequent quarrels with Jessie. Their differences finally resulted in divorce. Shortly afterward Jessie entered the first of several therapies for treatment of depression and help in managing her intensifying and often-displaced anger. She was very careful to censor what she said to her therapist about Jerry, afraid of being confronted with questions she dared not answer. Whenever the therapist probed too deeply, Jessie would begin to miss appointments, finally terminating after nine months with the excuse that her insurance had run out.

The second attempt at therapy, initiated for the same reasons, was equally short-lived although somewhat more successful. This time the therapist was able to point out to Jessie her considerable strengths and abilities, which she had wrongly been attributing to Jerry. Her normal self-esteem and self-confidence, severely diminished by Jerry's constant belittlement, were becoming strengthened, and she could take a more objective look at Jerry. This would be very helpful to her in coming years. Again, however, she resisted telling all and continued to protect herself from painful truths, wishing to go on believing in the person for whom she had sacrificed her marriage and several years of her life. Therapy ended with the scheduled retirement of her therapist.

The third attempt at treatment, begun eight years after meeting Jerry, was more successful, at least in the beginning. By this time, the pain of loving a man unwilling to and incapable of responding to her needs produced a stronger desire for resolution, though she was still plagued with ambivalent feelings about him.

The relationship came to a sudden end with news of Jerry's arrest for securities fraud. Although she was appalled at the news, Jessie was not surprised and felt a tremendous surge of relief. This event enabled Jessie finally to sever the relationship. Nine years of depression suddenly lifted. Returning to therapy that week, she told her therapist the truth about Jerry. She spoke of the small group of followers who obeyed him like a god. She described the marathon seminars where he used guided imagery and induced altered states to encourage his devotees to "get in touch with their fears and hang-ups and blockages to success." She revealed Jerry's sudden rages and sadistic baiting of group members to enhance job performance and increase sales, all to his benefit.

Jessie was now willing to look at the possibility that she had been taken in by a charismatic con man. She needed to know how he was able to take command of her life so suddenly and turn it around so drastically. The therapist, however, kept the focus on Jessie. He would halt her inquiries about the role Jerry played. He refused to discuss the voluminous literature she brought in about cults and mind control. Jessie ended therapy abruptly after two years, devastated when her therapist told her she was a "willing victim."

Several months later Jessie filed suit against Jerry in an attempt to sever lingering business ties and recoup some of her financial losses. In retaliation, Jerry threatened her. Fearful of him and at the same time enraged at the tremendous losses she had incurred, she found it difficult to contain her anger, displacing it onto friends and family. She had nightmares of Jerry taking over her life and became obsessed with incidents in the cult. Her life was marked by hypervigilance and fear of being followed and watched by Jerry. These unsettling feelings brought Jessie back into therapy.

This time she prudently interviewed several highly recommended therapists. The first asked her three times in the interview session whether she was molested in childhood. The second attempted to hypnotize her in the first session, repeatedly telling her how suggestible she was, then telling her she was safe now that she had entered his gates. The third—Dr. T.—agreed to help her identify the mind-control techniques employed by Jerry, and Jessie entered treatment again.

Dr. T. was well-known in the area for his skill with hypnosis and dissociative disorders. Jessie made it clear that she viewed herself as a partner in this therapy and saw the therapist as more of an ally. She was determined not to become dependent on the therapist and to retain as much control over the therapy session as she could. Throughout Jessie's brief therapy with Dr. T., hypnosis was used regularly: first to explore the cult, then to delve into childhood issues. At that point Jessie lost any control she thought she had over the therapy. Dr. T. stated firmly that there had to be some childhood trauma that would account for Jessie's vulnerability to Jerry. After four months of twice-weekly hypnotic regressions, episodes of depersonalization and derealization were occurring in between sessions. Jessie began to doubt all her perceptions about herself and all that she knew about her past. Her condition deteriorated rapidly and exacerbated a suspicion that she must have multiple personalities in order to have blocked such profound childhood trauma.

Jessie began to have trouble with concentration. She would frequently leave her job, unable to perform even routine tasks. She finally quit therapy with Dr. T. after he refused to look any further at events that had occurred during her years with Jerry. She felt much worse now than when she had started with him. She sought out and received an evaluation for dissociative disorders from a known expert on multiple personality who ruled out multiple personality disorder (MPD). Finally, Jessie began working with a competent therapist who slowly went through the layers of trauma starting with the most recent—her therapy with Dr. T.—until all issues of cultic and possible family abuse were resolved and Jessie was asymptomatic.

Therapeutic Errors

One common error made by Jessie's clinicians was to overlook the cultic experience and focus on early life experiences to explain the origin of presenting difficulties. By ignoring the influence of the group or leader and the use of sophisticated techniques of influence and persuasion, the clinicians missed the "therapeutic boat." By seeking explanations from childhood for current symptomatology, the therapist risked (1) ignoring or making light of the trauma of cultic involvement, (2) seriously confusing preexisting emotional disorders (if present at all) with current emotional difficulties, (3) considerably prolonging therapy, and (4) "blaming the victim" and potentially retraumatizing the client.

A second and more serious error was the misuse of hypnosis to "search" for prior vulnerabilities in childhood. This fishing expedition led to a deepening of already-expanded hypnotic capabilities, the iatrogenic production of a dissociative disorder, and a belief in nonexistent prior childhood sexual abuse. Some cult members certainly may have histories of childhood sexual abuse. It is inappropriate, however, to seek past abuse prior to a satisfactory resolution of the various cultic issues being presented. An intense hypnotic search for specific, previously unsuspected childhood abuse is likely to increase the possibility of induced, confabulated "memories," not to mention a growing dependence on the therapist. Unfortunately, this particular problem is being noted with increasing frequency at conferences and workshops attended by ex-members who report therapeutic difficulties following their cult experiences.

Jessie's first three therapists saw her while she was still involved with Jerry. She protected him by masking her presentation and withholding vital information about the abusiveness of the relationship and her belief in his superhuman capacities. This behavior of selective presentation is a protective necessity for someone still in a cult and is an aspect that is frequently misinterpreted, undervalued, or overlooked entirely.

Treatment of an Active Cult Member

For those still involved in a cultic system, therapy must move slowly. All three of Jessie's therapists acknowledged afterward that (1) they were aware that there was more to the relationship than Jessie was admitting, (2) they were afraid she would bolt out of therapy if they pushed too hard, and (3) they suspected, in spite of how little Jessie admitted, that Jerry had a severe character disorder, perhaps psychopathy.

Keeping an active cult member in therapy is a challenge. While the client may be presenting for other, ego-dystonic problems, the therapist must do the following:

- Work slowly to establish rapport and trust.

- Continually support and enhance ego strengths and other healthy aspects of the client's personality.

- Maintain good reality checking for the client.

- Gently confront cognitive distortions, which are perceived as reality by the client.

- Be prepared to examine countertransference with a peer or supervisor, as these clients sometimes evoke strong feelings of powerlessness, impatience, boredom, and anger.

- Look for opportunities to present another viewpoint, perhaps by means of an exit counseling.

Working with current cult members is similar to working with battered women. In reference to women in abusive relationships, psychologists Teresa Ramirez Boulette and Susan Andersen state, "One major challenge is that treatment for either partner is likely to remain unsuccessful while the couple remain together, yet their separation is, perhaps, the most difficult change to effect."(2) The same could be said for those who enter therapy while still involved in a cult. The cult involvement may be seen by the individual as ego-syntonic, appearing totally unconnected to presenting symptoms of depression, relational difficulties, and dissociative disorders.

A Framework for Ex-Member Therapy

Lorna Goldberg, a clinician who has worked with former cult members for more than 15 years, points out that not everyone recruited by a cultic group necessarily lives in a rigid thought-reform environment. "Conversely," she writes, "some individuals are involved in very controlling relationships that might not appear to be cults. It has become clear to me that what is important in terms of therapeutic intervention is not whether a person has left a group that fits within the definitional boundaries of a cult, but whether that individual reacted to involvement in that group in a particular way.... Ex-cultists need to know that their reactions usually are related to cultic suggestions, practices, and manipulations, and to their actual separation from the cult."(3)

Treatment of a former cult member might involve the following:

- an educational program to provide understanding of mind control and the cult experience

- counseling for adjustment difficulties in relationships, careers, and so on

- treatment of post-traumatic sequelae

- treatment of preexisting psychological and emotional difficulties

- medication for symptomatic relief of anxiety and depression, if necessary

The ability to see through the deceptive recruitment practices, understand the use of thought reform and manipulation, and dispel the magical thinking of the group is an important prerequisite to effective therapy. A client's capacity for this can sometimes be activated through an exit counseling session, either in an organized workshop with other ex-members or in private consultation with an exit counselor. Even if the therapist is very familiar with the cult in question, it may be less expensive, easier, and faster for the client to participate in an exit counseling session or use the in-house services of a rehabilitation center. (This will be clarified in the following case of "Christina.")

In therapy the clinician may find it helpful to explore with the ex-member the series of questions found at the end of Chapters 4 and 5. If the client is able to answer these questions, it indicates an understanding and acceptance of the cult experience. Even so, the clinician is in an important position to "normalize" the ex-member's confusion, emotional sequelae, identity issues, and cognitive distortions by helping the ex-member to consider these symptoms the result of a coordinated thought-reform program rather than an indication of psychopathology. Since former cult members are particularly vulnerable to authority figures, the clinician's stance can either enhance recovery or, by pathologizing the symptoms, increase the ex-member's discomfort and possibly produce iatrogenic damage, as happened to Jessie.

The clinician can be particularly helpful in assisting the ex-member to explore objectively his or her particular vulnerabilities, which may have existed prior to recruitment, as well as the recruitment tactics that exploited these vulnerabilities. This will help reduce guilt and shame while promoting insight and self-acceptance.

Major adjustment issues for the client, which the therapist can help the ex-member work through, include the following:

- emotional volatility

- dissociative symptoms

- depression

- loneliness

- guilt

- indecisiveness

- difficulty communicating

- fear of retribution (spiritual or physical)

- spiritual, philosophical, or ideological void

- conflicts with family(4)

The therapist must take an active stance in the therapeutic process. The client's normal thoughts and feelings have been reinterpreted and/or suppressed by the group or relationship, perhaps for many years. The former cult member in therapy needs active feedback from the therapist to help unravel cult-instilled distortions and beliefs and their residuals. The clinician needs to support the client's ability to sort through the consequences of newfound freedom, test reality, and correct cognitive distortions (see Chapters 6, 7, and 8).

Former cult members are sometimes extraordinarily sensitive to nonverbal cues, such as body language, voice intonation, and silences, and are apt to be hypervigilant for any signs of anger or rejection by the therapist. Lorna Goldberg reminds us of three important considerations:

1. The former member may fear being manipulated and controlled by the therapist, which is understandable after a cultic experience and is not an example of paranoid thinking.

2. The former member in therapy should be a participating member in a team of equals, with boundaries clearly spelled out.

3. The therapist should clarify that she or he has human limitations, no magical powers, and can make mistakes.(5)

Some ex-member clients may have magical expectations that therapy should facilitate a rapid recovery and are sometimes impatient with the slowness of their progress. The anticipation of a "magic bullet," or immediately getting on with their life, is unrealistic, especially if they experienced intense and long-term psychological abuse. At the same time, therapists should guard against prolonging therapy longer than necessary.

Postcult Emotional and Psychiatric Disorders

No one enters a cult expecting to become a psychiatric patient. Yet, as one significant study of 308 former members from 101 cults shows, symptoms of postcult psychological disorder are common. Here are the results of psychologist Michael Langone's survey:

83 percent felt anxiety/fear/worry.

76 percent were angry toward the group leader.

72 percent had low self-confidence.

71 percent had vivid flashbacks of the group experience.

70 percent received counseling after leaving.

67 percent reported depression.

67 percent had difficulty concentrating.

61 percent felt despair/hopelessness/helplessness.

56 percent felt guilty about what they did in the group.

55 percent experienced floating among very different states of mind.

51 percent felt as though they lived in an unreal world.

46 percent had conflicts with loved ones.

44 percent reported that the experience was very harmful.

42 percent reported that the group experience was very unsatisfying.

38 percent feared physical harm by the group.

34 percent experienced severe anxiety attacks after leaving.

11 percent were sexually abused in the group.(6)

Unfortunately, ex-members are occasionally misdiagnosed with having a psychotic disorder and may be heavily medicated due to behaviors related to their cult beliefs and practices, including lapsing into intense dissociative states. In fact, these persons are not hallucinating in the strict medical sense but are responding in ways they have learned in order to accommodate excessive meditative or trancelike states. In some cults it is expected that the initiate will have visions of the guru or demigods, see "heavenly sights," or hear "heavenly music," all of which is considered an indication of progress on the "path." Thus, a patient who is behaving in such a way is responding to training, not displaying a mental illness.

A number of clinicians have discussed cult-induced psychopathology, particularly dissociative, posttraumatic stress, and relational disorders.(7) In a special issue of *Psychiatric Annals* devoted solely to the cult phenomenon, Margaret Singer and Richard Ofshe note that there is a predictive quality to the type of psychiatric disorder found in ex-members of particular groups. Most commonly, Singer and Ofshe observed varying degrees of anomie among ex-members. Because of culture shock, anxiety, alienation, and disenchantment with both the cult and the larger society, they required a period of time to adjust and reevaluate goals, values, and identity. Singer and Ofshe also observed the following induced psychopathologies:

- reactive schizoaffective-like psychoses in individuals with no prior history of mental disorder, which on average lasted from one to five months

- posttraumatic stress disorders

- atypical dissociative disorders

- relaxation-induced anxiety

- miscellaneous reactions including anxiety combined with cognitive inefficiencies, self-mutilation, phobias, suicide and homicide, and a variety of physical ailments of psychogenic origin such as myocardial infarctions, strokes, asthma, peptic ulcers, and unexpected deaths(8)

Singer and Ofshe also point out that participation in a certain type of group will often precipitate aftereffects specific to that involvement. They write: "The techniques used to induce belief, change, and dependency by various thought-reform programs appear to be related to the type of psychiatric casualty the program tends to produce. Large-group awareness training programs appear more likely to induce mood and affect disorders. Groups that use prolonged mantra and empty-mind meditation, hyperventilation, and chanting appear more likely to have participants who develop relaxation-induced anxiety, panic disorder, marked dissociative problems, and cognitive inefficiencies .... Therapeutic community thought-reform programs appear more likely to induce enduring fears, self-mutilation, self-abasement, and inappropriate display of artificial assertiveness and emotionality."(9)

The following case study highlights some of the postcult dilemmas and disorders discussed here. "Christina" was in an Eastern cult for five years. Within a 12-month period she was subjected to an overwhelming array of diagnoses: bipolar disorder mixed with psychotic features, acute psychotic episode, depersonalization disorder, panic disorder, and temporal lobe epilepsy. Her case, however, is a good example of combining a treatment program with an exit counseling, using a team approach for diagnosis and therapy.

Christina: A Case Study

Christina was seeing a neuropsychiatrist weekly for the treatment of a possible Temporal Lobe Epilepsy (TLE). Though neurological testing (EEGs and an MRI) failed to show signs of this disorder, she was being medicated with Tofranil, Klonopin, and Depracote for control of a depersonalization disorder and anxiety states presumed to be caused by TLE. Christina was first diagnosed with TLE after hospitalization for an acute psychotic episode following five years of a strict regimen of up to four or more hours a day of meditation. Her meditation practice included the continual, silent repetition of her mantra, which produced a persistent dissociated state. The year prior to admission to the hospital she had spent six weeks at the group's ashram in India. After returning to the United States, Christina worked for a brief period, got fired from her job, and then spent several weeks wandering in California with people she had met in India.

Christina found it difficult to function, panicked easily, and then decompensated, whereupon she was hospitalized. When brought into the emergency room by her family, she stated that she felt disconnected from reality and was quite fearful. In the hospital an initial diagnosis of bipolar disorder was made, and she was treated with Lithium and Haldol. Upon discharge one month later there was no evidence of a bipolar or thought disorder and the medications were discontinued. TLE was suspected as causative of the dissociative states and anxiety attacks, and she was put on Tofranil, Klonopin, and Depracote. Later the Depracote was discontinued and replaced with Tegritol in an effort to control depersonalization. Up to now, her therapists made no connection between the dissociative states and her meditation.

Christina found and was able to keep a demanding and stimulating job in her field. She still had disturbing episodes of depersonalization and derealization, sometimes accompanied with or followed by anxiety attacks. Under the strict guidance of the cult, she watched her thoughts, feelings, and behaviors throughout the day. She felt a need to be perfect, adhere to a strict vegetarian diet, do four to five hours of meditation daily, and meet weekly with fellow members of the group. She never regarded herself as good enough. She felt numbed and her affect was flat and restricted.

Christina's family began to explore the possibility of an exit counseling as it had become increasingly difficult for her to deal with her moodiness, withdrawal, and the unrealistic expectations put on her by herself, her family, and her work. Her "spaciness," especially after meditating, worried her family considerably and was the basis for their seeking assistance from exit counselors. Her depersonalization disorder was causing distress and interfering with job functioning. In addition, Christina was convinced she did not have TLE and was subsequently not adhering to her medication regime.

The exit counselors supplied the family and the psychiatrist with information on relaxation-induced anxiety(10) and maintained active communication with the family before, during, and after the intervention. The psychiatrist proposed that he be the one to suggest to Christina that she have an evaluation from someone with expertise on meditation, altered states, and dissociation as a way of easing the tension between Christina and her family and allowing Christina to approach it as an adjunct to therapy, which it was. The exit counseling team's approach would be to use their usual educational model of information and dialogue, and add to the team a psychotherapist with expertise in both thought-reform techniques and dissociative disorders.(11)

Christina was eager to cooperate since her dissociative symptoms and anxiety were causing her severe distress. She was highly motivated to improve, though she had considerable difficulty controlling her dissociative states. The exit counseling went smoothly. Since one member of the team was a licensed psychotherapist, an evaluation of dissociative states was done using the Dissociative Experiences Scale (DES) and the Structured Clinical Interview for DSM-III-R Dissociative Disorders (SCID-D).(12) Christina's high scores on both were almost totally confined to the areas of depersonalization and derealization, with some short-term memory loss consistent with her dissociative states. She scored low for amnesia, identity confusion, and identity alteration. In this way, more pervasive and perhaps more serious dissociative disorders were tentatively ruled out.

By discussing dissociation with Christina, the team was able to also discuss altered states observed as a result of the abuse of meditation and hypnosis. At the end of three days of counseling, gently paced to meet her needs, Christina admitted to almost constant waking use of her mantras and was able to see the connections between her dissociative states and her meditating. Additional material was given to her regarding the history and current practices of her group and guru, which helped her to evaluate the group objectively and sever her ties to the cult.

Christina was encouraged to continue taking her medication and seeing her psychiatrist, as it would take time to determine if meditation alone was causing her depersonalization disorder and anxiety attacks. After the intervention Christina began counseling with someone familiar with cults and mind control and attended a local FOCUS support group. Family therapy was also strongly recommended. Continued testing with another neurologist confirmed that she did not have TLE and, slowly, under her doctor's supervision, she began to go off some of her medications.

Christina still had far to go in her recovery from her cult experience. She experienced floating episodes for several weeks, sometimes associated with severe anxiety. Episodes of depersonalization and derealization, however, were diminishing in frequency and duration. She continued to need help with her perfectionism, modulation of feeling states, and realistic planning for the future, such as moving out of her parents' home, new directions in her career, and coming to terms with her changing values and beliefs. Most of all she needed reassurance that what she was going through was normal for a person with her degree of cult experience, and that with patience she would pass through this difficult stage.

Christina's case illustrates the confusion in diagnosis that is likely to occur when the cult involvement is not taken into account. It also is a good example of the interplay of various agencies and resources in the recovery process once cult involvement is recognized as a considerable factor in the symptomatology.

Psychological Testing

There are many psychometric instruments that may prove helpful to the clinician working with cultists. In a study by Paul Martin and colleagues using the Millon Clinical Multiaxial Inventory (MCMI), the Beck Depression Inventory, the Hopkins Symptom Checklist, and clinical interviews of 111 clients at a rehabilitation facility, it was noted, not surprisingly, that former members exhibit considerable distress in the areas of anxiety, depression, and dissociation.(13) The DES and SCID-D have also proven useful in determining the degree and scope of dissociation, with SCID-D having the added ability of discerning specific dissociative disorders. It is heartening to note that treatment has shown demonstrable effectiveness in reducing postcult distress, as measured by pre- and posttreatment testing.

Hospitalization

There has been some study of the usefulness or necessity of psychiatric hospitalization in the treatment of former cult members. Some patients are self-referred while others are brought in by their families; yet others are dropped off at hospital emergency rooms when their symptoms become too severe for the cult to handle. As in Christina's case and as shown in other examples in previous chapters, decompensation may occur both during and after involvement in intensive thought-reform environments or programs.

Psychiatrist David Halperin writes, "If psychiatric intake workers are not sensitive to cult issues and do not bother to inquire about their patients' possible cultic involvements, they will not realize the extent to which a patient's presenting symptomatology may be related to powerful group pressures and their aftereffects. As a consequence, they will tend to overestimate and misunderstand the psychopathology and inappropriately treat the cult-involved individual. Sometimes such misdiagnosing can result in unnecessarily prolonged inpatient treatment."(14) Halperin suggests the following considerations in working with cultists who require hospitalization:

1. Careful assessment of the individual's preaffiliation status. Cult affiliation may precipitate a brief psychotic reaction. It may also be symptomatic of severe underlying pathology and chronic illness. Even in an otherwise intact individual the brief psychotic reaction may be surprisingly severe, with the patient manifesting agitated, suspicious, confused, and quasi-manic behavior. However, hospitalization, which places the individual in a structured and protected setting without further contact with members of the cultic group, is usually successful in terminating the brief psychotic reaction.

2. Treatment of an individual with a problematical preaffiliation history is often protracted and complex. Mood stabilizers, anxiolytic agents, and neuroleptics may be required.

3. Follow-up care in halfway houses and other supportive settings, in particular rehabilitation centers for former cultists, may be extremely helpful. In most cases follow-up care should include exit counseling, psychotherapy, family therapy, and pharmacotherapy.(15)

He also notes that it is sometimes appropriate to incorporate an exit counseling as part of inpatient treatment, with the exit counseling team also educating hospital staff about the realities and potential aftereffects of cult involvement.

Medication

There is a scarcity of data on the pharmacological treatment of ex-cult members as well as other victims of trauma.(16) Dr. John Clark points out the need for caution in the decision to prescribe medication since it is difficult at times to distinguish the ex-member's symptoms as a function of the thought-reform system versus true symptoms of psychiatric illness. Appropriate utilization of antidepressants and anxiolytic agents can be helpful in the acute stages of postcult recovery for some individuals. Some ex-members, especially those who have had no treatment following their exiting from the group, are tempted to self-medicate with alcohol and other substances. Distress levels can be extremely high, and short-term use of medication may be necessary while education, support, and counseling are instituted. Dr. Clark states that in his experience ex-members are more sensitive and responsive to medication and therefore should be monitored more closely.(17)

Complex Post-traumatic Stress Disorder

Judith Herman, along with other researchers and clinicians, proposes that people who have suffered prolonged, repeated trauma deserve recognition in an expanded category of the diagnosis of PTSD. Herman has given it a name: *complex post-traumatic stress disorder.* Because her understanding of the symptomatology encompasses so much of what has been experienced by former cult members, we include here the full diagnostic criteria as it is being considered for inclusion in the upcoming edition of the *Diagnostic and Statistical Manual of Mental Disorders* (DSM-IV).

1. A history of subjection to totalitarian control over a prolonged period (months to years). Examples include hostages, prisoners of war, concentration camp survivors, and survivors of some religious cults. [Authors' note: We would remove the word *religious* so as to include all systems of thought reform.] Examples also include those subjected to totalitarian systems in sexual and domestic life, including survivors of domestic battering, childhood physical or sexual abuse, and organized sexual exploitation.

2. Alterations in affect regulation, including

   - persistent dysphoria

   - chronic suicidal preoccupation

   - self-injury

   - explosive or extremely inhibited anger (may alternate)

   - compulsive or extremely inhibited sexuality (may alternate)

3. Alterations in consciousness, including

   - amnesia or hypermnesia for traumatic events

   - transient dissociative episodes

   - depersonalization/derealization

   - reliving experiences, either in the form of intrusive post-traumatic stress disorder symptoms or in the form of ruminative preoccupation

4. Alterations in self-perception, including

   - sense of helplessness or paralysis of initiative

- shame, guilt, and self-blame

- sense of defilement or stigma

- sense of complete difference from others (may include a sense of specialness, utter aloneness, belief no other person can understand, or nonhuman identity)

5. Alterations in perception of perpetrator, including

- preoccupation with relationship with perpetrator (includes preoccupation with revenge)

- unrealistic attribution of total power to perpetrator (caution: victim's assessment of power realities may be more realistic than clinician's)

- idealization or paradoxical gratitude

- sense of special or supernatural relationship

- acceptance of belief system or rationalizations of perpetrator

6. Alterations in relations with others, including

- isolation and withdrawal

- disruption in intimate relationships

- repeated search for rescuer (may alternate with isolation and withdrawal)

- persistent distrust

- repeated failures of self-protection

7. Alterations in systems of meaning

- loss of sustaining faith

- sense of hopelessness and despair(18)

We believe, along with Herman, that "naming the syndrome of complex post-traumatic stress disorder represents an essential step toward granting those who have endured prolonged exploitation a measure of the recognition they deserve. It is an attempt to find a language that is at once faithful to the traditions of accurate psychological observation and to the moral demands of traumatized people. It is an attempt to learn from survivors, who understand, more profoundly than any investigator, the effects of captivity."(19)

Resources for the Professional

With the growth of professional awareness of and increased research on cult phenomena, help is available for clinicians unfamiliar with treatment paradigms for victims of cultic thought-reform environments.

The American Family Foundation (AFF) has prepared information packets especially for the mental health professional. AFF also has an extensive bibliography and, through its catalogue, sells related books and periodicals including the *Cultic Studies Journal* and the *Cult Observer*. Information prepared for clergy, educators, and lawyers is also available.

A highly recommend book for the clinician is *Recovery From Cults: Help for Victims of Psychological and Spiritual Abuse,* edited by Michael D. Langone, executive director of the AFF. Published by W. W. Norton in 1993, this volume is a compendium of the latest research in the field of cult recovery and treatment issues.

AFF maintains a listing of mental health professionals, clergy, educators, exit counselors, and lawyers who are knowledgeable about cult issues and available as resources. It may be helpful for those who are new to treating clients who have had a cult experience to have the assistance of more experienced clinicians for supervision or consultation. Through AFF's standing committees, resources and information are available on, victim assistance, exit counseling, legal issues, group work, and psychotherapy.

Further resources and suggested reading can be found in the appendices at the end of this book.

Working with current or former members of a thought-reform environment can be challenging and thought provoking for the clinician. It provides a window into the study of victimization that, once opened, is hard to close. For those clinicians who are already involved in working with survivors of other types of emotional, physical, and sexual abuse, cult survivors will offer yet another disturbing example of how inhuman our species can be to its own kind. Fortunately, with the proper education and counseling, most former cult members recover and are able to lead productive, creative, and useful lives.

APPENDIX
A

CHECKLIST OF CULT CHARACTERISTICS*

Deception lies at the core of mind-manipulating cultic groups and programs. Many members and supporters of cults are not fully aware of the extent to which they have been abused and exploited. The following list of characteristics helps to define such groups. Comparing the descriptions on this checklist to aspects of the group with which you or a family member or loved one is involved may help you determine if this involvement is cause for concern. If you check any of these items as characteristic of the group, and particularly if you check most of them, you should reexamine the group and its relationship to you.

☐ The group is focused on a living leader to whom members seem to display excessively zealous, unquestioning commitment.

☐ The group is preoccupied with bringing in new members.

☐ The group is preoccupied with making money.

☐ Questioning, doubt, and dissent are discouraged or even punished.

☐ Mind-numbing techniques (such as meditation, chanting, speaking in tongues, denunciation sessions, debilitating work routines) are used to suppress doubts about the group and its leader(s).

☐ The leadership dictates—sometimes in great detail—how members should think, act, and feel (for example: members must get permission from leaders to date, change jobs, get married; leaders may prescribe what types of clothes to wear, where to live, how to discipline children, and so forth).

---

* This checklist was compiled by Dr. Michael Langone, executive director of the American Family Foundation, and is reprinted with permission.

☐ The group is elitist, claiming a special, exalted status for itself, its leader(s) and members (for example: the leader is considered the Messiah or an avatar; the group and/or the leader has a special mission to save humanity).

☐ The group has a polarized us-versus-them mentality, which causes conflict with the wider society.

☐ The group's leader is not accountable to any authorities (as are, for example, military commanders and ministers, priests, monks, and rabbis of mainstream denominations). The group teaches or implies that its supposedly exalted ends justify means that members would have considered unethical before joining the group (for example: collecting money for bogus charities).

☐ The leadership induces feelings of guilt in members in order to control them.

☐ Members' subservience to the group causes them to cut ties with family, friends, and personal group goals and activities that were of interest before joining the group.

☐ Members are expected to devote inordinate amounts of time to the group.

☐ Members are encouraged or required to live and/or socialize only with other group members.

APPENDIX
B

RESOURCE ORGANIZATIONS

The following resources may be of assistance with cult-related concerns or questions. We encourage people seeking help to explore a variety of points of view before making any decisions, drawing conclusions, or contracting for services. Do not be intimidated by professional or religious credentials. Cult-related problems can be complex and very personal. Thoroughness, perseverance, and caution are vital.

Organizations

American Family Foundation (AFF)
Director: Michael D. Langone
P.O. Box 2265
Bonita Springs FL 33959
(212) 249-7693

Christian Research Institute
P.O. Box 500
San Juan Capistrano CA 92693
(714) 855-9926

Commission on Cults & Missionaries
Jewish Federation Council of
Greater Los Angeles
Director: Rachel Andres
6505 Wilshire Blvd., Suite 802
Los Angeles CA 90048
(213) 852-1234, ext. 2813

Cult Awareness Network (CAN)
Director: Cynthia Kisser
2421 W. Pratt Blvd., Suite 1173
Chicago IL 60645
(312) 267-7777

FOCUS (Former cult members support network)
c/o CAN
2421 W. Pratt Blvd., Suite 1173
Chicago IL 60645
(312) 267-7777

Interfaith Coalition of Concern About Cults
711 Third Avenue, 12th Floor
New York NY 10017
(212) 983-4800

International Cult Education Program (ICEP)
Director: Marcia R. Rudin
P.O. Box 1232, Gracie Station
New York NY 10028
(212) 439-1550

Spiritual Counterfeits Project
Christian Research Organization
P.O. Box 4308
Berkeley CA 94704
(510) 540-0300

Task Force on Cults and Missionaries
Greater Miami Jewish Federation
4200 Biscayne Blvd.
Miami FL 33137
(305) 576-4000

Watchman Fellowship
P.O. Box 7681
Columbus GA 31908
(404) 576-4321

Counseling Services

In addition to the following, the AFF (listed above) has a list of mental health professionals around the country with cult-related expertise.

Cult Clinic & Hot Line
Jewish Board of Family and Children's Services
120 W. 57th Street
New York NY 10019
(212) 632-4640

Cult Clinic
Jewish Family Service
6505 Wilshire Blvd., 6th Floor
Los Angeles CA 90048
(213) 852-1234

Wellspring Retreat & Resource Center
Director: Paul R. Martin
P.O. Box 67
Albany OH 45710
(614) 698-6277

International Organizations

Concerned Christian Growth Ministries
Box 6
North Perth
Western Australia 6006
(61) 63-444-6183

Gesamtosterreichische Elterninitiative
Obere Augartenstrasse
A-1020 Wien
Austria

ADFI
Hertogenweg 8
1980 Tervuen
Belgium
(32) 27-675-421

Instituto Cristao de Pesquisas
Caixa Postal 5011
Agencia Central
01051 Sao Paolo
SP Brazil
(55) 11-256-4801

Info-Cult
5655 Park Avenue, 305
Montreal H2V 4H2
Canada
(514) 274-2333

The Dialog Center
Katrinebjergve 46
DK-8200 Aarhus N
Denmark
(45) 6-10-54-11

ADFI (Association pour la defense
de la famille et de l'individu)
10 rue du Pere Julien Dhuit
75020 Paris
France
(33) 47-97-96-08

EHSARE
P.O. Box 874
D-8000 Munchen 1
Germany

Pan-Hellenic Parents Union for the
Protection of the Family and the
Individual
14 Ioannou Gennadiou St.
Athens 11521
Greece

Concerned Parents
Box 1806
Haifa 31018
Israel
(972) 4-71-85-22

GRIS (Gruppo di Ricerca e di In-
formazione sulle Sette)
Via del Monte 5
40126 Bologna
Italy
(39) 51-26-00-11

Pascal Zivi
003 Sapporo shi, shiro ishi ku,
nango dori, 2 chome
minami 4 no 27
Orange House
Hokkaido
Japan
(81) 11-861-9338

S.O.S.
255G Graafsweg
5213 AJ S'Hertogenbosch
Netherlands
(31) 83-602-8773

Asociacion Pro Juventud, A.I.S.
(Asesoramiento e Informacion sobre
Sectas)
Aribau, 226
08006 Barcelona
Spain
(34) 32-014-886

Foreningen Radda Individen
Langholmsgatan 17
11733 Stockholm
Sweden
(46) 08-70-90-077

SADK (Schweizerische Arbeitsgeme-
inschaft gegen Destruktive Kulte)
Postfach 18
8156 Oberhasli
Switzerland
(41) 71-75-61-07

F.A.I.R. (Family Information and
Rescue)
BCM Box 3535, P.O. Box 12
London WC1N 3XX
United Kingdom
(44) 1-539-3940

Special Interest

False Memory Syndrome Foundation
3401 Market St., Suite 130
Philadelphia PA 19104
(215) 387-1865

Incest Survivors Resource Network,
Inc.
15 Rutherford Place
New York NY
(513) 935-3031

International Society for the Study
of Multiple Personality Disorder
5700 Old Orchard Rd., 1st Floor
Skokie IL 60077
(708) 966-4322

P.A.C.T. (People Against Cultic
Therapies)
P.O. Box 4011, Grand Central
Station
New York NY 10160
(212) 316-1560

The Sidran Foundation
(advocacy, education, and research
of catastrophe-induced trauma)
211 Southway
Baltimore MD 21218

STOP Abuse by Counselors
P.O. Box 68292
Seattle WA 98168

(206) 243-2723

SurvivorShip
(for survivors of ritual abuse, torture, and mind control)
3181 Mission St., #139
San Francisco CA 94110
(707) 279-1209

Task Force on Ritual Abuse
Los Angeles County Commission
for Women
383 Hall of Administration
500 W. Temple St.
Los Angeles CA 90012
(213) 974-1455

The Vineyard
(for satanic ritual abuse survivors)
P.O. Box 3475
Tega Cay SC 29715

Voices in Action
(information, referrals, and resources
for survivors and advocates)
P.O. Box 148309
Chicago IL 60614
(312) 327-1500

APPENDIX C

RECOMMENDED READING LIST

This is a partial listing of some of the most important books, articles, and publications related to cults, thought reform, and related topics. For further reading suggestions review the notes in this and related titles. For a complete bibliography contact the American Family Foundation, which also makes available back issues of the *Cultic Studies Journal,* selected reprints of articles, and information packets on specific groups and types of groups.

General

Andres, Rachel, and James Lane, eds. *Cults and Consequences.* Los Angeles: Commission on Cults and Missionaries, 1988.

Appel, Willa. *Cults in America: Programmed for Paradise.* New York: Holt, Rinehart & Winston, 1983.

Cialdini, Robert B. *Influence: The New Psychology of Modern Persuasion.* New York: Quill, 1984.

Conway, Flo, and Jim Siegelman. *Snapping: America's Epidemic of Sudden Personality Change.* New York: Dell, 1979.

Eisenberg, Gary D., ed. *Smashing the Idols: A Jewish Inquiry into the Cult Phenomenon.* Northvale, NJ: Jason Aronson, 1988.

Festinger, Leon, Henry W. Riecken, and Stanley Schachter. *When Prophecy Fails: A Social and Psychological Study of a Modern Group That Predicted the Destruction of the World.* New York: Harper & Row, 1964.

Ford, Wendy. *Recovery from Abusive Groups.* Bonita Springs, FL: American Family Foundation, 1993.

Giambalvo, Carol. *Exit Counseling: A Family Intervention.* Bonita Springs, FL: American Family Foundation, 1992.

Halperin, David, ed. *Psychodynamic Perspectives on Religion, Sect and Cult.* Boston: John Wright, 1983.

Hassan, Steven. *Combatting Cult Mind Control.* Rochester, VT: Park Street Press, 1988.

Keiser, Thomas W., and Jacqueline L. Keiser. *The Anatomy of Illusion: Religious Cults and Destructive Persuasion.* Springfield, IL: Charles C. Thomas, 1987.

Langone, Michael D., ed. *Recovery from Cults: Help for Victims of Psychological Abuse.* New York: W. W. Norton, 1993.

LeBar, Rev. James J. *Cults, Sects and the New Age.* Huntington, IN: Our Sunday Visitor, 1989.

Lifton, Robert Jay. *Thought Reform and the Psychology of Totalism.* New York: W. W. Norton, 1961.

———, ed. *The Future of Immortality and Other Essays.* New York: Basic Books, 1987.

Ross, Joan C., and Michael D. Langone. *Cults: What Parents Should Know.* Secaucus, NJ: Lyle Stuart, 1989.

Rudin, James, and Marcia R. Rudin. *Prison or Paradise: The New Religious Cults.* Philadelphia: Fortress Press, 1980.

Rudin, Marcia R., ed. *Cults on Campus: Continuing Challenge.* Bonita Springs, FL: American Family Foundation, 1991.

Schein, E., I. Schneier, and C.H. Barker. *Coercive Persuasion: A Sociopsychological Analysis of the "Brainwashing" of American Civilian Prisoners by the Chinese Communists.* New York: W. W. Norton, 1961.

Stoner, Carroll, and Cynthia Kisser. *Touchstones: Reconnecting After a Cult Experience.* Chicago: Cult Awareness Network, 1992.

Zimbardo, Philip G., and Michael R. Lieppe. *The Psychology of Attitude Change and Social Influence.* New York: McGraw-Hill, 1991.

Articles and Pamphlets

Clark, Charles, C. "Cults in America." *The CQ Researcher* 3,17 (7 May 1993): 385–408. (Available from AFF)

Clark, John G., Jr. "Cults." *Journal of the American Medical Association* 242,2 (20 July 1979): 279–80.

Clark, John G., Jr., et al. *Destructive Cult Conversion: Theory, Research, and Treatment.* Weston, MA: American Family Foundation, 1981.

Langone, Michael D. "Assessment and Treatment of Cult Victims and Their Families." In *Innovations in Clinical Practice: A Sourcebook,* ed. P. A. Keller and S. R. Hegman. Sarasota, FL: Professional Resource and Exchange, 1991.

———. *Cults: Questions and Answers.* Weston, MA: American Family Foundation, 1988.

———. "Psychological Abuse." *Cultic Studies Journal* 9,2 (1992): 206–18. Miller, Jesse S. "The Utilization of Hypnotic Techniques in Religious Cult Conversion." *Cultic Studies Journal* 3,2 (1986): 243–50.

Ofshe, Richard, and Margaret T. Singer. "Attacks on Peripheral versus Central Elements of Self and the Impact of Thought Reforming Techniques." *Cultic Studies Journal* 3,1 (1986): 3–24.

Psychiatric Annals 20,4 (April 1990): 171–216. Special Issue on Cults. (Available from AFF).

Singer, Margaret Thaler. "Coming Out of the Cults." *Psychology Today,* January 1979, 72–82.

———. "Cults: Where Are They? Why Now?" *Forecast for Home Economics,* May/June 1979, 37.

———. "Group Psychodynamics." In *The Merck Manual of Diagnosis and Therapy,* ed. Robert Berkow. Rahway, NJ: Merck Sharp & Dohme Research Laboratories, 1987.

Singer, Margaret T., and Richard Ofshe. "Thought Reform Programs and the Production of Psychiatric Casualties." *Psychiatric Annals* 20,4 (April 1990): 188–193.

Singer, Margaret T., Maurice K. Temerlin, and Michael D. Langone. "Psychotherapy Cults." *Cultic Studies Journal* 7,2 (1990): 101–25.

West, Louis J. "Persuasive Techniques in Contemporary Cults: A Public Health Approach." *Cultic Studies Journal* 7,2 (1990): 126–49.

West, Louis J., and Margaret Thaler Singer. "Cults, Quacks, and Nonprofessional Therapies." In *Comprehensive Textbook of Psychiatry/III,* eds. Harold I. Kaplan, Alfred M. Freedman, and Benjamin J. Sadock. Baltimore: Williams & Wilkins, 1980.

Books on Related Topics

Cleckley, Hervey. *The Mask of Sanity.* New York: New American Library/Plume, 1982.

Figley, Charles R., ed. *Trauma and Its Wake: The Study of Post-Traumatic Stress Disorder.* New York: Brunner/Mazel, 1985.

Fromm, Erich. *Escape from Freedom.* New York: Avon Books, 1965.

Hare, Robert D. *Without Conscience: The Disturbing World of the Psychopaths Among Us.* New York: Pocket Books, 1993.

Herman, Judith Lewis. *Trauma and Recovery: The Aftermath of Violence—From Domestic Abuse to Political Terror.* New York: Basic Books, 1992.

Hoffer, Eric. *The True Believer.* New York: Harper and Row, 1951.

Kaminer, Wendy. *I'm Dysfunctional, You're Dysfunctional: The Recovery Movement and Other Self-Help Fashions.* New York: Vintage Books, 1993.

Kanter, Rosabeth Moss. *Commitment and Community: Communes and Utopias in Sociological Perspective.* Cambridge, MA: Harvard University Press, 1972.

Kasl, Charlotte Davis. *Women, Sex, and Addiction: A Search for Love and Power.* New York: Ticknor & Fields, 1989.

Kolk, Bessel van der. *Psychological Trauma.* Washington, DC: American Psychiatric Press, 1987.

Lessing, Doris. *Prisons We Choose to Live Inside*. New York: Harper & Row, 1987.

Lifton, Robert Jay. *The Broken Connection: On Death and the Continuity of Life*. New York: Basic Books, 1983.

Magid, Ken, and Carole A. McKelvey. *High Risk: Children Without a Conscience*. New York: Bantam Books, 1989.

Milgram, Stanley. *Obedience to Authority*. New York: Harper & Row, 1974.

Orwell, George. *Nineteen Eighty-four*. New York: New American Library, 1983.

Reid, William H. et al., eds. *Unmasking the Psychopath: Antisocial Personality and Related Syndromes*. New York: W. W. Norton, 1986.

Reich, Wilhelm. *The Mass Psychology of Fascism*. New York: Pocket Books, 1976.

Shapiro, Shanti, and George Dominiak, eds. *Sexual Trauma and Psychopathology*. New York: Lexington Books, 1992.

Shengold, Leonard. *Soul Murder: The Effects of Childhood Abuse and Deprivation*. New York: Fawcett Columbine, 1989.

Terr, Lenore. *Too Scared to Cry*. New York: Basic Books, 1990.

Weber, Max. *The Sociology of Religion*. Boston: Beacon Press, 1963.

Special Interest

Arterburn, Stephen, and Jack Felton. *Toxic Faith: Understanding and Overcoming Religious Addiction*. Nashville: Thomas Nelson, 1991.

Atack, Jon. *A Piece of Blue Sky: Scientology, Dianetics, and L. Ron Hubbard Exposed*. New York: Carol, 1990.

Bussell, Harold L. *Unholy Devotion*. Grand Rapids, Mich: Zondervan, 1983.

Chandler, Russell. *Understanding the New Age*. Grand Rapids, MI: Zondervan, 1993.

Corydon, Bent, and L. Ron Hubbard, Jr. *L. Ron Hubbard: Messiah or Madman*. Fort Lee, NJ: Barricade Books, 1992.

Earley, Pete. *Prophet of Death: The Mormon Blood-Atonement Killings*. New York: Morrow, 1991.

Edwards, Christopher. *Crazy for God: The Nightmare of Cult Life*. Englewood Cliffs, NJ: Prentice-Hall, 1979.

Enroth, Ronald. *Churches That Abuse*. Grand Rapids, MI: Zondervan, 1992.

Goldstein, Eleanor, with Kevin Framer. *Confabulations: Creating False Memories, Destroying Families*. Boca Raton, FL: SIRS Books, 1992.

Gordon, Henry. *Channeling into the New Age: The "Teachings" of Shirley MacLaine and Other Such Gurus*. Buffalo, NY: Prometheus Books, 1988.

Hubner, John, and Lindsey Gruson. *Monkey on a Stick: Murder, Madness, and the Hare Krishnas*. San Diego: Harcourt Brace Jovanovich, 1988.

Langone, Michael, and Linda Blood. *Satanism and Occult-Related Violence: What You Should Know*. Weston, MA: American Family Foundation, 1990.

Olin, William. *Escape from Utopia: My Ten Years in Synanon.* Santa Cruz, CA: Unity Press, 1980.

Persinger, M. A., N. J. Cary, and L. A. Suess. *TM and Cult Mania.* North Quincy, MA: Christopher, 1980.

Pressman, Steven. *Outrageous Betrayal: The Dark Journey of Werner Erhard from est to Exile.* New York: St. Martin's Press, 1993.

Raschke, Carl. *Painted Black: From Drug Killings to Heavy Metal—The Epidemic of Satanic Crime Terrorizing Our Communities.* San Francisco: Harper and Row, 1990.

Reiterman, Tim, and John Jacobs. *Raven: The Untold Story of the Rev. Jim Jones and His People.* New York: Dutton, 1982.

Sakheim, David, and Susan Devine, eds. *Out of Darkness: Exploring Satanism and Ritual Abuse.* New York: Lexington Books, 1992.

Stoner, Carroll, and Jo Anne Parke. *All God's Children: The Cult Experience—Salvation or Slavery.* New York: Penguin, 1979.

Underwood, Barbara, and Betty Underwood. *Hostage to Heaven.* New York: Clarkson N. Potter, 1979.

Yeakley, Flavil, ed. *The Discipling Dilemma.* Nashville: Gospel Advocate, 1988.

Special Interest/One-on-One Cultic Relationships

Boulette, Teresa Ramirez, and Susan M. Andersen. "'Mind Control' and the Battering of Women." *Cultic Studies Journal* 3,1 (1986): 25–35.

Nievod, Abraham. "Undue Influence in Contract and Probate Law." *Journal of Questioned Document Examination* 1,1 (March 1992): 14–26.

Noel, Barbara. *You Must Be Dreaming.* New York: Poseidon, 1993.

Ofshe, Richard. "The Rabbi and The Sex Cult: Power Expansion in the Formation of a Cult." *Cultic Studies Journal* 3,2 (1986): 173–79.

———. "Coerced Confessions: The Logic of Seemingly Irrational Action." *Cultic Studies Journal* 6,1 (1989): 1–15.

Plasil, Ellen. *Therapist.* New York: St. Martin's Press, 1985.

Siegel, Shirley. *What To Do When Psychotherapy Goes Wrong.* Tukwila, WA: Stop Abuse by Counselors, 1991.

Singer, Margaret T. "What Causes the Damage in Sexual Abuse Cases: It's Not the Touching." Paper presented at the California Trial Lawyers Association, San Francisco, November 1992.

———. "Undue Influence and Written Documents: Psychological Aspects." *Journal of Questioned Document Examination* 1,1 (March 1992): 4–13.

Temerlin, Jane W., and Maurice K. Temerlin. "Some Hazards of the Therapeutic Relationship." *Cultic Studies Journal* 3,2 (1986): 234–42.

Turner, Tina, with Kurt Loder. *I, Tina: My Life Story.* New York: Avon Books, 1986.

Special Interest/Political Cults

There is abundant literature shedding light on the destructive nature of the combination of fanaticism and political power—whether from the Left or Right. From the rethinking of Stalin and Mao in the communist world, to the connections between Nazism and the occult, to the links between some cultic groups and the radical right in America, the entire political spectrum becomes open to evaluation from the point of view of the potential dangers of totalistic thinking and behavior. Much of this reading can be useful, in particular to former members of overtly political cults or of cults that insert themselves into political issues while on the surface touting a nonpolitical framework. The following are some works to consider:

Arendt, Hannah. *The Origins of Totalitarianism.* New York: Harcourt Brace Jovanovich, 1973.

Camus, Albert. *The Fall.* New York: Vintage Books, 1956.

———. *The Plague.* New York: Vintage Books, 1972.

Chang, Jung. *Wild Swans: Three Daughters of China.* New York: Doubleday/Anchor, 1991.

Cheng, Nien. *Life and Death in Shanghai.* New York: Viking Penguin, 1988.

Conway, Flo, and James Siegelman. *Holy Terror: The Fundamentalist War on America's Freedom in Religion, Politics, and Our Private Lives.* New York: Delta, 1982.

Corcoran, James. *Bitter Harvest: Gordon Kahl and the Posse Comitatus.* New York: Viking Penguin, 1991.

Diamond, Sara. *Spiritual Warfare: The Politics of the Christian Right.* Boston: South End Press, 1989.

Djilas, Milovan. *The Unperfect Society.* New York: Harcourt Brace Jovanovich, 1969.

Dostoyevsky, Fyodor. *The Possessed.* New York: New American Library, 1962.

Goodrick-Clarke, Nicholas. *Occult Roots of Nazism: Secret Aryan Cults and Their Influence on Nazi Ideology.* New York: New York University Press, 1992.

Hearst, Patricia Campbell, with Alvin Moscow. *Patty Hearst: Her Own Story.* New York: Avon Books, 1982.

King, Dennis. *Lyndon LaRouche and the New American Fascism.* New York: Doubleday, 1989.

Koestler, Arthur. *Darkness at Noon.* New York: New American Library, 1961.

Kundera, Milan. *The Farewell Party.* New York: Viking Penguin, 1977.

———. *The Joke.* New York: Viking Penguin, 1982.

———. *The Book of Laughter and Forgetting.* New York: Viking Penguin, 1986.

Lalich, Janja. "The Cadre Ideal: Origins and Development of a Political Cult." *Cultic Studies Journal* 9,1 (1992): 1–77.

Lifton, Robert Jay. *The Nazi Doctors*. New York: Basic Books, 1986.

————. *Revolutionary Immortality: Mao Tse-tung and the Chinese Cultural Revolution*. New York: Random House, 1968.

Methvin, Eugene. *The Rise of Radicalism: The Social Psychology of Messianic Extremism*. New Rochelle, NY: Arlington House, 1973.

Orwell, George. *Homage to Catalonia*. New York: Harcourt, Brace, 1952.

Rickett, Allyn and Adele. *Prisoners of Liberation: Four Years in a Chinese Communist Prison*. New York: Anchor Books, 1973.

Sklar, Dusty. *The Nazis and the Occult*. New York: Dorset Press, 1990.

Thompson, Jerry. *My Life in the Klan*. New York: Putnam, 1982.

Wheaton, Elizabeth. *Code Name: Greenkil: The 1979 Greensboro Killings*. Athens: University of Georgia Press, 1987.

Periodicals

CAN News. Published monthly by the Cult Awareness Network. Write: CAN, 2421 W. Pratt Blvd., Suite 1173, Chicago IL 60645.

The Cult Observer. Published 10 times yearly by the American Family Foundation. Write: AFF, P.O. Box 2265, Bonita Springs FL 33959.

Cultic Studies Journal. Published twice yearly by the American Family Foundation. Write: AFF, P.O. Box 2265, Bonita Springs FL 33959.

Dissociation. A journal of the International Society for the Study of Multiple Personality and Dissociation. Write: Ridgeview Institute, 3995 South Cobb Drive, Smyrna GA 30080-6397.

FMS Foundation Newsletter. Published 10 times yearly by the False Memory Syndrome Foundation. Write: FMS, 3401 Market St., Suite 130, Philadelphia PA 19104.

FOCUS News. A quarterly publication of the FOCUS organization. Write: c/o CAN National Office, 2421 W. Pratt Blvd., Suite 1173, Chicago IL 60645.

SCP Newsletter and *SCP Journal*. Published by the Spiritual Counterfeits Project. Write: SCP, Box 4308, Berkeley CA 94704.

SurvivorShip: A Forum on Survival of Ritual Abuse, Torture, & Mind Control. Published 6 times yearly. Write: SurvivorShip, 3181 Mission St. #139, San Francisco CA 94110.

TM-Ex. A newsletter by and for ex-members of Transcendental Meditation. Write: TM-Ex, P.O. Box 2520, Philadelphia PA 19147.

NOTES

Foreword

1. Michael D. Langone, "Helping Cult Victims: Historical Background," in *Recovery from Cults: Help for Victims of Psychological and Spiritual Abuse,* ed. Michael D. Langone (New York: W. W. Norton, 1993), 22–47.

Introduction

1. "Statement of Margaret T. Singer, Ph.D., to the Clinton Health Care Task Force," delivered to the White House, 16 March 1993. Dr. Margaret Thaler Singer, Emeritus Adjunct Professor, Department of Psychology, University of California at Berkeley, is considered to be the world's leading expert on cults, having counseled more than 3,000 former cult members in the past 24 years.

2. Charles S. Clark, "Cults in America," *The CQ Researcher* 3,17 (7 May 1993), 387, citing Cynthia S. Kisser, Executive Director of the Cult Awareness Network, a nonprofit group with 2,000 members.

3. Some of the material in Part Two was originally developed by Madeleine Landau Tobias for the American Family Foundation's Project Recovery. Entitled "Guidelines for Ex-Members," it was presented at the AFF's annual conference in Philadelphia, 11–12 May 1991. Portions were originally published in a chapter of the same name by Madeleine Landau Tobias in *Recovery from Cults,* ed. Langone, 300–324.

Chapter 1

1. *Webster's Ninth New Collegiate Dictionary,* s.v. "thrall."

2. Hannah Arendt, *The Origins of Totalitarianism* (New York: Harcourt Brace & World, 1966), 326.

3. In 1988 the American Family Foundation published *Cults: Questions and Answers* by Michael D. Langone. This pamphlet provides a basic understanding of cults and the issues surrounding them, including definitions, how cults are different from recognized authoritarian and hierarchical groups, an explanation of thought reform, and why cults are harmful to individuals and society. This pamphlet is available from AFF (see Appendix B).

4. American Family Foundation, "Cultism: A Conference for Scholars and Policy Makers," *Cultic Studies Journal* 3,1 (1986): 119–20.* This conference was sponsored by the Neuropsychiatric Institute of the University of California at Los Angeles, the Johnson Foundation, and the American Family Foundation.

5. Langone, *Cults: Questions and Answers,* (Weston, MA: American Family Foundation, 1988), 1.

---

* Note: All future references to the *Cultic Studies Journal* are abbreviated *CSJ*.

6. Margaret Thaler Singer, "Cults: Where Are They? Why Now?" *Forecast for Home Economics,* May/June 1979, 37.

7. Willa Appel, *Cults in America: Programmed for Paradise* (New York: Holt, Rinehart & Winston, 1983), 16–18.

8. Frances FitzGerald, *Cities on a Hill: A Journey through Contemporary American Cultures* (New York: Simon and Schuster, 1986), 390, 408.

9. The authors would like to acknowledge Joan Carol Ross and Michael D. Langone for the initial outline of cult categories presented in their book, *Cults: What Parents Should Know* (Secaucus, NJ: Lyle Stuart, 1989).

10. An excellent book describing the power a therapist can have over a client is Barbara Noel's *You Must Be Dreaming* (New York: Poseidon, 1993), a fascinating and detailed account of 18 years of alleged systematic sexual and emotional abuse while a patient of renowned psychoanalyst Jules Masserman. See Appendix C for other reading material relevant to this topic.

11. Teresa Ramirez Boulette and Susan M. Andersen, "'Mind Control' and the Battering of Women," *CSJ* 3,1 (1986): 26.

12. Judith Lewis Herman, *Trauma and Recovery: The Aftermath of Violence—From Domestic Abuse to Political Terror* (New York: Basic Books, 1992), 92.

13. Boulette and Andersen, "Battering of Women," 26–27.

14. Ibid., 31.

15. Tina Turner with Kurt Loder, *I, Tina: My Life Story* (New York: Avon Books, 1986), 137.

16. Ibid., 78–79.

17. Ibid., 138.

18. Ibid., 189–90.

19. Ibid., 247.

20. Samuel Klagsbrun, "Is Submission Ever Voluntary?" (Paper presented at annual conference of the Cult Awareness Network, Teaneck, NJ, November 1989).

21. Rachel [pseud.], written communication, June 1993.

Chapter 2

1. Janet Joyce, written communication, 20 June 1993. See Chapter 14 for her personal account.

2. Margaret T. Singer, "Group Psychodynamics," in *The Merck Manual of Diagnosis and Therapy,* ed. Robert Berkow (Rahway, NJ: Merck Sharp & Dohme Research Laboratories, 1987), 1468, 1470.

3. Louis Jolyon West, "Persuasive Techniques in Contemporary Cults: A Public Health Approach," *CSJ* 7,2 (1990): 131.

4. Ibid.; Langone, *Cults: Questions and Answers,* 5.

5. Langone, *Cults: Questions and Answers,* 6.

6. Rev. Wm. Kent Burtner, "Helping the Ex-Cultist," in *Cults, Sects, and the New Age,* ed. Rev. James J. LeBar (Huntington, IN: Our Sunday Visitor, 1989), 65.

7. This summary is derived from notes taken during Robert Cialdini's keynote speech, "The Powers of Ethical Influence," presented at the annual conference of the Cult Awareness Network, Los Angeles, 6 November 1992. Cialdini's presentation was based on his book *Influence: The New Psychology of Modern Persuasion* (New York: Quill, 1984).

8. Philip G. Zimbardo and Michael R. Leippe, *The Psychology of Attitude Change and Social*

Influence (New York: McGraw-Hill, 1991), 10.

9. Gary Scharff, "Autobiography of a Moonie," *CSJ* 2,2 (1985): 252–58.

10. Jesse S. Miller, "The Utilization of Hypnotic Techniques in Religious Cult Conversion," *CSJ* 3,2 (1986): 245.

11. Ibid. 247.

12. Jennie Sharma, M.S.W., a psychotherapist with a private practice in Connecticut, developed the original contract. She was delighted to see it adapted for former cult members. The authors would like to acknowledge her contribution and support.

13. Adapted from draft paper by Benjamin Zablocki, professor of sociology at Rutgers University, "Bill of Rights for Religious Communities and Their Members," 2 November 1992.

Chapter 3

1. Robert Jay Lifton, *Thought Reform and the Psychology of Totalism* (New York: W. W. Norton, 1961).

2. Ibid., 419.

3. Ibid., 435.

4. Richard Ofshe and Margaret T. Singer, "Attacks on Peripheral Versus Central Elements of Self and the Impact of Thought Reforming Techniques," *CSJ* 3,1 (1986): 3–24.

5. Ibid., 19.

6. Singer, "Group Psychodynamics," 1470.

7. Ibid.

8. Herman, *Trauma and Recovery*, 34–35, quoting Pierre Janet and Abram Kardiner.

9. Robert Jay Lifton, *The Future of Immortality and Other Essays for a Nuclear Age* (New York: Basic Books, 1987), 197.

10. I. Farber, H. Harlow, and L. J. West, "Brainwashing, Conditioning, and DDD," *Sociometry* 20 (1957): 271–85, cited in Langone, "Assessment and Treatment of Cult Victims and Their Families," in *Innovations in Clinical Practice: A Sourcebook*, ed. P. A. Kellerman and S. R. Hegman (Sarasota, FL: Professional Resource & Exchange, 1991), 264.

11. Langone, "Assessment and Treatment," 264.

12. *Webster's Ninth New Collegiate Dictionary*, s.v. "double bind."

13. Louis J. West and Margaret T. Singer, "Cults, Quacks, and Nonprofessional Therapies," in *Comprehensive Textbook of Psychiatry/III*, ed. Harold I. Kaplan, Alfred M. Freedman, and Benjamin J. Sadock (Baltimore: Williams & Wilkins, 1980), 3248.

14. Ibid., 3248–49.

15. Langone, *Cults: Questions and Answers*, 6.

16. Lifton, *The Future of Immortality*, 197–98.

17. Ibid., 200.

Chapter 4

1. Langone, *Cults: Questions and Answers*, 7.

2. Cynthia B. [pseud.], letter to M. L. T., November 1990.

3. See, for example, Shirley Landa, "Warning Signs: The Effects of Authoritarianism on Children in Cults," *Areopagus* 2,4 (1989): 16–22; Michael Langone and Gary Eisenberg, "Children and Cults," in *Recovery from Cults*, ed. Langone, 327–42; Arnold Markowitz and David Halperin, "Cults and Children: The Abuse of the Young," *CSJ* 1,2 (1984): 143–66.

4. Herbert L. Rosedale, Esq., telephone communication, 16 August 1993.

5. West, "Persuasive Techniques," 133.

6. Carroll Stoner and Cynthia Kisser, *Touchstones: Reconnecting After a Cult Experience* (Chicago: Cult Awareness Network, 1992), 2.

7. Gerald Renner et al., "Brother Julius followers exploited for empire's gain," *Hartford Courant,* 16 November 1987.

8. Patricia R. [pseud.], interview with M. L. T., 1989.

9. Hana Eltringham Whitfield, letter to M. L. T., 1991. Unless otherwise noted, all quotes in this book by Hana Whitfield are from this document. See Chapter 19 for her personal account.

10. Steven Hassan, *Combatting Cult Mind Control* (Rochester, VT: Park Street Press, 1988), 170.

11. At the 1990 conference of the Cult Awareness Network in Chicago, approximately 5 percent of the ex-members present had been exit counseled out of their groups. Almost all of the rest were walkaways.

12. Carol Giambalvo, *Exit Counseling: A Family Intervention* (Bonita Springs, FL: American Family Foundation, 1992), 3.

13. At the invitation of several ex-members, Joe Szimhart and Madeleine Tobias led an exit counseling weekend workshop.

Chapter 5

1. Edward Levine and Charles Shaiova, "Religious Cult Leaders as Authoritarian Personalities," *Areopagus* (Fall 1987): 19.

2. Portions of this chapter were originally presented at the 1989 national conference of the Cult Awareness Network in Teaneck, NJ. At that time, Madeleine Landau Tobias and Paul Martin presented a joint paper for a panel on "The Psychopathology of the Cult Leader."

3. Adapted from "Personality Structure and Change in Communist Systems: Dictatorship and Society in Eastern Europe" by Ivan Volgyes, in *The Cult of Power: Dictators in the Twentieth Century,* ed. Joseph Held (Boulder, CO: East European Monographs, 1983), 23–39.

4. Peter Suedfeld, "Authoritarian Leadership: A Cognitive-Interactionist View," in *The Cult of Power* ed. Held, 8–9.

5. *Webster's Ninth New Collegiate Dictionary,* s.v. "charisma."

6. Max Weber, *The Sociology of Religion* (Boston: Beacon Press, 1963), cited in *Charisma: A Psychoanalytic Look at Mass Society,* Irvine Schiffer (New York: Free Press, 1973), 3.

7. Schiffer, *Charisma,* 4.

8. Joachim C. Fest, *The Face of the Third Reich* (New York: Pantheon Books, 1960); Alexander Deutsch, "Tenacity of Attachment to a Cult Leader: A Psychiatric Perspective," *American Journal of Psychiatry* 137 (1980): 12; Benjamin B. Wolman, *The Sociopathic Personality* (New York: Brunner/Mazel, 1987); Leon J. Saul and Silas L. Warner, *The Psychotic Personality* (New York: Van Nostrand Reinhold, 1982); Levine and Shaiova, "Religious Cult Leaders."

9. Robert D. Hare, *Without Conscience: The Disturbing World of the Psychopaths Among Us* (New York: Pocket Books, 1993), xi.

10. American Psychiatric Association, *Diagnostic and Statistical Manual of Mental Disorders,* 3rd rev. ed. (Washington, DC: Author, 1987), 335–358.

11. Hervey Cleckley, *The Mask of Sanity* (New York: NAL/Plume, 1982), 204.

12. Robert D. Hare, "Twenty Years of Experience With the Cleckley Psychopath," in *Unmasking the Psychopath: Antisocial Personality and Related Syndromes,* ed. William H. Reid et

al. (New York: W. W. Norton, 1986), 18.

13. Richard M. Restak, *The Self Seekers* (Garden City, NY: Doubleday, 1982), 195.

14. Ken Magid and Carole A. McKelvey, *High Risk: Children Without a Conscience* (New York: Bantam Books, 1989), 21.

15. Darwin Dorr and Peggy K. Woodhall, "Ego Dysfunction in Psychopathic Psychiatric Inpatients," in *Unmasking the Psychopath,* ed. Reid et al., 128–29.

16. Larry H. Strasburger, "The Treatment of Antisocial Syndromes: The Therapist's Feelings," in *Unmasking the Psychopath,* ed. Reid et al., 191.

17. Magid and McKelvey, *High Risk,* 21.

18. Restak, *Self Seekers,* 289.

19. Magid and McKelvey, *High Risk,* 4.

20. Lifton, *The Future of Immortality,* 211.

21. Ethel Person, "Manipulativeness in Entrepreneurs and Psychopaths," in *Unmasking the Psychopath,* ed. Reid et al., 257.

22. Magid and McKelvey, *High Risk,* 98.

23. Scott Snyder, "Pseudologica Fantastica in the Borderline Patient," *American Journal of Psychiatry* 143,10 (1986): 1287.

24. See Magid and McKelvey, *High Risk.* For those interested in learning more about childhood factors and how they may influence a person's view of the world and his or her potential for violence, we recommend the work of Alice Miller, in particular, *The Drama of the Gifted Child* (New York: Basic Books, 1981) and *For Your Own Good: Hidden Cruelty in Child-Rearing and the Roots of Violence* (New York: Farrar Straus Giroux, 1984). In the latter is a fascinating study of Adolf Hitler's childhood.

25. Richard M. Restak, "If Koresh had been treated as a psychotic," *Hartford Courant,* 3 May 1993.

26. Charles W. Holmes, "Jerusalem syndrome victim?" *Atlanta Journal,* 13 March 1993.

27. The sources used for the information related to David Koresh's life are listed in chronological order, and include "Violent Cult Had Faith in Twisted Leader" by Mark England and Darlene McCormick, *San Francisco Chronicle,* 1 March 1993; "The Cult Leader's Seductive Ways" by Mark England and Darlene McCormick, *San Francisco Chronicle,* 2 March 1993; "Bloody Sunday's Roots in Deep Religious Soil" by Peter Applebome, *New York Times,* 2 March 1993; "'Messiah' Fond of Rock, Women and Bible" by Sam Howe Verhovek, *New York Times,* 3 March 1993; "The Siege, Waco Points Out, Isn't Exactly in Waco" by Sam Howe Verhovek, *New York Times,* 6 March 1993; "At the Whim of the Leader: Childhood in a Cult" by Melinda Henneberger, *New York Times,* 7 March 1993; "Thy Kingdom Come" by B. Kantrowitz et al., *Newsweek,* 15 March 1993; "The Zealot of God" by J. Treen et al., *People,* 15 March 1993; "In the Grip of a Psychopath" by Richard Lacayo, *Time,* 3 May 1993; "Oh, My God, They're Killing Themselves" by Nancy Gibbs, *Time,* 3 May 1993; "Death Wish" by A. Press et al., *Newsweek,* 3 May 1993; "Tragedy in Waco" by J. Smolowe et al., *Time,* May 3, 1993; "If Koresh had been treated as a psychotic" by Richard M. Restak, *Hartford Courant,* May 3, 1993; "U.S. Pleads with Cult Leader to Let His Followers Go" by Michael deCourcy Hinds, *New York Times,* 7 May 1993; "FBI Told Not to Attack Compound," *Hartford Courant,* 9 May 1993; "An Emotional Moonscape" by David Gelman, *Newsweek,* 17 May 1993; "911 Tape Reveals Koresh Knew of Planned ATF Raid," *San Francisco Chronicle,* 10 June 1993.

Chapter 6

1. Carol B. [pseud.], letter to M. L. T., 1990. Unless otherwise noted, all quotes in this book by Carol B. are from this document.

2. American Psychiatric Association, *Diagnostic and Statistical Manual,* 275–77.

3. Patrick Ryan and Joseph Kelly, "Coping with Trance States" (Workshop presentation at "After the Cult" conference, American Family Foundation, Stony Point, NY, 21 May 1993).

4. Robert Jean Campbell, *Psychiatric Dictionary* (New York: Oxford University Press, 1989), 492.

5. Wendy Ford, *Recovery from Abusive Groups* (Bonita Springs, FL: American Family Foundation, 1993), 41.

6. Aaron Beck et al., *Cognitive Treatment of Depression* (New York: Guilford Press, 1979); Gary Emery, *New Beginning* (New York: Simon and Schuster, 1981).

7. David Burns, *Feeling Good: The New Mood Therapy* (New York: Signet, 1981).

Chapter 7

1. Stoner and Kisser, *Touchstones,* 2–3.

2. Margaret T. Singer, "Coming Out of the Cults,"*Psychology Today,* January 1979, 72–82.

3. Ibid., 75.

4. Ibid., 76.

5. Derived from notes taken during a workshop led by Dr. Margaret Singer on "Triggers: How to Recognize and Deal with Them," Annual Conference of the Cult Awareness Network, Los Angeles, 6 November 1992; and from interviews with J. L., July and August 1993.

6. The authors would like to thank Patrick Ryan and Joseph Kelly for allowing us to reprint "Ex-Members' Coping Strategies," distributed at the Coping with Trance States workshop (see Chap 6., n. 3).

7. The worksheet originally appeared as the Reprogramming Worksheet in *SurvivorShip,* March 1990, in an article by founder and editor Caryn StarDancer, entitled "Recovery Skills for the Dissociatively Disabled: Reprogramming." It is reprinted here with permission of *SurvivorShip,* 3181 Mission Street #139, San Francisco CA 94110.

Chapter 8

1. Viktor Frankl, *Man's Search for Meaning: An Introduction to Logotherapy* (New York: Washington Square Press, 1984).

2. Willard Gaylin, *Feelings,* (New York: Ballantine, 1979), 145.

3. Janis and Martin [pseuds.], written communication, 19 July 1993.

4. Gaylin, *Feelings,* 54.

5. Herman, *Trauma and Recovery,* 68.

6. Hassan, *Combatting Cult Mind Control,* 45.

7. Kevin Garvey, written communication to M. L. T., 1991.

8. Herbert L. Rosedale, Esq., phone communication, 16 August 1993.

9. Ibid.

10. Anna Bowen, written communication, July 1993. Unless otherwise noted, all quotes in this book by Anna Bowen are from this document.

11. Michael D. Langone, "Psychological Abuse," *CSJ* 9,2 (1992): 213.

Chapter 9

1. *Nutrition and Your Health: Dietary Guidelines for Americans* (U.S. Department of Agriculture and U.S. Department of Health and Human Services), 1990. To receive a free copy of these guidelines, write to "Nutrition and Your Health: Dietary Guidelines for Americans," Consumer Information Center, Pueblo CO 81009.

2. Warren E. Leary, "If You Can't Run for Health, A Walk Will Do, Experts Say," *New York Times,* 30 July 1993.

3. Adapted from "A Bill of Assertive Rights," in *When I Say No I Feel Guilty* by Manuel Smith (New York: Bantam Books, 1975).

4. Singer, "Coming Out of the Cults," 80.

5. Kevin Crawley, Diana Paulina, and Ronald W. White, "Reintegration of Exiting Cult Members with Their Families: A Brief Intervention Model," *CSJ* 7,1 (1990): 37.

6. Ibid.

7. Ibid., 34–37.

8. Bill and Lorna Goldberg, "Questions and Answers," *FOCUS News,* Winter 1992, 2.

9. Lorna Goldberg and William Goldberg, "Family Responses to a Young Adult's Cult Membership and Return," *CSJ* 6,1 (1989): 86–100.

10. Arnold Markowitz, "The Role of Family Therapy in the Treatment of Symptoms Associated with Cult Affiliation," in *Psychodynamic Perspectives on Religion, Sect, and Cult,* ed. David Halperin (Boston: John Wright, 1983), 331.

11. Ginger Zyskowski, "Some Thoughts on Postcult Parenting," written communication, 14 June 1993.

12. Bill and Lorna Goldberg, "Questions and Answers," *FOCUS News,* Fall 1991, 3.

13. Frances Lief [pseud.], written communication, May 1993. See Chapter 15 for her personal account.

Chapter 10

1. Markowitz, "The Role of Family Therapy."

2. Adapted from a handout at an Al-Anon meeting in Hartford, Conn., July 1990.

3. Adapted with permission from "Typical Characteristics of Co-Dependent Relationships" by Jennie Sharma, M.S.W.

4. Burtner, "Helping the Ex-Cultist," 74–75 (see Chap. 2, n. 6).

5. Ibid., 76–77.

6. Ibid. See also Rev. William Dowhower, "Guidelines for Clergy," in *Recovery from Cults,* ed. Langone, 251–62.

Chapter 11

1. "After the Cult" workshop, American Family Foundation, Stony Point, NY, 21–22 May 1993. Attendance statistics provided by Marcia Rudin, International Cult Education Project, telephone communication to M. L. T., 23 July 1993. M. L. T. was the leader of the impromptu workshop which had been initiated by several of the attendees.

2. N. Gartrell et al., "Psychiatrist-Patient Sexual Contact: Results of a National Survey," *American Journal of Psychiatry* 143 (1984): 110–24; Annette Brodsky, "Sex Between Patient and Therapist: Psychology's Data and Response," in *Sexual Exploitation in Professional Relationships,* ed. Glen Gabbard (Washington: American Psychiatric Press, 1989), 18–19.

3. See, for example, Kevin Garvey, "The Importance of Information Collection in Exit Counseling: A Case Study," in *Recovery from Cults,* ed. Langone, 181–200.

4. Jane W. Temerlin and Maurice K. Temerlin, "Some Hazards of the Therapeutic Relationship," *CSJ* 3,2 (1986): 234–42.

5. Kim Boland and Gordon Lindbloom, "Psychotherapy Cults: An Ethical Analysis," *CSJ* 9,2 (1992): 137–62; Margaret T. Singer, Maurice Temerlin, and Michael D. Langone, "Psychotherapy Cults," *CSJ* 7,2 (1990): 101–25; Kenneth Pope and Jacqueline Bouhoutsos, *Sexual Intimacy Between Therapists and Patients* (New York: Praeger, 1986).

6. Kenneth Pope "Therapist-Patient Sex Syndrome: A Guide for Attorneys and Subsequent Therapists to Assessing Damage," in *Sexual Exploitation,* ed. Gabbard, 39–45.

7. "The Family," *The Sun* (Melbourne), 17 May 1990, cited in *Cult Observer,* September/October 1990.

8. Nick Cohen, "Sex guru's ex-aides face murder charges," *San Francisco Examiner,* 20 December 1992; Don Lattin, "Bhagwan's teachings survive his death," *San Francisco Chronicle,* 7 December 1992, "Two British Ex-Cultists Win Reprieve on U.S. Extradition," *New York Times,* 30 July 1993.

9. "Hunt praised for courtroom work," Los Angeles *Daily News,* 20 December 1992; Lois Timnick, "BBC Trial Traces Maze of 'Paradox Philosophy,'" *Los Angeles Times,* November 1986, cited in *Cult Observer,* 10,1 (1993): 3.

10. Tom Fennell, "The Cult of Horror," *Macleans,* 8 February 1993, cited in *Cult Awareness Network News,* April 1993, 3–4.

11. Janja Lalich, "The Cadre Ideal: Origins and Development of a Political Cult," *CSJ* 9,1 (1992): 28–30.

12. West, "Persuasive Techniques," 128 (see Chap. 2, n. 3).

13. Michael Langone and Linda Blood, *Satanism and Occult-Related Violence: What You Should Know* (Weston, MA: American Family Foundation, 1990), 13, citing B. R. Wheeler et al., "Assessment and Intervention with Adolescents Involved in Satanism," *Social Work* (Nov-Dec, 1988): 547.

14. Gelman, "Emotional Moonscape," 54 (see Chap 5., n. 27).

Chapter 12

1. Also from materials used in Anna Bowen's workshops and her paper in progress, "Journaling for Survivors of Ritual and Severe Childhood Abuse."

2. Heather Svoboda, "What Helped You to Heal?" *FOCUS News,* Spring 1993, 8.

3. Rosanne Henry, letter to M. L. T., 31 March 1991.

4. Lynda McCullogh, "Counselors Can Help Former Cult Members Adjust to Life Outside," *Guidepost,* May 1993, 8–9.

5. Margaret Singer, telephone communication with J. L., 5 August 1993.

6. Burtner, "Helping the Ex-Cultist," 70–78 (see Chap. 2, n. 6).

7. Lorna and Bill Goldberg, "Questions and Answers," *FOCUS News,* Summer 1992, 3.

8. Judith Bentley, *How to Choose a Therapist: A Checklist* (Chicago: Voices in Action, 1985). Adapted with permission.

9. "A Report of the National Legal Seminar II," *Cultism and the Law,* September 1986, in *Cults and Consequences: The Definitive Handbook,* ed. Rachel Andres and James R. Lane (Los Angeles: Commission on Cults & Missionaries, 1988), 8–7. For an excellent reference on legal issues and a useful legal checklist, see Herbert Rosedale, "Legal Considerations: Regaining Independence and Initiative," in *Recovery from Cults,* ed. Langone, 382–95.

10. Randy Frances Kandel, "Litigating the Cult-Related Child Custody Case," *CSJ* 5,1

(1988): 122–131.

11. Ford Greene, "Litigating Child Custody with Religious Cults," *CSJ* 6,1 (1989): 71.

12. For a description of some of these cases, see Sara Van Hoey, "Cults in Court," *CSJ* 8,1 (1991): 61–79; Lawrence Levy, "Prosecuting an Ex-Cult Member's Undue Influence Suit," *CSJ* 7,1 (1990): 15–25.

Chapter 20

1. Robert G. Kegan, "The Child Behind the Mask: Sociopathy as Developmental Delay," in *Unmasking the Psychopath*, ed. Reid et al., 45–77.

2. David Halperin, "The Dark Underside: Cultic Misappropriation of Psychiatry and Psychoanalysis," *CSJ* 10,1 (1993): 33–44; Singer et al., "Psychotherapy Cults" (see Chap. 11, n. 5).

3. Shippen [pseud.], excerpts from a presentation to the Jewish Board of Family and Children's Services Conference, Queens, NY, October 1989.

4. M. J. Gaines et al., "The Effects of Cult Membership on the Health Status of Adults and Children," *Health Values: Achieving High Level Wellness* 8(2): 13–17, cited in Langone and Eisenberg, "Children and Cults" (see Chap. 4, n. 3).

5. Joe Callahan, "Couple convicted in daughter's death," *Chicago Tribune,* 4 July 1992.

6. Robin Clark, "Measles abating, but city might still seek inoculations," *Philadelphia Inquirer,* 23 February 1991.

7. See for example, "Children: The Cults Most Innocent Victims," *Cult Awareness Network News,* April 1993, 1; Langone and Eisenberg, "Children and Cults"; Landa, "Child Abuse in Cults"; Markowitz and Halperin, "Cults and Children."

8. Gerald Renner, "Cult leader's son held on sex assault charges," *Hartford Courant,* 29 August 1991.

9. John Painter, Jr., "Seven Eccelsia members plead guilty, sentenced," *The Oregonian* (Portland), 18 January 1992.

10. Dick Tuchscherer, "L. R. Davis guilty of sex crimes," *The News-Sun* (Waukegan), 11–12 July 1992, 1.

11. Authors' note: Criminal charges were dropped after Fred successfully passed a lie detector test. Physical evidence of abuse had been present during an emergency room visit for rectal bleeding; however, no report was filed because Fred was able to convince the intern that the problem was induced by Jessica Kay. A civil suit was then filed against him.

12. Jessica Kay [pseud.], written communication, May 1993.

13. Gelman, "Emotional Moonscape," 54 (see Chap. 5, n. 27).

14. Herman, *Trauma and Recovery,* 96.

15. Lenore Terr, *Too Scared to Cry* (New York: Basic Books, 1990).

16. Rosanne Henry, written communication, June 1993.

17. Margaret T. Singer, "Cults, Coercion, and Society" (keynote speech, Annual Conference of the Cult Awareness Network, Los Angeles, 5 November 1992); Langone and Eisenberg, "Children and Cults," 337–39.

Chapter 21

1. Moishe Halevi Spero, "Therapeutic Approaches and Issues," in *Psychodynamic Perspectives,* ed. Halperin, 314.

2. Boulette and Andersen, "Battering of Women," 31 (see Chap. 1, n. 11).

3. Lorna Goldberg, "Guidelines for Therapists," in *Recovery from Cults,* ed. Langone, 239–40.

4. Langone, "Assessment and Treatment," 267 (see Chap. 3, n. 10).

5. Goldberg, "Guidelines for Therapists."

6. Michael D. Langone et al., "Results of a Survey of Ex-Cult Members," *CSJ,* in press.

7. Stephen Ash, "Cult-Induced Psychopathology, Part 1: Clinical Picture," *CSJ* 2 (1985): 2–16; Marvin Galper, "The Atypical Dissociative Disorder: Some Etiological, Diagnostic, and Treatment Issues," in *Psychodynamic Perspectives,* ed. Halperin; Herman, *Trauma and Recovery;* Mark I. Sirkin and Lyman C. Wynne, "Cult Involvement as Relational Disorder," *Psychiatric Annals* 20:4 (1990): 199–203.

8. Margaret T. Singer and Richard Ofshe, "Thought Reform Programs and the Production of Psychiatric Casualties," *Psychiatric Annals* 20,4 (April 1990): 191.

9. Ibid., 193.

10. F. J. Heide and T. D. Borkovec, "Relaxation-Induced Anxiety: Paradoxical Anxiety Enhancement Due to Relaxation Training," *Journal of Consulting and Clinical Psychology* 51 (1983): 171–82; Richard Castillo, "Depersonalization and Meditation," *Psychiatry* 53,2 (May 1990): 158–69.

11. See Carol Giambalvo, *Exit Counseling: A Family Intervention.* Also note that when the cult member has a psychiatric history it is sometimes advisable to have a mental health professional on the exit counseling team.

12. Richard Lowenstein and Frank Putnam, "A Comparison Study of Dissociative Symptoms in Patients with Complex Partial Seizures, MPD, and Post-traumatic Stress Disorder," *Dissociation* 1,4 (1988): 17–23; Marlene Steinberg et al., "The Structured Clinical Interview for DSM III-R Dissociative Disorders: Preliminary Report on a New Diagnostic Instrument," *American Journal of Psychiatry* 147,1 (January 1990): 76–81.

13. Paul Martin et al., "Post-Cult Symptoms as Measured by the MCMI Before and After Residential Treatment," *CSJ* 9,2 (1992): 219–50.

14. David Halperin, "Guidelines for Psychiatric Hospitalization of Ex-Cultists," in *Recovery from Cults,* ed. Langone, 263–74.

15. Ibid.

16. George Dominiak, "Psychopharmacology of the Abused," in *Sexual Trauma and Psychopathology,* ed. Shanti Shapiro and George M. Dominiak (New York: Macmillan, 1992).

17. John G. Clark, Jr., et al., *Destructive Cult Conversion: Theory, Research, and Treatment* (Weston, MA: American Family Foundation, 1981).

18. Herman, *Trauma and Recovery,* 119-121.

19. Ibid., 122.

INDEX

abuse; of cult children, 81, 170–71, 248, 249–53; effects of, 249–50; healing from, 181–82; physical, 16, 17–20, 50, 52, 76, 98, 142, 170–71; sexual, 16, 50, 52, 77, 98; spiritual, 11, 163; verbal, 20, 76;

acting out; cult children, 252, 256; cult leaders, 76–77

affect disorders, 268, 273

AIDS, 26, 142, 159, 240

Al-Anon, 227

alcohol abuse, 110, 134, 239, 256, 272

Alcoholics Anonymous (AA), 8, 9, 10, 50

altered states (see also dissociation, trancelike states); induced, 39, 46; involuntary, 40, 96–98, 189

ambiguity intolerance, 27, 227

ambivalence, 116, 176

American Family Foundation (AFF), xii, 12, 91, 152, 180, 184, 275, 276, 278

amnesia, 97, 273

anger; of children, 254; expression of, 214–15; pathological, 273; postcult, 49, 134–37, 266

anomie, 267

anticult activism, 136, 195–97

antisocial personality disorder, 69

anxiety; postcult, 96, 266, 267, 268; relaxation-induced, 268, 269–70

art, 185, 187, 209

assertiveness training, 136, 145–46

authoritarian personality, 64, 65–66

authoritarian system, 38

authority, 29, 36, 217, 221

autonomy; impairment, 93–94; recovery, 105, 160; of young people, 214

battered women; and mind control, 17–23; psychiatric treatment, 263; self-blame in, 65

Beck Depression Inventory, 271

beliefs (see also values); alterations in, 274; indoctrination of, 13; vs. methods, 5; redefining, 121, 145, 155, 163–65, 226

belonging, sense of; and conversion, 43; and recovery, 157; and recruitment, 29, 31–32

Bible-based cults, 15, 55, 94, 127, 140

black-and-white thinking, 36, 100, 101; recovery from, 100, 106, 119–20, 158, 213, 227

blackmail, 52, 178, 199

blame; and anger, 134–35; by cult leader, 77; on cult leader, 64–65; over loss of leader, 58; the victim, 190, 229

boredom, 124–25, 254

boundaries, 147–48, 159–61, 175, 176

Bowen, Anna, 133–34, 185–86, 249–50

brainwashing, 3, 35 (see also thought reform)

Burtner, Father Kent, 163–64, 191–92

career issues, 165–69, 208, 232–33

castaways, 56–57

celibacy, 158, 173

chanting, 39, 40, 42, 98, 268, 269

charisma, 67–68, 72

Checklist for Evaluating Relationships, 162–63

Checklist of Cult Characteristics, 276–77

childraising; in neo-christian cult, 213–14; in political cult, 217–18; in psychotherapy cult, 207, 209, 245

children, cult, 120, 155, 244–45; abuse of, 15, 81, 170–71, 249–53; adjustment difficulties, 253–56; effects of cult on, 50, 249–50, 251–53; exit style of, 253; health/medical issues, 141, 247–48; identity issues, 215, 257; manipulation of, 43; reconnecting with, 151–53, 219–20; recovery of, 251, 253–56; recovery story, 211–15; relating to outside world, 245–57; separation from parents, 245

Children of God, 155, 175, 211–15, 245–46

Church of the International Society of Divine Love, Inc. (ISDL), 87–90

Cialdini, Robert, 29–30, 41

Cleckley, Hervey, 69, 70, 72

closed logic, 38

cognitive problems; of children, 255; concentration, 89, 96, 262, 266; confusion, 45–46, 49, 98–99; distortion, 101–103; indecisiveness, 93–94, 265; intellectual impairment, 177; memory loss, 49, 86, 98–99, 233, 270; recovery from, 104–111; and sexual abuse, 177; slow thinking, 46;

cognitive therapy, 101

commercial cults, 16, 127

commitment, as manipulation technique, 29, 30, 42

communication (see also talking, writing); cult control of, 36, 45; postcult difficulty, 265

Communism, 35, 41, 238

compassion, 188, 204

compliance, principles for eliciting, 29–30

conclusions, jumping to, 102

conferences, 87–88, 91, 188, 227–28

confession technique, 36, 42, 45, 147–48

confidence erosion, 38

confusion; induction, 45; postcult, 45–46, 49, 98–99; sexual, 176

contract for cult membership, 32–33

conversion (see also recruitment, thought reform), 34; and cult pseudopersonality, 44–47; elements, 44–45; process, 41–43

counseling (see also psychotherapy); career, 166, 169; choosing a counselor, 193–95; conditions requiring, 189; couples, 151; cult awareness in, 189–90; ethics in, 172; family, 150; pastoral, 164, 191–92; postcult, 54; psychological, 192

countertransference, 263

creativity, 184–87, 241

criminal activity; and children, 245; legal ad-

exit counseling, 54, 59, 60–61, 149, 153, 190–91 263, 269–70, 272,

failure, feeling like a, 125–26
family; conflicts with, 265; in cults, 244; cutting off, 25–26, 42, 45, 50; grieving loss of, 119, 121–22; prior problems with, 149–50, 160; reconnecting with, 121–22, 149–53, 208; as recovery factor, 53, 54; watchfulness of, 146–47
fatigue, 40
fear; in children, 252; postcult, 46, 52, 130–34, 230–31, 231–32, 233, 252; and dependency, 44; and dissociative state, 40; induction, 17, 19, 43, 45, 117, 130; prevalence in ex-members, 266; of retribution, 265, 267; and sexual abuse, 173
female subservience, 172, 173
financial resources; manipulation of, 19, 39, 88; postcult, 142, 232
First Amendment protections, 247
fishbowl effect, 146–47
floating (see also dissociation and triggers); postcult, 90, 96–98, 231, 270; prevalence in ex-members, 267; recovery from, 107–8; symptoms, 107; triggers, 108–13
FOCUS, 130, 187–88, 197, 226, 270, 278
forgiveness, 137–39
freedom; of former cult member, 9–10; of movement within cult, 14; of thought, 118
friends; within cult, 29, 119, 153–54; cutting off, 42; grieving loss of, 121–22; making new, 90–91; reconnecting with, 121–22, 149, 150–51, 210; as recovery factor, 53, 54; watchfulness of, 146–47
front organizations, 41, 168–69
fun, 124, 144

Garvey, Kevin, 131–33
Giambalvo, Carol, 60, 191
God-consciousness, 17, 87
Goldberg, Bill, 148, 154
Goldberg, Lorna, 148, 154, 264, 266
grieving, 93, 118–24; allowance for, 123–24; of children, 253; loss of family/friends, 121 22; loss of group, 119–20; loss of idealism, 120–21; loss of meaning in life, 121, 265; loss of pride/self- esteem, 122–23; loss of time, 49, 89, 119, 120, 233
guilt feelings; of castaways, 56; of cult leaders, 74, 127; postcult, 46, 49, 51, 65, 233, 265; prevalence in ex-members, 266; recovery from, 126–28, 137–38, 228–29, 230–31; reasons for, 126; and sexual abuse, 176, 251
guilt induction, 31, 36, 45, 102–3, 117, 127, 277
gullibility, 27

hallucinogenic drug use, 28
hallucinations, 96, 97, 267
harassment, protection against, 131–34
Hare, Robert, 69, 70, 72

Hassan, Steven, 9, 56, 131
health issues; of children, 247–48, 256; of cult leaders, 78–79; postcult, 110, 141–44; resources, 142–43
Herman, Judith Lewis, 18, 127–28, 182, 252, 273, 274
Hippocratic oath, 172
Hopkins Symptom Checklist, 271
hospitalization, 271–72
human potential cults, 16 (see also mass transformational cults, psychotherapy cults)
humiliation, 38, 122–23
humor, 241
hypervigilance, 266
hypnotic techniques; cognitive difficulties from, 97; in psychotherapy, 190, 194, 261, 262; in conversion, 31–32, 42

idealism; grieving loss of, 104, 119, 120–21, 223–24; manipulation of, 72, 78, 220; as predisposing factor, 28, 91
idealization, 91, 175–76, 274
identification, with abuser, 176, 272
identity issues, 2, 120; for cult children, 215, 257; resolving, 155–56
ideological totalism, 35
illness; anger-induced, 134; cult attitudes toward, 53, 79; medical treatment for, 141–42
immunization, 247, 248
indecisiveness, 93–94, 105, 265
individuation, 50
indoctrination sessions, 30–31, 39, 42
influence, principles of, 29
information control, 36, 39, 42, 45
informed consent, 32–33
innocence, loss of, 120–21
intimacy, 157–63, 274
intimidation tactics, 179
isolation; of castaways, 56–57; of children, 245; as manipulation technique, 17, 30–31, 38, 39, 42, 43, 44, 117, 122; as psychiatric symptom, 274; in recovery, 53, 157–58, 231; and sexual abuse, 176

jargon (see language)
Jonestown (People's Temple), x, 70, 73
journalkeeping, 99, 118, 125–26, 128, 135, 184–86, 228, 232
judgmentalism, 66, 106

Kashi Ranch, 234–36
Klagsbrun, Samuel, 19–20
Koresh, David, x, 4, 72, 79–82, 117

Langone, Michael, xiii, 28, 41, 45, 135, 154, 180, 266, 275, 276
language; of cult leaders, 72; distrust of, 239; loaded (jargon), 36–37, 94–96, 106; relearning, 95–96, 106, 226–27, 231
leaving cults; castaways, 54, 56–57; children, 253; counseled out, 54, 59–61; loss of leader/group, 54, 57–59, 238; walkaways, 54, 55, 222